Contents

An Introduction to Economics

Right, here we go... and we'll start with microeconomics. Microeconomics is all about individual people, individual firms and individual markets (as opposed to macroeconomics, which is about the economy as a whole). First off... the basic economic problem — everyone wants lots of stuff, but the resources to make it are limited. **These pages are for AQA, Edexcel and OCR.**

Economics — how best to satisfy *Infinite Desires* using *Limited Resources*

1) Everyone has certain basic **needs** in life — e.g. food, water, a place to live, and so on.
   Everyone also has an infinite list of things they **want** — e.g. designer clothes, smartphones, holidays, houses.

2) However, there's a **limited** amount of **resources** available to satisfy these needs and wants (i.e. resources are **scarce**).

3) These facts lead to the **basic economic problem**:

   > **How** can the available **scarce resources** be used to satisfy **people's infinite needs and wants** as effectively as possible?

There are *Four Factors of Production*

The scarce resources (inputs) used to make the things people want and need (outputs) can be divided into four **factors of production**. These factors are: **Land**, **Labour**, **Capital** and **Enterprise**.

Land: including all the *Natural Resources* in and on it

As well as actual 'territory', **land** includes all the Earth's **natural resources**:

- **non-renewable** resources, such as natural gas, oil and coal
- **renewable** resources like wind or tidal power, or wood from trees
- **materials** extracted by mining (e.g. diamonds and gold)
- **water**
- **animals** found in an area

Non-renewable resources will eventually run out if we carry on using them.

Renewable resources can regrow or regenerate. But some renewable resources have to be used carefully if they're not to run out — e.g. to be sustainable, enough trees need to be planted to replace those that are used.

1) Nearly all things that fall under the category of 'land' are **scarce** — there **aren't enough** natural resources to satisfy the demands of everyone.

2) One exception is **air**, but even this isn't as simple as it first looks...

   - Air is **not** usually considered a scarce resource — there's enough for **everyone** to have as much as they want.
   - But this **doesn't** mean all air is equally good — air can be **polluted**, as can be seen in a lot of big cities.
   - In fact, the **environment** is considered by some people to be a **scarce resource**.

   Because there's enough air for everyone to have as much as they want, in theory it's **impossible** to **sell** it. (*Why would anyone **buy** it when they can get it for free?*) Economists call things like this **free goods**.

   Things that are **scarce** and which can therefore be traded are known as **economic goods**.

Labour: the *Work* done by *People*

1) Labour is the **work done** by those **people** who contribute to the production process. The available population who are available to do work is called the **labour force**.

2) There's usually also a number of people who **want** to work and who are **old enough** to work, but who **don't** have a job. Economists refer to these people as **unemployed**.

3) There are also people who **aren't** in **paid employment** but still provide things people need or want, e.g. homemakers.

4) Different people have different levels of education, experience or training. These factors can make some people more 'valuable' or productive in the workplace than others — they have a greater amount of **human capital**.

In the UK, the number of people of working age with a job is around 30 million.

Capital: *Equipment* used in producing goods and services

1) **Capital** is the equipment, factories and schools that help to produce goods or services.

2) **Capital** is different from **land** because capital has to be **made** first.

3) Much of the capital in an economy is **paid for** by the **government** — e.g. a country's road network is a form of capital.

Enterprise: willingness to take a *Risk* to make a *Profit*

Enterprise refers to the people (**entrepreneurs**) who take **risks** and create things from the other three factors of production.

1) They set up and run **businesses** using any of the factors of production available to them.

2) If the business **fails**, they can **lose** a lot of money. But if the business is a **success**, the **reward** for their risk-taking is **profit**.

An Introduction to Economics

Scarcity requires the Careful Allocation of Resources

1) **Economic activity** involves **combining** the factors of production to create **outputs** that people can **consume**. The **purpose** of any economic activity is to **increase** people's **economic welfare** by creating outputs that **satisfy** their various **needs** and **wants**.

2) In Economics a wide range of things count as **economic activity**.

3) One form of economic activity is the making of **goods** and the provision of **services** (i.e. creating outputs).

> - **GOODS:** 'Physical' products you can **touch** — such as washing machines, books or a new factory.
> - **SERVICES:** 'Intangible' things — such as medical checkups, teaching, or train journeys.

4) **Consumption** (i.e. buying or using) is also a form of **economic activity**. When you consume something, you're trying to satisfy a **need** or a **want**. You can consume both goods and services.

Lots of other things are also classified as economic activity, such as doing housework, DIY and bringing up children (even though you might not get paid for doing it).

5) Since there's an **endless** array of things that could be produced and consumed, but only **limited resources**, this leads to three fundamental questions:

> - **What** to produce?
> - **How** to produce it?
> - **Who** to produce it **for**?

Economic Agents react to Incentives

1) The **agents** ('participants') in an economy can usually be thought of as:

> **Producers** — firms or people that make goods or provide services.
>
> **Consumers** — people or firms who buy the goods and services.
>
> **Governments** — a government sets the rules that other participants in the economy have to follow, but also produces and consumes goods and services.

2) Each of these **economic agents** has to make **decisions** that affect how resources are allocated. For example:
   - **Producers** decide what to make, and how much they're willing to sell it for.
   - **Consumers** have to decide what they want to buy, and how much they're willing to pay for it.
   - **Governments** have to decide how much to intervene in the way producers and consumers act.

3) In a **market economy** (see next page), all economic agents are assumed to be **rational**, which means they'll make the decisions that are best for **themselves**. These decisions will be based on economic **incentives**, such as making profit or paying as little as possible for a product.

4) Considering people's incentives helps to answer those fundamental questions above.
   - **What to produce?** This will be those goods that firms can make a profit from.
   - **How to produce it?** Firms will want to produce the good in the most efficient way they can, in order to maximise their profits.
   - **Who to produce it for?** Firms will produce goods for consumers who are willing to pay for those goods.

So in effect consumers decide what is to be produced. Producers won't want to produce things that nobody wants to buy.

Practice Questions

Q1 What is the basic economic problem?

Q2 What are the four factors of production? Give an example of each.

Q3 Give three different types of economic agent.

Exam Question

Q1 State and explain three factors of production which would be necessary for someone opening a new restaurant. [6 marks]

Learn the facts about factors of production...

Economics is a funny one... you might think it's going to be all about banks and money and stuff. But there's a bit of groundwork to do before you get to all that. It's interesting though, and getting your head round all this will definitely help you later on. Those four factors of production are at the heart of everything in economics, by the way... so learn them well.

Markets and Economies

Markets are a way to allocate resources to different economic activities. But sometimes governments decide that things would work out better if things weren't left entirely up to the market. **These pages are for all boards.**

Markets are a method for Allocating Scarce Resources

1) **Markets** are a way of **allocating resources**. They **don't** have to be a place, or involve the exchange of physical objects.

2) Each **buyer** or **seller** in a market **chooses** to exchange something they have for something they'd prefer to have instead. For example, someone's labour (their 'work') is a resource. If they have a job, they exchange their labour for a salary.

3) Since everyone is considered to be **rational** (see p.5), an economist would assume that:
   - the worker would **prefer** to have their wages, but less free time,
   - the employer would **prefer** to have less money, and to know that there's someone there to do some work.

   Any exchange can only happen because different people or organisations value things differently.

4) Exchanging things in this way eventually results in a particular **allocation of resources**.

Mixed Economies combine Free Markets and Government Intervention

1) In a **planned** economy, it's the **government** (not markets) that decides how resources should be allocated. Nowadays, planned economies are rare, though they still exist in countries like North Korea.

2) A **free market** on the other hand allocates resources based on **supply and demand** and the **price mechanism**. In other words, **anything** can be sold at **any price** that people will pay for it.

   See Section 2 for more about the workings of a free market.

3) **Free market economies** have a number of advantages... but there are also some downsides.

> **PROS of a Free Market Economy**
>
> - **Efficiency**
>   As **any** product can be bought and sold, only those of the **best value** will be **in demand**.
>   So firms have an **incentive** to try to make goods in as efficient a way as possible.
>
> - **Entrepreneurship**
>   In a market economy, the **rewards** for good ideas (e.g. new, better products, or better ways to make existing products) can make entrepreneurs a lot of money. This encourages risk-taking and innovation.
>
> - **Choice**
>   The **incentives** for innovation can lead to an increase in **choice** for consumers.
>   (And in a free market, consumers aren't restricted to buying only what the government recommends.)

> **CONS of a Free Market Economy**
>
> - **Inequalities**
>   Market economies can lead to huge **differences in income** — this can be controversial, since many people think particularly large differences are **unfair**. And in a completely free market, anyone who is unable to work (even if it's not their fault) would receive no income.
>
> - **Non-profitable goods may not be made**
>   For example, drugs to treat **rare** medical conditions may never sell enough for a firm to make any profit, so these would not be made.
>
> - **Monopolies**
>   Successful businesses can become the only supplier of a product
>   — this **market dominance** can be abused (see p.53).

4) **Market failure** happens when free markets result in **undesirable outcomes** — for example, traffic congestion is seen as a market failure.

   See Section 3 for more about market failure.

5) **Governments** often intervene when there's a market failure.
   - They might **change the law**, or **offer tax breaks** (e.g. reduce taxes for anyone carrying out particular activities), or create some other kind of **incentive** to try to influence people's behaviour.
   - Governments can also intervene in the economy by **buying** or **providing** goods or services.

6) When both the **government** and **markets** play a part in allocating resources, this is called a **mixed economy**.

Markets and Economies

A *Mixed Economy* has a *Public Sector* and a *Private Sector*

1) In a mixed economy, the government is known as the **public sector**.

2) Businesses that are privately owned make up the **private sector**.

3) Private-sector organisations usually have to **break even** or make a **profit** to survive.

4) **Most** countries have a mixed economy, including the UK — there are **no** purely free market economies where the government doesn't intervene in some way.

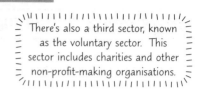
There's also a third sector, known as the voluntary sector. This sector includes charities and other non-profit-making organisations.

There are *Two Kinds* of economic statement

Before moving on to more specific things, you need to know about the **two** kinds of **statements** you can make in economics.

POSITIVE statements

Positive statements are **objective** statements that can be **tested** by referring to the available **evidence**.

- For example:
  "A reduction in income will increase the amount of people shopping in pound shops."

- With suitable data collected over a period of time, you should be able to tell if the above claim is true or false.

Positive statements are important in economics because they're a way of testing whether **economic ideas** are **correct** — they're '**testable**'.

NORMATIVE statements

Normative statements are **subjective** statements which contain a **value judgement** — they're **opinions**.

- For example:
  "The use of fossil fuels should be taxed more highly than the use of renewable fuels."

- It's not possible to say whether the above statement is true or not — only whether you agree or disagree with it.

Normative statements are also important in economics, because **value judgements** influence **economic decision-making** and **government policy**.

Practice Questions

Q1 Explain briefly how resources are allocated by a market.

Q2 Give two advantages and two disadvantages of a free market economy.

Q3 Explain what is meant by the terms: 'mixed economy', 'public sector' and 'private sector'.

Exam Question

Q1 Statement 1: Increased government spending during a recession generally leads to a quicker recovery.
Statement 2: Governments should spend more during a recession to prevent unemployment getting too high.

Choose the option below that best describes the above two statements. Explain your answer.

A) Both are positive statements.
B) Statement 1 is positive and statement 2 is normative.
C) Statement 1 is normative and statement 2 is positive.
D) Both are normative statements.

[4 marks]

Do some economics exam practice — but don't forget to market...

Free markets are one of those things that sound really good in theory, but in practice one or two problems tend to crop up. This is why mixed economies are currently all the rage in world economics (apart from in a couple of places).

Production Possibility Frontiers

Production possibility frontiers (PPFs) — also known as production possibility curves (PPCs) or production possibility boundaries (PPBs) — show the maximum amount of two goods or services an economy can produce. **For all boards.**

Production Possibility Frontiers show the Maximum possible output

The basic problem in Economics is how best to allocate scarce resources. A **production possibility frontier** (PPF) shows the options that are available when you consider the production of just **two types** of goods or services.

1) The PPF below shows the **maximum** number of **houses** (on the horizontal axis) and **vehicles** (on the vertical axis) that can be made, using the **existing** level of resources in an economy.

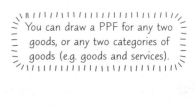

You can draw a PPF for any two goods, or any two categories of goods (e.g. goods and services).

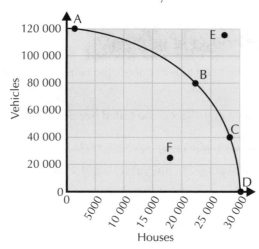

2) Points A, B, C and D (and every other point on the PPF) are all achievable **without** using any **extra** resources. However, they are **only** achievable when **all** the available resources are used as **efficiently** as is actually possible.

- Notice how, as you move along the curve from A to B, you're building **more houses** (about 22 500 instead of 1000) but **fewer vehicles** (80 000 instead of 120 000).

- Moving along the curve from A to B like this corresponds to allocating **more resources** to the production of houses, and **fewer resources** to the production of vehicles.

All the different points on the PPF represent a different choice about how to use the available scarce resources.

- In other words, there's a **trade-off** between 'building more houses' and 'making more vehicles' — to do **more** of one, you have to do **less** of the other.

> A **trade-off** is when you have to choose between conflicting objectives because you **can't** achieve all your objectives at the **same time**. It involves **compromising**, and aiming to achieve **each** of your objectives **a bit**.

3) Point E lies **outside** the PPF, so it **isn't achievable** using the **current level** of resources in the economy. To build that many houses and vehicles at the same time, **extra** (or **better**) **resources** would need to be found.

4) Point F lies **inside** the PPF (rather than **on** it) — this means making this mix of goods is **productively inefficient**. With the current level of resources, you could build more houses **without** making fewer vehicles (or more vehicles **without** making fewer houses).

Opportunity Cost is the next best thing that you're forced to give up

1) The trade-off described above involves an **opportunity cost**.

2) An opportunity cost is what you **give up** in order to do something else — i.e. it's the cost of any choice that's made.

3) So moving from A to B on the PPF above means you have the opportunity to build 21 500 extra houses as long as you **give up** the opportunity to make 40 000 vehicles. In other words, the **opportunity cost** of building 21 500 extra houses is the lost production of 40 000 vehicles.

> The **opportunity cost** of a decision is the **next best alternative** that you **give up** in making that decision.

Production Possibility Frontiers

Economic Growth shifts the PPF

1) A PPF shows what's possible using a **particular level** of resources (e.g. a particular number of people, a particular amount of capital and raw materials, and so on).

2) If this level of resources is **fixed**, then movements **along** the PPF just show a **reallocation** of those resources.

3) However, if the total amount of resources **changes**, then the PPF itself **moves**.

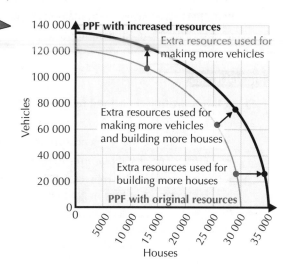

- For example, **increased resources** (e.g. an increase in the total number of workers) would mean that the total possible **output** of that economy would also **increase** — so the PPF **shifts outward**.

- For the economy shown by this PPF, the extra output could be **either** more houses **or** more vehicles **or** a combination of both.

4) **Improved technology** or **improvements** to **labour** (e.g. through training) can also shift the PPF outwards, because it allows **more output** to be produced using the **same resources**.

5) An **outward shift** of the PPF shows **economic growth**.

6) When **fewer** total resources are available (e.g. after some kind of **natural disaster**), the opposite happens — the PPF **shifts inwards**, showing that the total possible output has **shrunk**. This shows **negative economic growth**.

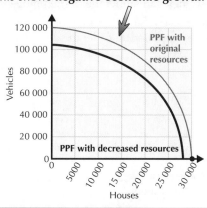

7) In this example, the possible output has **grown** because of improved technology. However, this particular technology can only help with **house-building** — this means the PPF has been stretched in only the **horizontal direction**.

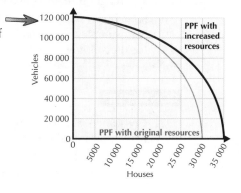

Practice Questions

Q1 Explain what a production possibility frontier (PPF) shows.

Q2 What is meant by a trade-off?

Q3 Describe why a PPF might move outwards. What does it mean if it moves inwards?

Exam Questions

Q1 Look at the diagram on the right. Which of the following combinations of cars and butter cannot currently be produced in this economy using the existing resources? Explain your answer.

A) Only W

B) Only X

C) Only W, Y and Z

D) Only Y and Z   [4 marks]

Q2 Use the diagram on the right to explain the term opportunity cost.   [5 marks]

Decisions, decisions, decisions...

It's important to get your head round these PPFs. Think of different points on a PPF as representing different decisions you could make about how you want to allocate your all-too-scarce resources. Then they don't seem (quite) as bad.

Economic Objectives and Specialisation

Economic objectives are targets set by either individuals, firms or the government that they would like to achieve.
This page is for AQA only, but is useful for Edexcel and OCR students.

Different **Economic Agents** will have different **Economic Objectives**

1) **Economic agents** (e.g. producers, consumers, governments) will usually have different **objectives**.

2) Quite often, these objectives are to **maximise** a particular quantity (e.g. profit).

3) This page describes the usual **assumptions** made about the objectives of economic agents.

They won't be true for everyone, but they should be 'quite good' for 'quite a lot of people'.

PRODUCERS

1) A firm's **profit** is their **total revenue** (money received by the firm, e.g. from sales) minus their **total costs**.

2) Firms are often assumed to want to maximise **profit** — this could be for **various** reasons:

   • Profit means the firm can **survive** — loss-making firms might eventually have to close.

   • Greater profits allow firms to offer better **rewards** to the **owner** (or **shareholders**) and **staff**...

   • ...or profit can be **reinvested** in the business in the hope of making even more profits later. For example, a firm might want to invest in order to **expand**.

3) But firms may want to maximise other quantities instead, such as **total sales** or the firm's **market share**.

   • A large **market share** could lead to some **monopoly power** (see p.52) — this would mean that the firm could charge higher prices due to a lack of competition.

   • Bigger firms are often considered more **prestigious** and **stable**, so they can attract the best employees.

4) Some firms may also have **ethical objectives** — i.e. 'doing some good', even if it **doesn't** increase profits. For example, a firm may decide to buy all its raw materials from nearby suppliers in order to support the **local economy**, even if cheaper alternatives are available elsewhere.

CONSUMERS

1) **Consumers** are assumed to want to **maximise** their **utility**, while not spending more than their income (i.e. while living within their means).

   Utility is a hard-to-measure quantity that roughly means 'well-being', 'happiness' or 'satisfaction'.

   • **Utility** will involve **different things** for different people — e.g. some people might value the **security** of making large pension contributions, while others might want to **spend** their money on things like fast cars and holidays.

   • But whatever someone spends their money on, you'd assume they're acting **rationally** to increase their utility in the way that makes most sense to them.

2) Consumers can also act as workers — **workers** are assumed to want to **maximise** their **income**, while having as much **free time** as they need or want.

GOVERNMENTS

1) **Governments** try to balance the **resources** of a country with the **needs and wants** of the population — i.e. economists assume that governments try to **maximise the 'public interest'**.

2) This is likely to include some or all of the following:

   • **Economic growth** — usually measured by growth in a country's **GDP**.

   Gross domestic product — see p.72.

   • **Full employment** — everybody of a working age, who is capable of working, having a job.

   • **Equilibrium in the balance of payments** — a balance between the payments **into** the country over a period of time and the payments **out**.

   There's a lot more about government economic objectives in Section 6.

   • **Low inflation** — keeping prices under control, as high inflation can cause serious problems.

3) In practice, these are **competing objectives** — policies that help achieve one objective may make it **more difficult** to achieve another (e.g. extra government spending may help create jobs, but it could lead to higher inflation). See p.108-109 for more information.

Economic Objectives and Specialisation

By specialising, we don't have to spend all our time making what we want or need. **This page is for all boards.**

Specialisation leads to a Division of Labour

1) It would (in **theory**) be possible for almost everyone to **make** all the things they need and want **themselves**. People could grow their own **food**, make their own **clothes**, build their own **computers**, and so on.

2) In **practice** though, this is very hard, so it rarely happens. What usually happens is that people and firms **specialise** — some people grow food, other people make clothes, others build computers, and so on.

3) The **division of labour** is a **type** of **specialisation** where production is **split** into **different tasks** and **specific people** are **allocated** to each task, e.g. in making a stool — one person could make the legs and one person could make the seats.

4) There are **advantages** and **disadvantages** to specialisation, but overall an economy can produce **more stuff** (i.e. make more goods and provide more services) if people and firms **specialise**.

5) It's not just individuals and firms that can specialise — whole **regions** and even entire **countries** can specialise to some extent. For example, there are loads of technology companies based in Silicon Valley in California.

Advantages of Specialisation

- People can **specialise** in the things they're **best** at. (Or by doing it, they learn to become better at it.)
- This can lead to **better quality** and a **higher quantity** of products for the same amount of effort overall — i.e. increased **labour productivity**.
- Specialisation is one way in which firms can achieve **economies of scale** (see p.14). For example, a **production line** (where each person may have just one or two tasks to perform) is a form of specialisation.
- Specialisation leads to **more efficient** production — this helps to tackle the problem of **scarcity**, because if **resources** are used more efficiently, **more output** can be produced **per unit** of **input**.

Disadvantages of Specialisation

- Workers can end up doing **repetitive** tasks, which can lead to **boredom**.
- Countries can become **less self-sufficient** — this can be a problem if **trade** is **disrupted** for whatever reason (e.g. a war or dispute). For example, if a country specialises in **manufacturing**, and **imports** (rather than produces) all its **fuel**, then that country could be in trouble if it falls out with its fuel **supplier**.
- It can lead to a **lack** of **flexibility** — for example, if the companies eventually move elsewhere, the workforce left behind can struggle to **adapt**.

Coal mining in the UK is an example of this. When pits closed, many miners had non-transferable skills (this is structural unemployment — see p.99).

Trade means everyone can Buy the stuff they're no longer making Themselves

1) Specialisation means that **trade** becomes absolutely vital — economies (and individual people and firms) have to be able to **obtain** the things they're no longer making for themselves.

2) This means it's **necessary** to have a **way** of **exchanging** goods and services between countries.

3) **Swapping** goods with other countries is one way a country can get what it needs, for example, a country which mines diamonds may want oil, while another country which produces oil may want diamonds.

4) The most **efficient** way of exchanging goods and services between countries is using **money** (with the use of **exchange rates** where necessary — see p.104-105). Money is a **medium of exchange** — it's something both buyers and sellers value and that means that countries can buy goods, even if sellers don't want the things that the buying country produces.

Practice Questions

Q1 Describe two economic objectives a firm might have.
Q2 Give two advantages and two disadvantages of specialisation.
Q3 What's a medium of exchange? Why is it useful?

Exam Question

Q1 Explain why the use of money as a medium of exchange enables an economy to benefit from specialisation and the division of labour. [4 marks]

Learn this, and achieve maximum utility...

Not many people know this, but Mick Jagger studied at the London School of Economics, and in fact the title of the Rolling Stones' biggest hit was actually intended to be "I can't get no economic utility". Which is actually very interesting. Though not true.

Production, Productivity and Efficiency

Economists sometimes seem to use terms which sound similar, but which mean quite different things. These pages cover three of the most confusing: production, productivity and productive efficiency. **These pages are for AQA and OCR only.**

Production means *Manufacturing* something in order to *Sell* it

1) Production involves converting **inputs** (e.g. raw materials, labour) into **outputs** (things to sell).

2) The inputs can be any of the four **factors of production** — land, labour, capital and enterprise.
   Inputs can be:

   > • **tangible** — things you can touch, like raw materials or machines.
   > • **intangible** — 'abstract' things that can't be touched — like ideas, talent or knowledge.

3) The **outputs** produced should have an **exchangeable value** — they need to be something that can be sold.

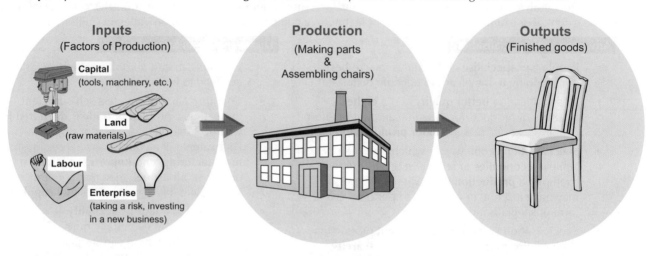

Productivity is the output *per Factor Employed*

1) **Productivity** is a way of measuring how efficiently a company or an economy is producing its output.

2) It's defined as the **output per unit of input employed**. So if one company could take the same amount of inputs as another company, but produce more stuff, their productivity would be **greater**.

3) You can work out an **overall** level of productivity (involving all four possible inputs).

4) But you can also calculate productivity for **any one** of the four individual factors of production, such as labour (see below). Improving the productivity of any one of these **separate** factors should lead to an increase in **overall productivity**.

Labour Productivity is the output *per Worker* or output *per Hour Worked*

1) **Labour productivity** is one example of measuring productivity for one factor.
   It's the amount of output produced **per worker** (or **per worker-hour**).

2) To calculate labour productivity:
   • Take the amount of output produced in a particular time.
   • Divide this by the **total** number of workers (or the total **hours worked** by all the workers).

3) Labour productivity allows workers to be **compared** against other workers.
   For example, labour productivity is calculated for **whole economies**, so that the productivity of the different labour forces can be compared.

4) Improvements in labour productivity can come about as a result of better **training**, more **experience**, improved **technology**, and so on. **Specialisation** is also a good way to improve labour productivity — if each worker concentrates on performing tasks that they're **good at doing**, have **practised a lot** or have been **trained** to do, then they'll be able to **produce more** than if they did lots of different tasks.

A fitter workforce is a more productive workforce.

Production, Productivity and Efficiency

Productive Efficiency occurs at the lowest point on the Average Cost Curve

1) **Productive efficiency** means outputting the desired amount of goods or services for the **lowest average cost** of production. A firm's average cost is calculated by **dividing** its **total cost** by its **output**.

2) This diagram shows a firm's **average cost curve**. It shows how a firm's **average cost of production** of a good changes as the firm's **level of output** varies (i.e. as it makes more or fewer goods).

   - At **very low** levels of output, the average cost is **high**.
   - As the level of output **increases** (and the firm takes advantage of **economies of scale** — see p.14) the firm's **average cost** of production **falls** — the firm becomes more **efficient**.
   - As the level of output **continues to increase**, the firm's **average cost** of production starts to **increase** again (as the firm starts to encounter **diseconomies of scale** — see p.15).

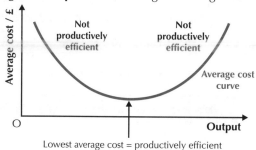

3) This means that the firm is **productively efficient** when it produces the level of output shown at the **lowest point** on the average cost curve.

Productive Efficiency happens on a PPF

1) To be productively efficient, an economy as a whole **must** be producing on its **production possibility frontier**.

2) One way to understand why this must be the case is to think about the amount of resources (e.g. land or labour) that are **wasted**.

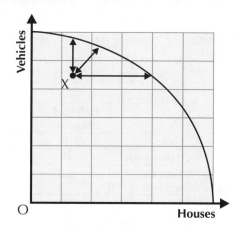

- Productive efficiency can only be achieved when waste is **eliminated** from the production process (else you could **stop** wasting those resources, **reduce** your average cost, and so **increase** your productive efficiency).
- But 'working without wasting resources' is exactly what it means to be on the **production possibility frontier**.
- On the production possibility frontier, you **can't** just reduce waste and make more of something — you can only **make more** of something by **making less** of something else.

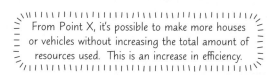

Practice Questions

Q1 What is meant by the term productivity?
Q2 How is labour productivity calculated?
Q3 At which point on an average cost curve is a firm being productively efficient?

Exam Question

Q1 Which one of the following is most likely to lead to improvements in labour productivity? Explain your answer.
A) An increased supply of labour
B) More specialisation
C) Adopting low-tech methods of production
D) Less division of labour
[4 marks]

That's not an average cost curve — that's a really nice one...

If you want my honest opinion... those diagrams can get a bit confusing. So if you're getting a bit bothered and bewildered by them, you won't be the only one. But they're worth persevering with, because they come up time and again in Economics. Remember... the PPF shows the maximum possible output, so any point on it is as efficient as it can possibly be.

Economies and Diseconomies of Scale

Economies and diseconomies of scale are the pros and cons of getting bigger. **These pages are for AQA only.**

Economies of Scale can be Internal or External

1) The **average cost** to a firm of making something is usually quite high if they **don't** make very many of them.

2) But the more of those things the firm makes, the more the average cost of making each one falls. These falls in the cost of production are due to **economies of scale**.

> Economies of scale — the cost advantages of production on a large scale.

See the average cost curve on p.13.

3) Economies of scale can be divided into two categories — **internal** and **external**.

Internal economies of scale involve changes Within a firm

Technical Economies of Scale

- **Production line** methods can be used by large firms to make a lot of things at a very low average cost.
- Large firms may also be more able to purchase other **specialised equipment** to help reduce average costs.
- Workers can **specialise**, becoming more efficient at the tasks they carry out. This might not be possible in a small firm with few employees.
- Another potential economy of scale arises from the **law of increased dimensions**. For example:
  - The **price** you pay to build a new warehouse might be closely related to the **total area of the walls and roof**, say.
  - If you make the dimensions of the walls and roof **twice as big**, the total **area** of the walls and roof will be **4 times greater** — so the warehouse will **cost about 4 times as much** to build.
  - But the **volume** of the warehouse will be **8 times greater**, meaning that you're getting more storage space for each pound you spend.
  - The same is true of things like **oil tankers** — e.g. bigger tankers reduce the cost of transporting each unit of oil.

Warehouse 1: Area = 20 m², Area = 24 m², 4 m, 5 m, 6 m
Volume = 5 × 4 × 6 = 120 m³

Warehouse 2: Area = 120 m², Area = 96 m², Area = 80 m², 8 m, 10 m, 12 m
Volume = 10 × 8 × 12 = 960 m³

Purchasing Economies of Scale

- **Large firms** making lots of goods will need **larger quantities** of raw materials, and so can often **negotiate discounts** with suppliers.
- This isn't just the large firm driving a hard bargain — **suppliers' costs** are lower if they deliver **larger amounts** of goods.
- This table shows the general idea — the **cost per unit** to the supplier changes massively (since the **supplier's delivery costs** don't increase much even when the size of the order **doubles**).

	Half load (50 units)	Full load (100 units)
Fuel	£50	£60
Driver costs	£100	£100
Tax / wear and tear	£20	£20
Total	£170	£180
Cost per unit	£3.40	£1.80

Managerial Economies of Scale

- **Large firms** will be able to employ **specialist** managers to take care of different areas of the business (e.g. finance, production, customer service). These specialist managers gain **expertise** and **experience** in a specific area of the business, which usually leads to better **decision-making** abilities in that area.
- And the number of managers a firm needs **doesn't** usually depend directly on the amount of **goods** produced — for example, a firm probably won't need twice as many managers to produce twice as many goods. This **reduces** the management cost per unit of output.

Financial Economies of Scale

- Larger firms can often **borrow money** at a **lower** rate of **interest**, because lending to them is seen by banks as less risky (i.e. the banks are more likely to get their money back).

Risk-bearing Economies of Scale

- Larger firms can **diversify** into different **product areas** (e.g. make different things) and different **markets** (e.g. sell in different countries). Although demand for any one product in any one market can **vary**, this diversification actually leads to a **more predictable overall demand** (basically, if demand for one product in one country falls, there's likely to be a different product whose demand somewhere increases).
- This also means large firms are able to take **risks** (e.g. by launching products that may or may not prove popular). If the product is unsuccessful, a large firm's other activities allow it to **absorb** the cost of **failure** more easily.

Economies and Diseconomies of Scale

Still a bit more to cover about economies of scale — bear with me...

External economies of scale involve changes Outside a firm
...but within that firm's industry.

- Local colleges may start to offer **qualifications** needed by **big local employers**, reducing the firms' training costs.
- Large companies locating in an area may lead to improvements in **road networks** or **local public transport**.
- If lots of firms doing **similar** or **related** things locate near each other, they may be able to **share resources** (e.g. research facilities). **Suppliers** may also decide to locate in the same area, reducing transport costs.

Extremely successful companies can gain Monopoly Power in a market

1) As a firm's **average cost** for making a product **falls**, it can sell that product at a **lower price**, undercutting its competition.

2) This can lead to a firm gaining a bigger and bigger **market share**, as it continually offers products at prices that are lower than the competition.

3) In this way, a firm can eventually force its competitors out of business and become the **only supplier** of the product — i.e. it has a **monopoly**.

Undercutting means selling something at a lower price.

Diseconomies of Scale — Disadvantages of being big

1) Becoming bigger and bigger isn't always good though — as a firm increases in size, it can start to encounter **diseconomies of scale** (i.e. 'disadvantages of being big'). This happens when **average cost increases** as **production increases**.

2) Diseconomies can be **internal** or **external**:

INTERNAL

- **Wastage** and **loss** can increase, as materials might seem in plentiful supply. Bigger warehouses might lead to more things getting **lost** or **mislaid**.
- **Communication** may become more difficult as a firm grows, affecting staff morale.
- Managers may be less able to **control** what goes on.

EXTERNAL

- As a **whole industry** becomes bigger, the price of raw materials may **increase** (since demand will be greater).
- Buying large amounts of materials **may not** make them less expensive per unit. If local supplies aren't sufficient, more expensive goods from further afield may have to be bought.

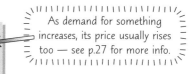
As demand for something increases, its price usually rises too — see p.27 for more info.

Practice Questions

Q1 What's meant by the term 'economy of scale'?

Q2 Give two examples of diseconomies of scale.

Q3 What's the difference between an internal economy of scale and an external one?

Exam Question

Q1 Explain why companies may find that their average cost of production increases as their output increases. [4 marks]

Diseconomies of scale — when big isn't beautiful...

There are all sorts of economies of scale. But it's not all plain sailing for big firms — they can have their fair share of difficulties too. This is why someone, somewhere invented the term 'diseconomy of scale'. I know, 'diseconomy' doesn't sound like a real word, but the effects are very real indeed. You know the drill... learn the stuff, cover the page, try to recall it all, and then try the questions.

Demand

Section 2 is all about markets, and to understand markets you'll need to know everything there is to know about demand and supply. Working out what demand is seems like a good place to start — so go on, get reading... **These pages are for all boards.**

Markets *are where* Goods *and* Services *are* Bought *and* Sold

1) A **market** is anywhere **buyers** and **sellers** can exchange **goods** or **services**.

2) The **price charged** for and **quantity sold** of each good or service are **determined** by the levels of **demand** and **supply** in a market.

3) The levels of demand and supply in a market are shown using **diagrams**. These diagrams demonstrate the price level and quantity demanded/ supplied of goods or services.

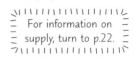
For information on supply, turn to p.22.

Demand *for* Goods *or* Services *is* Different *at* Different Prices

1) **Demand** is the **quantity** of a good or service that consumers are **willing and able** to buy at a **given price**, at a **particular time**.

2) A **demand curve** shows the relationship between **price** and **quantity demanded**. At any given point along the curve it shows the **quantity** of the good or service that would be bought at a particular **price**.

3) Here's an example of a demand curve:

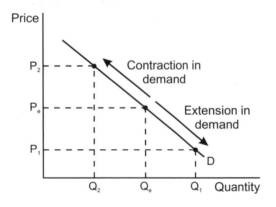

- At price P_e the quantity Q_e is demanded.
- A **decrease** in price from P_e to P_1 causes an **extension** in demand — it **rises** from Q_e to Q_1.
- An **increase** in price from P_e to P_2 causes a **contraction** in demand — it **falls** from Q_e to Q_2.
- So, **movement along** the **demand curve** is caused by **changes in price**.

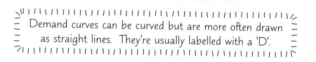
Demand curves can be curved but are more often drawn as straight lines. They're usually labelled with a 'D'.

4) Demand curves usually **slope downwards**. This means that the **higher** the **price** charged for a good, the **lower** the **quantity demanded** — as shown by the diagram above.

5) In general, consumers aim to pay the **lowest price possible** for goods and services. As prices decrease **more consumers** are **willing and able** to purchase a good or service — so **lower prices** means **higher demand**.

Changes *in* Demand *cause a* Shift *in the* Demand Curve

1) A demand curve moves to the **left** (e.g. D_1) when there is a **decrease** in the **amount demanded** at **every price**.

2) A demand curve shifts to the **right** (e.g. D_2) when there is an **increase** in the **amount demanded** at **every price**.

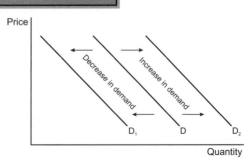

Demand

There are lots of *Factors* that can *Cause* a *Shift* in the *Demand Curve*

1) Changes in tastes and fashion can cause demand curves to shift to the **right** if something is **popular** and to the **left** when it is **out of fashion**.

2) Changes to people's **real income**, the amount of goods/services that a consumer can afford to purchase with their income, can affect the **demand** for **different types** of goods differently.

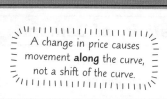

A change in price causes movement **along** the curve, not a shift of the curve.

- **Normal goods** (e.g. DVDs) are those which people will demand **more** of if their **real income increases**. This means that a **rise** in real income causes the **demand curve** to **shift** to the **right** — people want to buy more of the good at each price level.

- **Inferior goods** (e.g. cheap clothing) are those which people demand **less** of if their real income increases. This means that a **rise** in real income causes the **demand curve** to **shift** to the **left** — people demand less at each price level since they'll often switch to more expensive goods instead.

- A more **equal distribution** of income (i.e. a reduction in the difference between the incomes of rich and poor people) may cause the demand curve for **luxury goods** (e.g. sports cars) to shift to the **left** — and the demand curve for other items to shift to the **right**. This is because there'll be **fewer** really **rich** people who can afford **luxury** items, and **more** people who can afford **everyday** items.

Changes in demand in *One Market* can affect demand in *Other Markets*

Some markets are **interrelated**, which means that changes in **one** market **affect** a **related** market.

- **Substitute goods** are those which are alternatives to each other (see previous page) — e.g. beef and lamb. An **increase** in the **price** of one good will **decrease** the **demand** for it and **increase** the **demand** for its **substitutes**.

- **Complementary goods** are goods that are **often used together**, so they're in **joint demand** — e.g. strawberries and cream. If the **price** of strawberries **increases**, demand for them will **decrease** along with **demand** for cream.

- The introduction of a **new product** may cause the demand curve to shift to the **left** for goods that are **substitutes** for the new product and to the **right** for goods that are **complementary** to it.

- **Derived demand** is the demand for a good or a factor of production used in making another good or service. For example, an **increase** in the demand for **fencing** will lead to an **increased** derived demand for **wood**.

- Some goods have more than one use. For example, oil can be used to make plastics or for fuel — this is **composite demand**. Changes in the **demand curve** for **oil** could lead to changes in the **demand curve** for **plastic**.

Practice Questions

Q1 What causes a movement along a demand curve?

Q2 What causes a shift in a demand curve?

Q3 What are normal goods?

Q4 Give four examples of complementary goods.

Exam Questions

Q1 The decline in the housing market experienced in the UK during the period 2008-2012 led to building firms reducing their workload and to many tile retailers cutting down or delaying expansion plans. Discuss the likely impacts of the decline of the UK housing market on tile manufacturers. [4 marks]

Q2 Cheese and crackers are complementary goods. Analyse the likely impacts on the demand for crackers if the price of cheese dramatically increases. [4 marks]

I love complementary goods — always make me feel good about myself...

A market determines the price of a certain good (or service), and price will often affect demand. Demand links to the quantity sold — greater demand will tend to lead to a greater quantity sold. There are loads of different factors that can influence demand, so make sure you learn how these affect the demand curve — those that change the level of demand cause the curve to shift.

Price, Income and Cross Elasticities of Demand

Elasticity of demand is a measure of how much the demand for a good changes with a change in one of the key influences on demand — the price of the good, the level of real income and the price of another good. **These pages are for all boards.**

Price Elasticity of Demand *shows how* Demand Changes *with* Price

1) **Price elasticity of demand** (**PED**) is a measure of how the quantity **demanded** of a good **responds** to a **change** in its **price**.

2) PED can be **calculated** using the following formula:

$$PED = \frac{\text{percentage change in quantity demanded}}{\text{percentage change in price}}$$

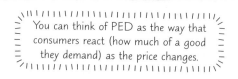 You can think of PED as the way that consumers react (how much of a good they demand) as the price changes.

3) Have a look at this example:

> - When the **price** of a type of toy car **increased** from **50p** to **70p** the **demand** for them **fell** from **15** cars to **10** cars.
>
> - The **percentage change** in **quantity demanded** would be: $\frac{\text{change in demand}}{\text{original demand}} \times 100 = \frac{-5}{15} \times 100 = \textbf{-33.33\%}$
>
> - The **percentage change** in **price** would be: $\frac{\text{change in price}}{\text{original price}} \times 100 = \frac{20}{50} \times 100 = \textbf{40\%}$
>
> - So **PED** $= \frac{-33.33\%}{40\%} = \textbf{-0.83}$

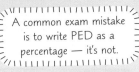 A common exam mistake is to write PED as a percentage — it's not.

4) Price elasticity of demand is **usually negative** because **demand falls** as **price increases** for most goods.

PED *can be* Elastic, Inelastic *or* Unit Elastic

< means 'less than'
> means 'greater than'

Elastic Demand: PED > 1

1) If the value of PED (ignoring any minus signs) is **greater than 1** (**> 1**), demand for the good is **elastic**. This means a **percentage change** in **price** will cause a **larger percentage change** in **quantity demanded**.

2) The **higher** the value of PED, the **more elastic** demand is for the good.

3) In diagram 1, price falls from **£50** to **£40** and an extra **45** units are demanded, which gives an **elastic** PED of -7.5.

$$PED = \frac{45/30 \times 100}{-10/50 \times 100} = -7.5$$

So a 1% change in price leads to a 7.5% change in demand.

4) **Perfectly elastic demand** has a PED of ± infinity and any **increase** in **price** means that **demand** will **fall** to **zero** — see diagram 2. Consumers are willing to buy all they can obtain at P, but **none** at a **higher price** (above P).

Inelastic Demand: 0 < PED < 1

1) The value of PED for goods with inelastic demand (ignoring any minus signs) is **between 0 and 1** (**0 < PED < 1**). This means a **percentage change** in **price** will cause a **smaller percentage change** in **quantity demanded**. The **smaller** the value of PED, the **more inelastic** demand is for the good.

2) In diagram 3, price falls from **£50** to **£40** (**20% decrease**) and only an extra **4** units (**8% increase**) are demanded. This gives an **inelastic** PED of -0.4 which means for every 1% change in price there's a 0.4% change in demand.

3) **Perfectly inelastic demand** has a PED of **0** and any **change** in **price** will have **no effect** on the **quantity demanded** — see diagram 4. At any price (e.g. P_1 or P_2), the **quantity demanded** will be the **same**.

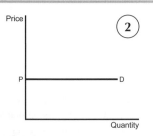

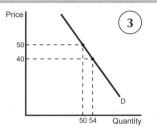

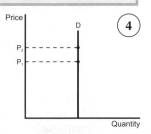

Unit Elasticity of Demand: PED = ±1

1) A good has **unit elasticity** (PED = ±1) if the size of the **percentage change** in **price** is **equal** to the size of the **percentage change** in **quantity demanded** — see diagram 5.

2) For example, here a **20% decrease** in price will lead to a **20% increase** in quantity demanded.

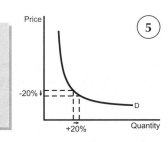

Jim's demand for bungee cord elasticity was at an all-time high.

Price, Income and Cross Elasticities of Demand

Income Elasticity of Demand *shows how* Demand Changes *with* Income

1) **Income elasticity of demand** (**YED**) measures how much the **demand** for a good changes with a **change in real income**.

2) YED can be **calculated** using the following formula:

$$YED = \frac{\text{percentage change in quantity demanded of a good}}{\text{percentage change in real income}}$$

3) Here's an example:

> If **real incomes increased** by **10%** and because of this the **demand** for **cameras** **increased** by **15%**, the income elasticity of demand for cameras would be: $\quad YED = \frac{15\%}{10\%} = 1.5$

4) Here are examples of the meanings of different values of YED (ignoring any minus signs):

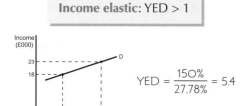

| Income elastic: YED > 1 | Income inelastic: YED < 1 | Perfectly inelastic: YED = 0 |

$$YED = \frac{150\%}{27.78\%} = 5.4$$

$$YED = \frac{25\%}{27.78\%} = 0.9$$

An increase in income of **£5000** leads to an increase in demand for the good of **6 units**. This gives an **elastic** YED of **5.4**. So for every 1% increase in incomes, demand increases by 5.4%.

An increase in income of **£5000** leads to an increase in demand for the good of only **1 unit**. This gives an **inelastic** YED of **0.9**.

No matter how high incomes rise, **demand remains constant**.

You need to know about Cross Elasticity of Demand *too*

1) **Cross elasticity of demand** (**XED**) is a measure of how the **quantity demanded** of one good **responds** to a **change** in the **price** of another good.

2) XED can be **calculated** using the following formula:

$$XED = \frac{\text{percentage change in quantity demanded of good A}}{\text{percentage change in price of good B}}$$

3) If two goods are **substitutes** their XED will be **positive** and if they're **complements** their XED will be **negative**. For example:

> **Toy cars** and **teddy bears** are **substitutes**. If the **price** of toy cars **rose** by **40%**, the **demand** for teddy bears may **increase** by **20%**. $\quad XED = \frac{20\%}{40\%} = 0.5$

> **Tennis rackets** and **tennis balls** are **complementary goods**. If the **price** of tennis rackets **rose** by **50%**, the **demand** for tennis balls may **fall** by **30%**. $\quad XED = \frac{-30\%}{50\%} = -0.6$

Practice Questions

Q1 Give the formula for PED.

Q2 What is income elasticity of demand?

Exam Question

Q1 The price of chococakes was reduced from £3 to £1.50, causing an increase in demand from 200 to 400.
What is the price elasticity of demand for chococakes?

    A) –1.0   B) –2.0   C) –0.5   D) +2.0

Explain your answer.

                                                      [4 marks]

Cross elasticity of demand — it's elasticity of demand on a bad day...

I'm sorry, I know that's pretty terrible. Anyway, the key things to pick up here are that there are three elasticities of demand that you need to understand. Their names should give you a clue about what affects them. Well, except XED, which is a bit less obvious — it's like PED, but it's about two different goods (or services) rather than just the one. Read it over until it's all clear in your head.

Uses of Elasticities of Demand

Different factors influence the different elasticities of demand. Some factors influence more than one type of elasticity, so make sure you study them well. PED also has implications for a firm's revenue. **These pages are for all boards.**

Many Factors Influence the Price Elasticity of Demand

1) **Substitutes**

   The **more substitutes** a good has, the **more elastic** demand is — if there are many substitutes available then consumers can easily **switch** to something else if the price rises. The **number of substitutes** a good has depends on how closely it's **defined**. For example, peas have a number of substitutes (e.g. carrots, sweetcorn), but vegetables as a group have fewer.

   The most important influence on elasticity is the number of substitutes a good has, but in the exam you'll be expected to know lots of influences.

2) **Type of good (or service)**

   - **Essential items** (e.g. milk) are price **inelastic**, but **non-essential** items (e.g. tablet computers) tend to be price **elastic**.
   - Goods that are **habit-forming** (e.g. alcohol and tobacco) tend to be price **inelastic**.
   - Purchases that **cannot be postponed** (e.g. emergency plumbing services) tend to be price **inelastic**.
   - Products with **several different uses** (e.g. water is used in cooking, building, washing) tend to be price **inelastic**.

3) **Percentage of income spent on good**

   Demand for products that need a **large proportion** of the **consumer's income** (e.g. a fridge) is **more elastic** than demand for products that only need a **small proportion** of **income** (e.g. toothpaste). Consumers are more likely to shop around for the **best price** of an expensive good.

4) **Time**

   In the **long run** prices become **more elastic** as it becomes **easier** to change to **alternatives** because consumers have had the time to shop around. Also, in the long run, habits and loyalties can change.

Total Revenue and Price Elasticity of Demand

1) It's important for firms to understand the relationship between **total revenue** (price per unit × quantity sold) and a product's **price elasticity of demand**.

2) Elasticity **changes** along a **straight-line demand curve**:

   - PED changes along the demand curve from minus **infinity** at **high price/zero demand**, through an elasticity of minus **one** at the **midpoint**, to an elasticity of **zero** at **zero price/high quantity** demanded.
   - The n-shaped graph underneath shows how the **total revenue changes** as the point **moves along the demand curve** — i.e. as the price and quantity demanded change.
   - **Total revenue is maximised when PED = ±1** — the nearer a firm sets a product's price to the **mid-point** of the demand curve, the **higher** its **total revenue** will be.

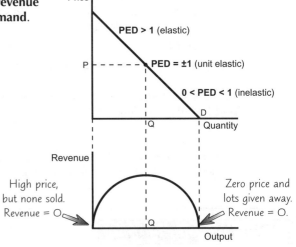

3) If a good has **elastic** demand, then:

   - A **reduction** in **price** will **increase** the firm's **total revenue**.
   - An **increase** in **price** will **reduce** the firm's **total revenue**.

   For example, a good has an **elastic** PED of -2.5. When the good's price is £5, 20 units are sold, giving a total revenue of **£100**. When **price falls** to £4, **demand rises** to 30 units and **total revenue increases** to **£120**.

4) However, if a good has **inelastic** demand, then:

   - A **reduction** in **price** will **reduce** the firm's **total revenue**.
   - An **increase** in **price** will **increase** the firm's **total revenue**.

   For example, a good has an **inelastic** PED of -0.5. When the good's price is £5, 20 units are sold, giving a total revenue of **£100**. When **price falls** to £4, **demand rises** to 22 units and **total revenue falls** to **£88**.

Uses of Elasticities of Demand

Income Elasticity of Demand is different for Normal and Inferior goods

Normal Goods

These goods have a **positive YED**. As **incomes rise, demand increases**. The size of the demand increase is dependent on the product's elasticity.

Normal goods are the most common type of good.

Income | D | Quantity

Inferior Goods

These goods have a **negative YED**. As **incomes rise, demand falls**. A rise in income will lead to the **inferior good** being **replaced** with one considered to be of **higher quality**.

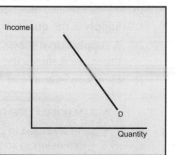

Cross Elasticities of Demand show if goods are Substitutes or Complements

1) **Substitutes** have **positive** cross elasticities of demand (XEDs). A **fall** in the **price** of **one substitute** (e.g. rice) will **reduce** the **demand** for **another** (e.g. pasta). The **closer** the substitutes, the **higher** the **positive XED**. For example, ballpoint pens and fountain pens will have a **higher XED** compared to ballpoint pens and pencils.

2) Goods that are **complements** have **negative** XEDs. An **increase** in the **price** of a good (e.g. cheese) will lead to a **reduction** in **demand** for its **complements** (e.g. chutney).

3) Goods which have a **XED of zero** are **independent goods** and **don't** directly affect the demand of each other — for example, bananas and slippers.

Knowledge of Elasticities of Demand is Useful for Firms and Governments

1) Information about **YED** can be used in **sales forecasting** — if the YED of a product and likely **changes** in **income** are known, then **sales levels** can be **predicted**. YED can also be used in **pricing policy** — a **reduction** in price for a normal good, when there's an **expected fall** in incomes, may **limit** the **expected reduction** in **demand** for the good.

2) A firm may choose to supply a **range** of goods with **various YEDs**. During a boom **demand** for a product with a **high YED** will **increase**, but demand for that product will **decrease** when the economy is in a recession. So a firm may also supply products with a **low YED** so that they can still **earn revenue** during a **recession**.

3) It's also useful for firms to know the **XEDs** of their goods because that will tell them how to **react** to **changes** in the **price** of **related products** to ensure they **maximise demand** for their products. For example, if a firm sells a product that has a close substitute and the substitute's price **drops**, they may choose to **lower** the price of their product to **reduce** the possible **fall** in demand for it.

4) It'd be very useful for governments to know how **demand** for goods might change during **booms** and **recessions** when they're setting their **policies**. For example, **demand** for **bus services** may **increase** with **falling incomes** in a recession, so a government would have to make sure that sufficient bus services were provided.

Practice Questions

Q1 List four influences on PED.

Q2 What is the PED when a firm's revenue is maximised?

Q3 Do complements have positive or negative XED?

Exam Question

Q1 A firm produces two goods: A and B. Recent market research shows that the products have a negative cross elasticity of demand.
Discuss how the firm may use this information to maximise sales. [6 marks]

Inferior? How dare you call my bespoke carrier bag raincoats inferior...

Well, who'd have thought it? If you charge too much for an elastic good you can actually reduce revenue. If firms and governments had perfect knowledge of all the different elasticities of demand then they'd be laughing. Unfortunately, though, they don't, which means there's a bit of guesswork involved and getting it wrong can lead to some pretty costly mistakes.

Supply

*Like demand, supply is a key part of the market mechanism. But whereas demand is all about what consumers are willing and able to pay for, supply is all about firms' willingness to supply goods/services at different prices. **These pages are for all boards.***

Supply of Goods or Services is Different at Different Prices

1) **Supply** is the **quantity** of a **good or service** that **producers supply** to the **market** at a **given price**, at a **particular time**.

2) A **supply curve** shows the **relationship** between **price** and **quantity supplied**. At any given point along the curve it shows the **quantity** of the good or service that would be supplied at a particular **price**.

3) Here's an example of a supply curve:

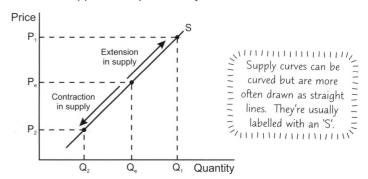

- At price P_e the quantity Q_e is supplied.
- An **increase** in price from P_e to P_1 causes an **extension** in supply — it **rises** from Q_e to Q_1.
- A **decrease** in price from P_e to P_2 causes a **contraction** in supply — it **falls** from Q_e to Q_2.
- So, **movement along** the **supply curve** is caused by **changes in price**.

Supply curves can be curved but are more often drawn as straight lines. They're usually labelled with an 'S'.

4) Supply curves usually **slope upwards**. This means that the **higher** the **price** charged for a good, the **higher** the **quantity supplied** — as shown by the diagram above.

5) **Producers** and **sellers** aim to **maximise** their **profits**. Other things being equal, the **higher** the **price** for a good or service the **higher** the **profit**. **Higher profit** provides an **incentive** to **expand production** and **increase supply**, which explains why the **quantity supplied** of a good/service **increases** as **price increases**.

6) However, increasing **supply** increases **costs**. Firms will only **produce more** if the **price increases** by **more** than the costs.

7) **Increased prices** mean that it will become **profitable** for **marginal firms** (these are firms that are just breaking even) to **supply** the **market** — increasing **market supply** levels.

Changes in Supply cause a Shift in the Supply Curve

1) A supply curve moves to the **left** (e.g. S_1) when there's a **decrease** in the **amount supplied** at **every price**.

2) A supply curve shifts to the **right** (e.g. S_2) when there's an **increase** in the **amount supplied** at **every price**.

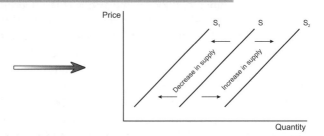

There are lots of Factors that can Cause a shift in the Supply Curve

Changes to the costs of production

An **increase** in one or more of the **costs of production** (e.g. raw materials, wages etc.) will **decrease producers' profits** and cause the supply curve to **shift** to the **left**. If a cost of production **decreased**, the **supply curve** would shift to the **right**. For example, an **increase** in the cost of **cocoa** will lead to a **reduction** in the **supply** of **chocolate**, but a **decrease** in the cost of **packaging** will lead to an **increase** in **supply**.

Improvements in technology

Technological improvements can **increase** supply as they **reduce** the **costs of production**. For example, improvements in the **energy efficiency** of commercial freezers could **reduce** the **energy costs** of a food company.

Changes to the productivity of factors of production

Increased productivity of a factor of production means that a company will get **more output** from a unit of the factor. For example, **more productive staff** will lead to an **increase** in **output** and shift the supply curve to the **right**.

Supply

Indirect taxes and subsidies

An **indirect tax** on a good effectively **increases costs** for a **producer** — this means that the **supply** is **reduced** and the supply curve is shifted to the **left**. A **subsidy** on a good encourages its production as it acts to **reduce costs** for **producers** — this leads to an **increased** level of supply and the supply curve **shifts right**.

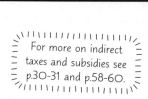
For more on indirect taxes and subsidies see p.30-31 and p.58-60.

Changes to the price of other goods

If the **price** of **one product** (A) made by a firm **increases**, then a firm may **switch production** from a **less profitable** one (B) to **increase production** of **A** and make the most of the higher price that they can get for it. This **increases** the supply of **product A**.

Number of suppliers

An **increase** in the number of **suppliers** in a market (including new firms) will **increase** supply to the market, shifting the supply curve to the **right**. A **decrease** in the **number of suppliers** will shift the curve to the **left**.

AQA ONLY

EDEXCEL ONLY

Joint Supply is when Goods or Services are Supplied Together

1) **Joint supply** is where the **production** of **one good** or **service** involves the **production** of **another** (or several others) — it's another example of when markets are **interrelated**. For example, if **crude oil** is **refined** to make **petrol** this will also increase the supply of **butane** (another product that's made as a result of this process).

2) If the **price** of a product **increases**, then **supply** of it and any **joint products** will **also increase**. For example, if the **price** of **petrol increases**, the level of drilling for oil will rise and the **supply** of **petrol** and its **joint products** will **increase**.

Producer Cartels can really affect the Level of Supply in a Market

1) A **cartel** is a group of **producers** who **agree** to **limit production** (restrict supply) and **control** the price of goods or services.

2) Cartels can have a **significant influence** over **supply levels** if their **output** is a **large enough proportion** of the total **market supply**.

Producers in a cartel can include particular firms or whole countries.

3) The **amount** of a product that **each member supplies** to the market is often determined by **output quotas** or some other **negotiated system**. Limiting the output of cartel members helps to keep **prices high**.

4) **OPEC** (**The Organisation of Petroleum Exporting Countries**) is one example of a cartel — its members include some of the **major oil exporting nations**, such as Saudi Arabia and Venezuela.

Practice Questions

Q1 What does a supply curve show?

Q2 What causes a contraction of supply?

Q3 Describe two factors that can cause a supply curve to shift.

Exam Questions

Q1 Which of the following would cause a movement along a supply curve? Explain your answer.
A) A cut in the price of the product.
B) A new entrant into the market.
C) An improvement in the technology used to make the product.
D) An increase in the costs of the raw materials used to make the product.
[4 marks]

Q2 Which of the following would most likely lead to an increase in the supply of dolls' houses? Explain your answer.
A) An increase in the cost of wood-cutting machinery.
B) The exit from the market of a major toy maker.
C) A new doll's house construction method is introduced which speeds up production by 25%.
D) An increase in the cost of glue.
[4 marks]

Personally, I've always thought Supply was a bit shifty...

Ah supply, that's just like demand but the line goes a different way... No, no, no, wait, don't be fooled into thinking it's really similar to demand — it's still important that you learn all about supply. Although learning about it should be made easier if you're well acquainted with demand, as you've got to learn about what happens when prices change and the curve shifts.

Price Elasticity of Supply

These pages cover price elasticity of supply and the factors that can affect it. Be careful not to confuse it with price elasticity of demand (p.18) — it might seem similar but there are some differences to look out for. **These pages are for all boards.**

Price Elasticity of Supply *shows how* Supply Changes *with* Price

1) **Price elasticity of supply** (**PES**) is a measure of how the **quantity supplied** of a good **responds** to a **change in its price**.

2) PES can be **calculated** using the **following formula**:

$$PES = \frac{\text{percentage change in quantity supplied}}{\text{percentage change in price}}$$

You can think of PES as the way that suppliers react (how much of a good they supply) as the price changes.

3) Here's an example calculation:

- When the **price** of a smartphone **increased** from **£449** to **£485** the **supply** of them **increased** from **15000** to **21500**.

- The **percentage change** in **quantity supplied** would be: $\frac{\text{change in supply}}{\text{original supply}} \times 100 = \frac{6500}{15000} \times 100 = \textbf{43.33\%}$

- The **percentage change** in **price** would be: $\frac{\text{change in price}}{\text{original price}} \times 100 = \frac{36}{449} \times 100 = \textbf{8\%}$

Don't forget that PES has no units — it's not a percentage.

- So **PES** $= \frac{43.33\%}{8\%} = \textbf{5.42}$

4) PES is **generally positive** since the **higher** the **price** the **greater** the **supply**.

PES *can be* Elastic, Inelastic *or* Unit Elastic

Elastic Supply: PES > 1

1) If the value of PES is **greater than 1** (**> 1**), supply of the good is **elastic**. This means a **percentage change** in **price** will cause a **larger percentage change** in **quantity supplied**.

2) The **higher the value** of PES, the **more elastic** supply is for the good.

3) In diagram 1, price increases from **£5** to **£7** and an extra **7** units are supplied, which gives an **elastic** PES of **8.75**.

$$PES = \frac{7/2 \times 100}{2/5 \times 100} = \textbf{8.75}$$

So a 1% change in price leads to an 8.75% change in supply.

4) **Perfectly elastic supply** has a PES of **± infinity** and any **fall** in **price** means that the **quantity supplied** will be reduced to **zero** — see diagram 2.

Inelastic Supply: 0 < PES < 1

1) The value of PES for an inelastic good is **between 0 and 1** (**0 < PES < 1**). This means a **percentage change** in **price** will cause a **smaller percentage change** in **quantity supplied**. The **smaller** the value of PES, the **more inelastic** supply is.

2) In diagram 3, price increases from **£2000** to **£6000** (**200%**) and only an extra **2000** units (**100% increase**) are supplied. This gives an inelastic PES of 0.5 which means for every 1% change in price there is a 0.5% change in supply.

3) **Perfectly inelastic supply** has a PES of **0** and any **change** in **price** will have **no effect** on the **quantity supplied** — see diagram 4. At any price (e.g. P_1 or P_2), the **quantity supplied** will be the **same**.

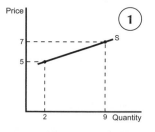

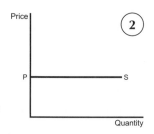

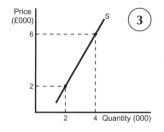

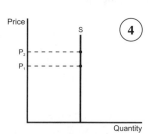

Unit Elasticity of Supply: PES = 1

1) A good has **unit elasticity** (PES = 1) if the percentage change in **quantity supplied** is **equal** to the percentage change in **price** — see diagram 5.

2) For example, a **50% increase** in price will lead to a **50% increase** in quantity supplied.

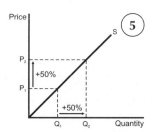

Supply of this floral outfit was low. Most people were glad about this.

Price Elasticity of Supply

A High PES is Important to Firms

1) Firms aim to **respond quickly** to **changes in price and demand**.

2) To do so they need to make their **supply** as **elastic** (i.e. responsive to price change) as possible.

3) Measures undertaken to **improve** the **elasticity** of **supply** include **flexible working patterns**, using the **latest technology** and having **spare production capacity**. For example, if a firm has spare production capacity it can quickly increase supply of a good without an increase in costs (e.g. the cost of building a new factory).

Supply is Price Inelastic in the Short Run

Over short periods of time firms can find it **difficult** to **switch production** from one good to another. This means that **supply** is likely to be **more price inelastic** in the **short run** compared to the **long run**.

SHORT RUN
- The **short run** is the **time period** when a firm's **capacity** is **fixed**, and at least one **factor of production** is **fixed**.
- **Capital** is often the factor of production that's **fixed** in the **short run** — a firm can recruit **more workers** and buy **more materials**, but it takes **time** to build additional production facilities. This means that it can be **difficult** to **increase production** in the **short run**, so supply in the short run is **relatively inelastic**.

LONG RUN
- In the **long run** all the factors of production are **variable** — so in the **long run** a firm is able to **increase** its **capacity**.
- This means that supply is **more elastic** in the long run because firms have **longer** to react to **changes** in **price** and **demand**.

The distinction between **long run** and **short run** varies with **different industries** because **production times** and levels of **capital equipment** vary between industries. For example, the **long run** for a firm that makes sandwiches will be a **shorter time** than that of a firm that builds ships — to change production levels in ship building requires **more capital equipment**, **more planning** etc. Because ships take longer to produce than sandwiches, the **supply** of ships is more **inelastic**.

There are Several Other Factors that affect PES

Agricultural products are more price inelastic in the short run than manufactured goods — plants take time to grow and livestock need nurturing over several years.

1) During periods of **unemployment** supply tends to be **more elastic** — it's **easy to attract new workers** if a firm wishes to expand.

2) **Perishable goods** (e.g. some fresh fruit and flowers) have an **inelastic supply** as they cannot be stored for very long.

3) Firms with **high stock levels** often have **elastic supply** — they're able to increase supply quickly if they want to.

4) Industries with more **mobile factors of production** (e.g. those that find it easy to expand their labour force and don't have production machinery/facilities that are difficult to relocate) tend to have **more elastic supply**. For example, industries that employ lots of unskilled workers may find it easy to increase their labour force.

Practice Questions

Q1 What is the formula used to calculate PES?

Q2 What is perfectly elastic supply?

Q3 In the short run is supply price elastic or price inelastic?

Exam Questions

Q1 It has been calculated that bananas have a price elasticity of supply (PES) in the short run of 0.62. Suggest two reasons for this inelastic short run PES. [4 marks]

Q2 Explain why a company that specialises in making hand-made furniture with a small highly skilled workforce could find it difficult to increase supply in the short run. [4 marks]

My morning exercise is a jog around the block — I call it the short run...

So, for PES, the diagrams are similar to the ones for PED (apart from the major difference of the line being a supply curve rather than a demand curve). However, remember that the one for unit elasticity is very different — it's a straight line rather than a curved one. It's important that you understand why firms are interested in PES and how time impacts on PES — it's all about the short and long run.

Market Equilibrium

Here comes a key topic. On these pages you'll cover what it means when you have a pair of axes with both a demand and a supply curve on them and what they show about a market. **These pages are for all boards.**

A *Market* is in *Equilibrium* when *Supply Equals Demand*

1) At **equilibrium**, **price** and **output** are **stable** — there's a **balance** in the market and **supply** is **equal** to **demand**. **All products** that are presented for sale are **sold** and the market is **cleared**.

2) In a **free market**, **supply** and **demand** determine the **equilibrium price** and **quantity**.

3) This **free interaction** of supply and demand is known as **market forces**.

4) The **equilibrium point** can be found at the point where the **supply curve** and **demand curve meet**. This is shown in the example below:

When a market is cleared, the amount sellers wish to sell is equal to the amount that buyers demand.

The table below shows the **supply** and **demand** for 'Teddy-for-you' at various prices.

Price (£)	Quantity demanded per fortnight	Quantity supplied per fortnight
10	7000	1000
20	6000	2000
30	5000	3000
40	4000	4000
50	3000	5000
60	2000	6000
70	1000	7000

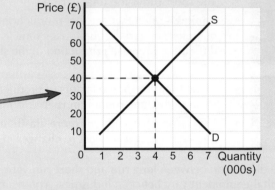

By looking at the data in this table you can see that the **equilibrium price** is **£40** — this is where the units **demanded** (4000) is **equal to** the units **supplied** (4000).

The equilibrium price and quantity are clear in the diagram above — it's at the point where the **supply** and **demand curves meet**.

5) When **supply** and **demand** aren't **equal** the market is in **disequilibrium**.

6) If there's **excess supply** or **excess demand** the market will be in **disequilibrium**.

Excess Supply and *Demand* won't exist in a *Free Market* for long

Market forces act to remove **excess supply** or **demand**.

EXCESS SUPPLY

1) **Excess supply** is when the **quantity supplied** to a market is **greater** than the **quantity demanded**.

2) If the price for 'Teddy-for-you' is set **above** the **equilibrium** (e.g. **£60**) there would be **excess supply** (a surplus) of **4000 units** (6000 supplied minus the 2000 demanded). This would cause the **price** to be **forced down**, **supply** to **contract** and **demand** to **extend** until the **equilibrium** was reached (£40 price and 4000 units supplied/demanded).

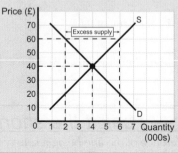

EXCESS DEMAND

1) **Excess demand** is when the **demand** for a good/service is **greater** than its **supply**.

2) If the price for 'Teddy-for-you' is set **below** the **equilibrium** (e.g. **£20**) there would be **excess demand** of **4000 units** (6000 units demanded minus 2000 supplied). This would cause the **price** to be **forced up**, **demand** to **contract** and **supply** to **extend** until the **equilibrium** was reached (again, £40 price and 4000 units supplied/demanded).

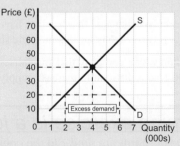

Market Equilibrium

Shifts in Demand or Supply Curves will change the Market Equilibrium

1) If the **demand curve shifts**, assuming no change in the supply curve, then this will affect supply and price in the following ways:

- If **demand increases** from D to D_1 then the **price** will **increase** from P_e to P_1 and **supply** will **extend** from Q_e to Q_1, creating a new equilibrium.
- If **demand decreases** from D to D_2 then the **price** will **fall** to P_2 and **supply** will **contract** to Q_2, again creating a new equilibrium.

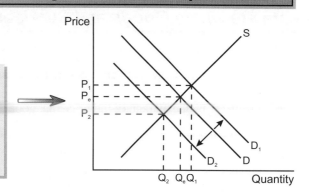

2) If the **supply curve shifts**, assuming no change in the demand curve, then this will affect demand and price in the following ways:

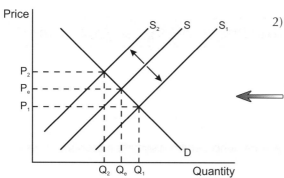

- If the **supply increases** from S to S_1 then the **price** will **fall** to P_1 and **demand** will **extend** to Q_1, creating a new equilibrium.
- If the **supply decreases** from S to S_2 then the **price** will **rise** to P_2 and **demand** will **contract** to Q_2, again creating a new equilibrium.

Elasticity will affect the Point of the New Equilibrium

1) **Price elasticity of supply** and **price elasticity of demand** influence the **size** of changes in the equilibrium price and quantity caused by supply and demand curve shifts.

2) For example, if the **demand curve** shifts to the **right** along an **elastic supply curve**, this will have a **larger effect** on **quantity** than price. The **opposite** is true for an **inelastic supply curve**.

Elasticity of PES/PED	Shifts in demand/supply curve has greater impact on:
Price **inelastic** supply or demand	Price
Price **elastic** supply or demand	Quantity

Practice Questions

Q1 When is a market in equilibrium?

Q2 What is market disequilibrium?

Q3 What is excess supply?

Exam Question

Q1 Complete the following sentence. The equilibrium point in a free market
A) is purely dependent on supply.
B) will stay the same if there's a fall in supply.
C) determines supply and demand.
D) will move with a shift in the demand curve.
Explain your answer.

[4 marks]

In my experience there's never an excess supply of cake...

...there's always a shortage. How sad. Anyway, it's important to get your head round what a market equilibrium is and how they can be shifted. Remember, disequilibrium can exist, but in free markets the price and quantity demanded (or supplied) will head back towards equilibrium levels. A key thing to remember is that equilibrium is where the supply and demand curves cross.

Price and the Allocation of Resources

Prices are crucial for determining how resources are allocated within a market. **This page is for all boards.**

Markets *are where* Goods *and* Services *are* Bought *and* Sold

1) A **market** is anywhere **buyers** and **sellers** exchange **goods** or **services**. **Competitive markets** exist under certain conditions:

   - When there are a **large number** of **buyers** (consumers) and **sellers** (producers).
   - When **no single consumer** or **producer** (or group of either) can **influence** the **allocation** of **resources** by the market, or the **price** that goods and services can be bought at.

2) In a competitive market:
   - **Consumers** aim to **maximise** their **welfare** by buying goods and services to **maintain** or **improve** their **quality of life**.
   - **Producers compete** with each other to provide consumers with what they **want**, at the **lowest possible price** — so the producers can **maximise** their **profit** by selling to the **most customers**.

Price *is the main way of* Allocating Resources *in a* Market Economy

1) The **value** at which a good or service is **exchanged** is known as its **price**.

2) Changes in the **demand** or **supply** of a good/service lead to changes in its **price** and to the **quantity bought/sold** — this is known as the **price mechanism**.

3) The price mechanism **allocates** goods and services by ensuring that **equilibrium** is achieved — prices change until **supply equals demand**. The price mechanism also **co-ordinates** the decisions of **buyers** and **sellers** — for example, how expensive something is will influence whether someone buys it.

4) The price mechanism has the following **three functions**:
   - It acts as an **incentive** to firms — **higher prices** allow firms to produce more goods/services and **encourage increased production** and **sales** by providing **higher profits**.
   - It acts as a **signalling device** — **changes** in **price** show **changes** in **supply and/or demand** and act as a **signal** to producers and consumers. For example, a price increase is a **signal** to producers that demand is high, so this will encourage them to **increase production**.
   - It acts to **ration scarce resources** — if there's **high demand** for a good/service and its supply is **limited**, then the price will be **high**. Supply of the good will be **restricted** to those that can afford to pay a **high price** for it. The **opposite** applies for goods that are in **low demand** but in **high supply** — they will have a **low price** and **many** will be sold.

5) The price mechanism is also used to **allocate** the **resources used** to **produce goods** and **services**.

   For example: if **demand** for **curtains increases**, the market will allocate, through the price mechanism, **more curtains** to **consumers**, **more labour** (e.g. seamstresses) for making curtains, and **more commodities** (e.g. cotton) to **curtain manufacturers** for producing curtains.

Allocative Efficiency *is when supply* Equals *demand*

OCR ONLY

1) In a **perfectly competitive market**, all resources are **efficiently allocated**. When allocative efficiency exists, the price of a good is equal to the price that consumers are happy to pay for it.

2) To achieve **allocative efficiency** resources need to be allocated in a way that **maximises consumer satisfaction**. This means that the **price** of a good or service should **match** the **consumer's valuation** of it — so the **quantity supplied** of the good should be **equal** to the **quantity demanded** (supply = demand).

Practice Questions

Q1 What is meant by the term 'price'?

Exam Question

Q1 Explain how prices can act as an incentive to firms. [4 marks]

So producers compete with low prices? Pretty sure some don't really try...

Prices are really important for allocating resources in a market — they determine the levels of supply and demand for different goods and services. Remember, you only need to know about allocative efficiency if you're doing the OCR exam.

Consumer and Producer Surplus

The consumer and producer surplus are about the size of the benefit to consumers and producers from a given price level. When prices change, consumer and producer surpluses change. **This topic is for Edexcel and OCR.**

Consumer and *Producer Surpluses* are above and below the *Equilibrium Price*

Consumer Surplus

1) Everyone has **different** tastes, incomes and views on how much they're prepared to pay for a good/service.

2) When a consumer **pays less** for a good than the amount that they're **prepared** to **pay** for it, this **amount** of **money** is known as the **consumer surplus**. For example, if someone was prepared to pay £10 for a good and bought it for £8 then there would be a consumer surplus of **£2**.

3) So, the **consumer surplus** is the **difference** between the **price** that a consumer is **willing** to pay for a good or service and the **price** that they **actually pay** (the equilibrium price).

Producer Surplus

1) Different producers have **different** costs when making goods/services.

2) If a producer **receives more** for a product or service than the **price** they're **willing** to **accept**, the **extra earnings** are known as the **producer surplus**. For example, if the equilibrium price of a good is £15 but a supplier would be happy to sell for £10 then the producer surplus would be **£5**.

3) So, the **producer surplus** is the **difference** between the **price** that a **producer** is **willing** to supply a good or service at and the **price** that they **actually receive** for it (the equilibrium price).

The consumer and producer surplus can be shown on a diagram:

- **Consumer surplus** — the area **below** the demand curve and **above** the equilibrium price line.
- **Producer surplus** — the area **above** the supply curve and **below** the equilibrium price line.

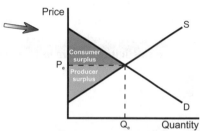

Changes in *Supply* and *Demand* affect *Consumer* and *Producer Surplus*

1) Anything that causes a **shift** in the **supply** or **demand curve** can lead to a **change** in the **price** of a good.

2) A change in price will bring a good **closer to**, or **further away from**, the **amount** the **buyer** was **willing** to **pay** or the **supplier** was **willing** to **sell** for — and this will **change** the **consumer** and **producer surpluses**.

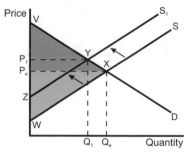

A shift in the **supply curve** from **S** to **S₁** means the **price** will **increase** from **Pₑ** to **P₁** and **quantity** will **decrease** from **Qₑ** to **Q₁**. The **consumer surplus** changes from **VPₑX** to **VP₁Y** and the **producer surplus** changes from **PₑWX** to **P₁ZY**.

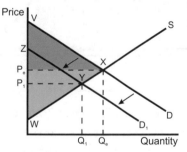

A shift in the **demand curve** from **D** to **D₁** means the **price** and **quantity** will **decrease** from **Pₑ** to **P₁** and **Qₑ** to **Q₁** respectively. The **consumer surplus** changes from **VPₑX** to **ZP₁Y** and the **producer surplus** changes from **PₑWX** to **P₁WY**.

Practice Questions

Q1 What is consumer surplus?

Q2 What is producer surplus?

Sir Plus — King Arthur's trusty accountant...

Consumer and producer surplus — it's all about you buying stuff for less than you're prepared to and producers selling stuff for more than they need to in order to cover their costs. When you find a bargain you have a big consumer surplus, which is awesome.

Subsidies and Indirect Taxes

Subsidies and indirect taxes result in gains or losses for producers and consumers. **This topic is for Edexcel only.**

Subsidies *and* Indirect Taxes *can affect* Consumers *and* Producers

1) Governments sometimes provide **subsidies** to **encourage demand** for a good (e.g. energy-saving home insulation). A subsidy is money paid by the government to the **producer** of a good to make it **cheaper** than it would be otherwise.

2) Governments can also place a **tax** on a good (these are called **indirect taxes**) to **reduce** the **demand** for it (e.g. cigarettes and alcohol). The presence of a tax on a good aims to **discourage** people from buying it as the tax **raises** its **market price**.

3) **Taxes** and **subsidies** lead to **shifts** in the **supply curves** of **goods/services**, which cause **prices to change**.

4) The changes in price lead to an **extension** or **contraction** in **demand**.

Government subsidies for make-up increased Coco's demand.

The Benefit *of* Subsidies *is divided between* Consumers *and* Producers

1) Subsidies encourage **increased production** and a **fall** in **price**, which leads to an **increase in demand**. So, a subsidy **shifts** the **supply curve** to the **right**.

2) The **benefit** of a subsidy is received partly by the **producer** and partly by the **consumer**.

3) The relative amounts gained by producers (**producer gain**) and consumers (**consumer gain**) are dependent on the **price elasticities** of **demand** and **supply**. Here are a couple of examples:

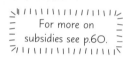

For more on subsidies see p.60.

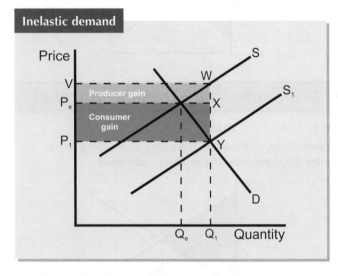

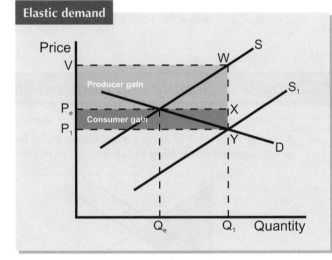

- The market is in **equilibrium** at P_e and Q_e **before** the subsidy is granted.
- The subsidy causes the supply curve to **shift** to S_1, the price to fall to P_1 and the quantity to increase to Q_1.
- The **cost** of the **subsidy** to the **government** is given by P_1VWY (the entire shaded-in box). This subsidy can be split into two parts: the **consumer gain** and the **producer gain**.

> The **consumer gain** is the fall in price from P_e **to** P_1 — they gain by **paying less** for the good than they would have if there was no subsidy (this would be P_e). The area of the consumer gain is P_1P_eXY (dark purple).

> The **producer gain** is equal to the difference between **V and** P_e — they gain by receiving **extra revenue** from the government that they can keep. The area of the producer gain is P_eVWX (light purple).

4) By comparing the two diagrams above it's clear that:
- The **more inelastic** the **demand** curve is, the **greater** the **consumer's gain** is from the subsidy.
- The **more elastic** the **demand** curve, the **greater** the **producer's gain** is from the subsidy.

Subsidies and Indirect Taxes

Indirect Taxes also affect both *Consumers* and *Producers*

1) Taxes **increase** the **price** of a good, which leads to a **reduction** in **demand**.
   Taxation **shifts** the **supply curve** to the **left**.

2) As with subsidies, taxation has an impact on both the **producer** and the **consumer** of a good.
   The **relative proportion** borne by producers and consumers is again **dependent** on
   the **price elasticities** of **demand** and **supply**. Here are a couple of examples:

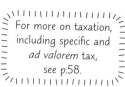

For more on taxation, including specific and *ad valorem* tax, see p.58.

Inelastic demand

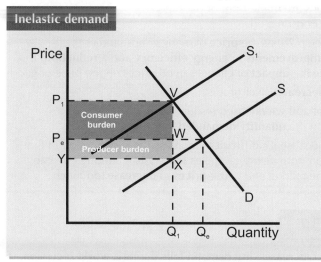

Elastic demand

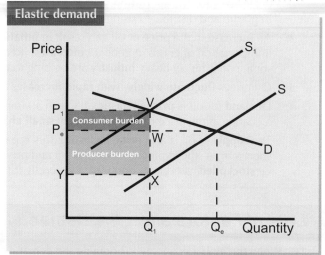

- With **no taxation** the market is in **equilibrium** at P_e and Q_e.
- The tax causes the supply curve to shift to S_1, the price to increase to P_1 and the quantity to decrease to Q_1.
- The **revenue** for the **government** generated by the **tax** is given by P_1YXV (the entire shaded-in box).
  This tax can be split into two parts: the **consumer burden** and the **producer burden**.

> The **consumer burden** is the rise in price from P_e to P_1 — they lose out by **paying more** for the good than if the tax wasn't in place (this would be P_e). The area of the consumer burden is P_1P_eWV (dark purple).

> The **producer burden** is equal to the difference between Y and P_e — they lose out by paying some of the revenue to the government. The area of the producer burden is P_eYXW (light purple).

3) By comparing the two diagrams above it's clear that:
   - The more **inelastic** the **demand curve**, the **greater** the **tax burden** for the **consumer**.
   - The more **elastic** the **demand curve**, the **greater** the **tax burden** for the **producer**.

Practice Questions

Q1 A subsidy is introduced for a good with elastic demand.
   Will the producer or consumer gain be larger?

Exam Questions

Q1 The diagram on the right shows the granting of a subsidy on a good.
   Which of the following areas represents the producer gain? Explain your answer.
   A) EGIK
   B) GOHL
   C) FGIJ
   D) EFJK

[4 marks]

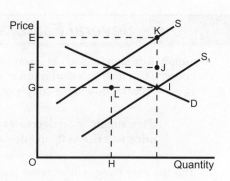

Q2 If a government places a tax on a product, explain the effect it will have on the product's price and demand. [8 marks]

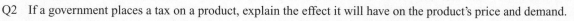

Indirect taxis — a burden on your holiday money...

Well, I bet you're glad you're doing the Edexcel exam, you lucky people, otherwise you'd miss out on all of this lovely stuff.
Learn how to draw the diagrams for subsidies and taxes and which way round the producer and consumer gain/burden goes.

Demand and Supply — Oil

A lot of Section 2 is theoretical, but now here are some pages that apply the theory to some real-world markets. The first market is the market for oil, which is a very important global resource. **Pages 32-33 are for AQA and Edexcel, but students of all boards will find pages 32-42 useful as they provide examples of how demand and supply is applied in real markets.**

The **Price** of **Oil** is **Very Important** for an **Economy**

1) Oil is used in the **production** of a huge variety of different **goods** and it's also **used** extensively for **transportation**. For example, many goods are made from or packaged in plastic and distributed using modes of transport that consume oil.

2) An **increase** in the **price** of oil can result in **inflation** (see p.74) as the **price** of many goods (and of the transportation of goods in general) **increases**. Recent **improvements** in **energy efficiency** and a **reduction**, in some countries, in **heavy industry** are helping to **reduce** the **impact** of changes in oil prices on the price of goods.

3) Oil prices **fluctuate widely**, with **rapid increases** and **decreases** over time.

4) **Demand** for oil is **price inelastic**. It's such an important and widely used resource that a change in the price causes a relatively **small change** in the **quantity demanded**.

5) The **supply** of oil is also **price inelastic**. This is partly because it's **difficult** to increase the supply of oil in the short term — the exploration for new oil and production from new wells takes **time**. Also, although oil can be **stockpiled**, producers don't want to supply lots to the market and cause **prices** to **decrease** too much.

Lots of **Factors** affect the **Demand** for **Oil**

1) When the global economy is **booming** the **demand** for oil **increases**, but **demand falls** during a **world recession**. This is because oil is used in **most economic activity**, so its demand increases during booms and decreases during recessions.

2) **Speculators** can affect the demand for oil because they buy and sell oil in the hope of making a **profit** from **fluctuations** in its **price**. For example, they could buy oil at **$100** per barrel **today** with the **hope** of selling it **next week** when they predict the price will have risen to **$120** per barrel — however, prices can fall and speculators can make large losses.

3) The **value** of the **US dollar** can affect the demand for oil. This is important because **oil** is priced in **US dollars** — if the **value** of the dollar is **low** then **more oil** can be **purchased** by speculators holding **other currencies**.

4) If the **demand** for **products made** from **crude oil** (e.g. plastics) **increases** then the **derived demand** for oil **increases** (see p.17 for more about derived demand).

5) The **attractiveness** of **buying oil substitutes**, e.g. biofuel, impacts demand for oil. As substitutes to oil become **cheaper**, **more reliable** and **more readily available**, this has a **negative impact** on **demand** for oil.

> The growth of emerging economies is increasing the demand for oil. For example, countries such as China and India are becoming increasingly large oil consumers.

6) **Weather conditions** in major oil using countries can affect oil demand. For example, in cold conditions **more oil** is needed for **heating**.

7) As **living standards improve** then the **demand** for oil **increases** — this can be linked to an **increased consumption** of goods and services. Many of these goods/services will use oil in their manufacture and delivery. For example, people with a high income can afford to own a large house and several cars — this involves **higher oil consumption** than people with small houses who don't own a car.

There are **Several Factors** affecting the **Supply** of **Oil** in the **Short Run**

1) **Supply-side shocks**, such as a **war** in a major oil producing country, can lead to a **disruption** of **oil supplies**. This would cause a **contraction** in the **supply of oil** as shown on the diagram.

> If the **supply** of oil **decreases** from S to S_1 then the **price will rise** to P_1 and **demand** will **contract** to Q_1.

2) This price increase will **increase costs** to firms where oil is an important factor of production. These firms might **increase prices** to maintain their **profits** and this could have a knock-on effect on **demand** (it would **decrease**).

3) The **Organisation of Petroleum Exporting Countries (OPEC)** also has a **major influence** on the world **supply** of oil (see p.23 for more). This means that the cartel can exert **significant control** over the **price** of oil.

4) OPEC members can agree to **cut** oil production levels (reduce supply), which causes oil **prices** to **increase**. Alternatively they can **increase production** levels (increase supply) to cause oil **prices** to **decrease**.

Demand and Supply — Oil

Different Factors affect the Supply of Oil in the Long Run

1) The **size** of remaining **oil reserves** — the **bigger** the remaining oil reserves, the **higher** the **supply** of oil will be in the **long run**. The estimates of the size of world oil reserves vary.

2) The **cost** of **extracting oil** from reserves — some reserves are **too expensive** to extract oil from at the moment, but if **demand** and **oil prices increase** then it might become **worth extracting** this harder to reach oil. Also an increase in price and demand could cause an **increase** in the **exploration** for new oil reserves.

3) The **efficiency** and **cost** of **technology** used in **exploiting** and **refining** the **oil** — the **cheaper** and **more efficient** the technology, the **lower** the cost of the oil due to the increased level of supply.

Michelle couldn't hide her excitement about the discovery of a new oil well.

Examples of changes to Demand and Supply of Oil

A large increase in the demand for oil

1) The **growth** of **emerging economies** is driving an **increased global demand** for oil.

2) This increase in demand can be shown on a diagram.
   - The **increase** in **demand** shifts the **demand curve** to the **right**.
   - The increase in demand can lead to an **increase** in **supply**.

3) Oil producers (e.g. OPEC) might **restrict** the use of **reserves** to keep the **price high**.

4) The **signalling effect** of the **price increase** can encourage an **increase** in **production**.

5) There will be a **delay** before this **additional supply** is **available** on the market.

6) **Demand** for oil in the **short run** is **price inelastic** — so this, with the inelastic supply curve, will lead to a large **increase** in price.

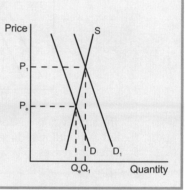

An expansion of fracking for oil

1) An **increase** in the scale of **fracking** activities (extraction of shale oil and gas) could lead to a **large increase** in the **supply** of oil.

2) This increase in supply can be shown on a diagram.
   - The **increase** in **supply** shifts the **supply curve** to the **right**. This increases output and causes the price to fall.
   - The **inelasticities** of supply and demand would lead to a **larger reduction** in **price** than the **increase** in **quantity**.

3) However, shale oil is **not a direct substitute** for **crude oil**, so the increase in its availability may not have a major effect on global oil prices.

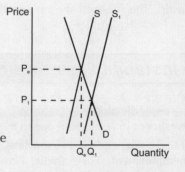

Practice Questions

Q1 Is the price elasticity of demand for oil elastic or inelastic?

Q2 Give two factors that affect demand for oil.

Q3 What factors affect the supply of oil in the long run?

Exam Question

Q1 Biofuel is a substitute for crude-oil-derived fuels and it's marketed in many countries as an alternative to diesel. How would a large subsidy granted to UK biofuel suppliers affect the demand for crude oil? [12 marks]

Crude oil — it tells the most inappropriate jokes...

In the exam you'll get extracts about different markets and you'll need to use the theory that you've learnt about demand and supply to explain what happens in them. If you learn the factors that affect the demand and supply of oil, then you'll have no trouble if you're asked about the market for oil. Remember, factors affecting supply can be split into short run and long run factors.

Demand and Supply — Agriculture

Many agricultural products (e.g. rice and wheat) suffer from price instability — the reasons for this can be explained using knowledge of supply and demand. **These pages are for AQA and Edexcel.**

Agricultural Products display short run Price Instability

1) **Supply** of agricultural products can be affected by **disease** and **weather** — both of which can be **unpredictable**.

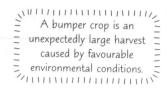
A bumper crop is an unexpectedly large harvest caused by favourable environmental conditions.

2) If **supply** is **reduced** then the price mechanism will **force** the **price up**. The opposite happens when there's an **increased level** of **supply** (e.g. when weather conditions are favourable and there's a bumper crop). These two situations are demonstrated in the diagrams below:

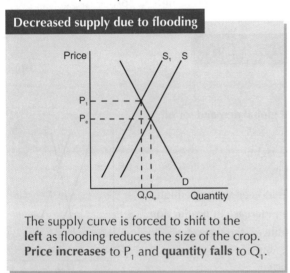

Decreased supply due to flooding

The supply curve is forced to shift to the **left** as flooding reduces the size of the crop. **Price increases** to P_1 and **quantity falls** to Q_1.

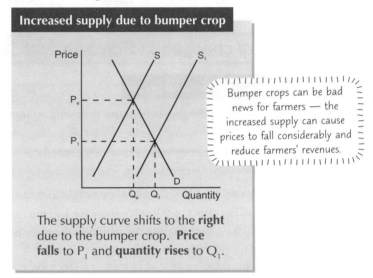

Increased supply due to bumper crop

The supply curve shifts to the **right** due to the bumper crop. **Price falls** to P_1 and **quantity rises** to Q_1.

Bumper crops can be bad news for farmers — the increased supply can cause prices to fall considerably and reduce farmers' revenues.

3) Agricultural products on the whole have **inelastic** price elasticities of **demand** (because food is a necessity) and **supply** (because, for example, it's difficult to store agricultural products).

4) **Price instability** can be a feature of markets for agricultural products because the **demand** for these products is fairly **price inelastic**. This means that even a **small increase** or **decrease** in the quantity supplied can have a **large impact** on **price**.

Price Instability has several effects

1) The **unpredictability** in the supply of agricultural products can reduce or prevent **investment** in agriculture due to the **uncertainties** about **returns** on any investment.

2) Countries **dependent** on **exporting** agricultural products can have periods of **low income** and **high unemployment**. For example, a country will receive **export revenue** after crops are harvested, but at other times of the year the revenue will be **much less**. Also, **workers employed** to harvest a crop are **only needed** when it's ready to be harvested. After this period they're **not needed** and will be made **redundant** (this is known as **seasonal unemployment**, see p.99 for more on this).

3) Buying food is a major part of people's monthly expenditure. When **food prices rise**, people become **worse off**. This has more of an impact on people on a **low** or **fixed income**.

4) Higher food prices can also have a **negative impact** on the economy as a whole. Increased prices leave **less income** to spend on other goods, which can lead to a **recession**.

Changes in Income have little impact on Demand for Agricultural Products

1) **Demand** for agricultural products is generally **income inelastic**. For example, as your income changes, your demand for food products isn't likely to change that much — you still need to buy enough food to survive.

2) **Increases** in **income** can lead to **changes** in the **quality** of agricultural products **demanded**. For example, consumers might switch to steak from mince or from concentrated fruit juice to freshly-squeezed juices.

Demand and Supply — Agriculture

Long Run Prices for Agricultural Products are Declining

1) Factors that affect the **long run supply** of agricultural products include **technological change**, the **supply of good quality land** and **changes to the climate** (e.g. caused by global warming).

> For example, **technological improvements** may lead to an **increase** in the **supply** of **corn** as there will be an **increase** in the **efficiency of corn production**. This would cause the **supply curve** to **shift** to the **right**, and result in a **fall in price**.

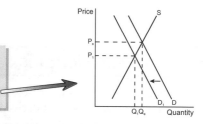

2) Factors that affect the **long run demand** for agricultural products include **changing incomes** and **consumer preferences**.

> For example, the **demand** for **meat** may **fall** in the long run because of an **increase** in the number of people choosing a **vegetarian diet**. This would result in the **demand curve** shifting to the **left** and a **fall in price**.

Buffer Stocks also affect the Price of Agricultural Products

1) **Buffer stocks** involve a government (or its agency) setting a **minimum** and **maximum price** for a product (e.g. wheat). The aim of buffer stocks is to **stabilise** market prices for particular products and **prevent shortages**.

See p.62 for more about buffer stocks.

2) If the price mechanism causes the price of the product to go **outside** of the **agreed price range** (i.e. too high or too low), then the government will **buy** or **sell** the product until the **price** returns to the **agreed range**.

> For example, if the **price falls too low**, the government will **buy** some of the product in order to **raise** the **price** — this shifts the **demand curve** to the **right** and restores the price to an acceptable level. This intervention stops prices plummeting in times of **high levels** of supply (e.g. after a bumper crop).

"No, no, I said buffer."

3) Buffer stocks of a product are **stored** and **sold** if the **price** rises **above** the **maximum allowed price**. This will **increase** the **supply** and **shift** the **supply curve** to the **right** — lowering the price.

4) A downside of buffer stock schemes is that they can be **difficult** to manage **effectively** and can be **expensive**.

Practice Questions

Q1 What are the causes of short run price instability for agricultural products?
Q2 What are the effects of short run price instability for agricultural products?
Q3 Are agricultural products income elastic?
Q4 Give two reasons for the long run downwards trend in agricultural prices.

Exam Question

Q1 Recent reports have suggested that UK consumers must expect continuing increases in the price of food. Reasons for this rise include an increasing world population and rising incomes in the developing world (in particular in China and India).
Using a diagram, explain how a rise in global demand for rice has caused prices to rise. [6 marks]

Here a moo, there a moo, everywhere a moo moo...

More about how supply and demand affect a market, in this case the market for agricultural products. Price instability is a key concept here, so make sure you understand what this means. Increasing prices for agricultural products is bad news for everyone really, as we all consume agricultural products as food. If all food prices rocketed tomorrow we'd have to pay them. Sad times.

Demand and Supply — Labour

Labour is an important resource. Firms need to employ workers in order to produce goods and deliver services. There are several different factors that affect the supply and demand for workers. **These pages are for Edexcel.**

Labour Markets are affected by Supply and Demand

1) In a labour market the **wage rate** of workers is **determined** by **demand** and **supply**. **Demand** comes from **firms**, who **need workers**, and **supply** comes from the **country's population** of **working age**.

2) There are **many labour markets**. For example, there are markets for different **professions** such as accountants, engineers, models, nurses and teachers.

The Demand for Labour is a Derived Demand

1) If the **demand** for a product increases, then **demand** for **workers** to make that product **increases too** — so the demand for labour is a **derived demand** (see p.17 for more about derived demand).

2) When an economy is **expanding** the total demand for labour **increases**.

3) Increases in demand **raise** the wage rate (increases in supply **lower** it).

4) For example, the diagrams below show how an **increase** in **demand** for **new cars** leads to an **increase** in the **demand** for **car production workers**.

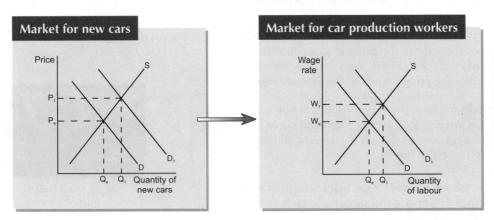

The **increased demand** for car production workers will mean that the **wage rate** of car production workers will **rise** to W_1 and the **number** of **workers** employed will **increase** to Q_1.

There are Several Factors influencing the Demand for Labour

1) The level of **demand** for a product will determine the **demand** for the **labour** that produces it.

2) A **rise** in the **wage rate** could lead to a **contraction** in demand for labour — firms may reduce their demand for labour if it costs more to pay each worker. But increasing wage rates can also **increase** the demand for labour — the increase in wage rates could lead to increased demand for goods and services, as employees have more income to spend, and this could increase **derived demand** for labour.

3) An **increase** in the **other costs** of employing labour (i.e. costs that aren't wages) will lead to a **reduction** in the number of workers demanded — e.g. the cost of employers' National Insurance contributions.

4) If it's **easy** for employers to **recruit** and **lay off staff**, this might stimulate **increased** demand for labour.

5) An **increase** in the **productivity** of a workforce may encourage a company to recruit more staff to maximise output, **increasing** the demand for labour.

6) An **increase** in the **cost** of a **substitute** factor of production (e.g. a machine used for production instead of a worker) would **increase** the demand for labour.

7) An **increase** in the **cost** of a **complementary** factor of production (e.g. tools used by a worker in production) would **reduce** the demand for labour.

8) The **greater** the **elasticity** of **demand** for labour, the **greater** the **fall** in the demand for labour caused by an **increase** in the **wage rate**.

The elasticity of demand for labour is a measure of how much the demand for labour changes with a change in the wage rate.

Demand and Supply — Labour

There are also **Several Factors** influencing the **Supply** of **Labour**

1) The **higher** the **wage rate**, the **greater** the supply of labour — as wage rates increase people are **more willing** to work.

2) The **greater** the **price elasticity** of supply of labour, the **greater** the impact of a **wage rate change** on the supply of labour.

3) The ability to **improve earnings** through things like bonus schemes or overtime will **increase** the supply of labour, as will improvements in the **benefits** of working, such as pensions or health insurance.

The supply of labour to an individual firm will also be affected by factors such as location, reputation and job security.

4) **Government regulations** (rules imposed by the government) that **improve** an employee's position, such as the National Minimum Wage (see below) or Health and Safety at Work regulations, **increase** the supply of labour. However, other government regulations may have the opposite effect — for example, the Working Time Directive **limits** the supply of labour per employee by restricting the number of hours they're allowed to work per week.

5) A **reduction** in **income tax** or **unemployment benefits** encourages more people to work and **increases** the supply of labour.

6) **Trade union** activities to **improve working conditions** and **increase wage rates** will **increase** the supply of labour.

7) The supply of labour might be increased by encouraging more **immigration**, **raising** the **retirement age** or increasing a country's **birth rate**. Making it **easier** for **parents** to work (for example, by making childcare more affordable) may also **increase** the supply of labour.

The **National Minimum Wage (NMW)**

1) The NMW sets a legal **minimum hourly rate of pay** for different age groups.

2) Using supply and demand diagrams it could be argued that **increasing the wage rate** would lead to a **contraction** in **demand** for **labour**.

- Introducing a minimum wage would **raise** the **wage rate** from W_e to **NMW**. This would cause the supply of labour to increase from Q_e to Q_s and demand to fall from Q_e to Q_d.

- This could cause unemployment of Q_s to Q_d because there's an **excess supply of labour**.

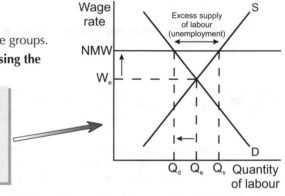

3) An **increase** in **wage rates** may have knock-on effects which help to **increase** demand for labour (see previous page).

4) In addition, an increase in wages might **increase** the **motivation of workers** and make them **more productive**. It can also act as an **incentive** for people to work and help **reduce** the **poverty** of those who gain from the increase in wages.

5) On the other hand, an NMW could **increase unemployment** if firms find it too expensive to employ staff. Also, the NMW might **not** act to **reduce poverty** as many of the poorest people don't work (e.g. because they're too old or sick).

Practice Questions

Q1 What happens to the demand for workers if the demand for the product they make increases?

Q2 Give two factors that affect the demand for labour and two different factors that affect the supply of labour.

Exam Question

Q1 A firm makes toys. Which one of the following situations is most likely to increase the firm's demand for labour? Explain your answer.
   A) New government legislation that requires new safety equipment for every worker.
   B) A decrease in demand for the firm's products.
   C) An increase in the productivity of the workforce.
   D) The firm increasing the benefits given to its workers. [4 marks]

The supply of labour — very important for midwives...

The demand for labour is a good example of derived demand — if people demand more of a good or service this is going to mean that there's an increase in the demand for people that produce it. There are lots of factors affecting the demand and supply of labour, but it's not too hard to come up with things that would encourage people to work and firms to hire more staff.

Demand and Supply — Housing

*The housing market is really important for an economy — there's always lots of demand for places to live and it's important to have a sufficient supply of housing in order for an economy to be successful. **This page is for AQA.***

Buying a House is an Investment

1) Houses can **rise** in value **over time** and they're seen as an **investment** — it's possible to invest in houses and make a **return** on the investment in the future.

2) However, a **fall** in house prices can result in **negative equity** — where the value of a property's **mortgage** is **greater** than the property's **market value**. This is **bad** for **home owners** — what they sell their house for won't pay off the amount they owe on it (the remainder of the mortgage). Unless they can pay off the remainder of their mortgage they can't move house.

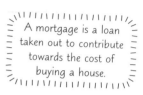
A mortgage is a loan taken out to contribute towards the cost of buying a house.

The Supply of Houses is the variety of houses available at a given time

1) The supply of houses is made up of **new build** and **pre-owned** houses that are available for a range of prices.

2) The supply of **new build houses** is partially dependent on the **costs** of building them (including labour, materials, land, and legal and planning costs). The supply also depends on the **number** and **size** of **building firms** and any **government policies** that encourage (or discourage) building new houses.

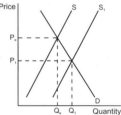

- An **increase** in the number of **new houses** built should lead to a **fall** in the **price** of houses. This is shown in the diagram on the right.

- The **supply curve** will shift to the **right**, leading to **more houses** being supplied at each price, a **fall** in the **equilibrium price** and a **rise** in the **equilibrium quantity**.

The Price of Housing is determined mainly by Demand Factors

1) The **state** of the **economy** has a big impact on the housing market — in areas of **high unemployment** houses have **lower prices** and **lower demand** (e.g. in some parts of north east England), but areas with **low unemployment** tend to have **high demand** and **high house prices** (e.g. parts of south east England).

2) **Economic growth**, high levels of **consumer confidence** and high **living standards** increase demand for housing.

3) The **substitute** for buying a house is **renting** one. A **fall** in the **cost** of renting may **decrease** the **demand** to **buy houses**, but falling rents could **reduce** the **supply** of properties for rent if landlords are **unwilling** to offer low rents.

4) Most properties are bought using a **mortgage**, so if, for example, **interest rates rise**, the cost of a **mortgage** will increase and **reduce** the **demand** for house purchases.

Short Run PED and PES for housing are Inelastic

1) There are **no close substitutes** for housing. This means the price elasticity of demand is **inelastic** — so a **rise** in **price** causes a **smaller reduction** in **demand**.

2) The price elasticity of supply is **inelastic** too. The **supply** of houses **can't** be quickly increased because it takes **time** to build new houses. Supply can also be **restricted** by the availability of **building materials**, **construction workers** and **suitable land**, and by **government regulations**.

3) Because supply can't increase much in the **short run**, an increase in demand can make **prices rise sharply**.

Dave was shocked to discover his builder's idea of 'minor refurbishment'.

House Prices have many Knock-on Effects

1) If house prices **rise** and lots of houses are bought and sold, then this might create more jobs in the **construction industry**.

2) **Higher** house prices **increase** the value of **people's assets** and can **increase consumer confidence** — this confidence can **encourage spending** and increase **investment**.

3) **Increased** house **sales encourage spending** on furniture, decorating and other household goods.

Demand and Supply — Metals

Some metals attract a high price — an example is copper. Demand for copper is high because of its wide variety of applications, which include its use for wiring and in electrical circuitry. **This page is for AQA and Edexcel.**

Copper has an Inelastic Supply in the Short Run

1) The **extraction** of copper (by mining) has **high fixed costs**, and the **development** of **new mines** takes a **long time** — so **short run supply** is **inelastic**.

2) **Demand** for copper is **inelastic** as there are **few** close substitutes available.

> If **demand** for copper **rises**, the **demand curve** will **shift right** from D to D_1, stocks will be depleted in an attempt to meet the demand (the quantity supplied will rise to Q_1) and the **price** will **rise considerably** (to P_1) because of **price inelastic demand** and **supply**.

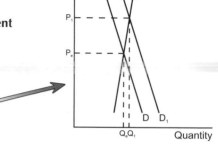

Effects of Increasing Demand for Copper

1) Copper has **many different applications**, including electronics, plumbing (e.g. copper pipes) and industrial machinery.

2) A lot of the demand for copper is **derived demand**. If demand for a product that uses copper **increases**, then demand for copper will **also increase**.

3) **Increasing copper prices** will have wider implications, such as:

- The **demand** for **scrap copper** will **increase**.
- The **demand** for **substitutes** (e.g. aluminium and plastics) will also **increase**.
- There will be an **increased effort** to find **new supplies** of copper, especially if the price is expected to remain high, as this gives companies an incentive to seek new sources of copper so they can supply it for a high price.

China is the World's Major Producer of Rare Earth Metals

1) Rare earth metals (e.g. yttrium) are used in many everyday electronic products. China currently dominates the **extraction** and **processing** of these metals — it provides **over 80%** of the world's supply.

2) The Chinese government has **restricted** its **export** of these metals — this reduction in supply has led to an **increase** in their **prices**, and therefore an **increase** in the **costs of production** in other countries of products they're used to make. However, recently these export restrictions have started to be **reduced** after complaints from other countries that they were unfair.

3) China's domination of the market for rare earth metals has meant that it could **sell** them to the rest of the world at a **high price**. It's also meant that it could keep **prices** of the metals within China **low**, which **benefits Chinese manufacturers** who are able to produce goods that use these metals **cheaper** than **international competitors**.

Practice Questions

Q1 Give three factors which influence the demand for housing.

Q2 Is the supply of housing in the short run price elastic?

Q3 If copper prices rise what will be the impact on the price of copper substitutes?

Q4 If the prices of the rare earth metals fall what will be the impact on the prices of electronic products?

Exam Questions

Q1 Discuss reasons why average house prices might vary between two areas of a country. [8 marks]

Q2 The market for an expensive metal is dominated by two suppliers: country A and country B.
The supply from country A is declining as reserves of the metal run out.
Use a diagram to describe the effect of this decline in supply on the price of the metal. [6 marks]

Useless CGP fact #1374 — a rise in crime will increase copper demand...

Hmm, your demand for better jokes is probably pretty high now too. So, here are two very different markets, but in the end it all comes down to how the market forces act. One very important thing you should learn is how important price elasticity of demand and supply are in determining price and output levels. Look back at earlier parts of the section for a reminder if anything isn't clear.

Demand and Supply — Health Care

The National Health Service (NHS) is a major provider of health care as well as a major employer in the UK.
This page will cover how the NHS affects the market for health care provision in the UK. ***This page is for AQA.***

The NHS is the Main Provider of Health Care in the UK

1) Private health care is available in the UK, but the **largest** health care provider is the **publicly-funded NHS**.

2) A lot of the health care provided by the NHS is **free** at the **point of delivery**. This means that patients don't pay for treatments when they receive them — they're paid for by the government (which funds the NHS from taxes).

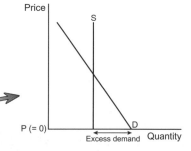

3) Free health care creates **excess demand**:

   - The **supply curve** for free health care is **vertical** — it's **perfectly inelastic**.
   - There's no price charged for the health care so **P** is equal to **zero**.
   - Price being zero leads to **demand being greater than supply**, causing an **excess demand** (a **shortage**).

4) The **zero price** (at point of delivery) means that the **price mechanism** can't act to **ration resources** or as a **signalling device**. If the market price was charged for treatments, this could massively **reduce demand** as many medical treatments are **expensive**.

5) However, the **excess demand** for free health care can be **managed** by **rationing out** the available health care. One way of doing this is to use **waiting lists**.

Supply of Health Care is Not Sufficient to meet the Growing Demand

1) **Growth** in **demand** for health care is **increasing** at a **greater rate** than **growth** in **supply**.

2) There are several reasons that contribute to the **shortage of health care** provided by the **NHS**. These include:

   - **People's expectations** of health care have **increased** — people expect to be treated for **more problems** as their **standard of living** improves. For example, some people expect that the NHS should offer laser eye surgery to anyone who has poor eyesight, but the NHS only offers this treatment to people who would develop severe problems (e.g. blindness) without the surgery.
   - **Advances in medicine** (e.g. improvements in techniques and medical technology) that allow **more conditions** to be treated and be treated **more effectively** also act to **increase demand**. For example, when improvements are made in fertility treatment, people expect them to be made available.
   - There's a **limited supply** of health care services in the UK — there are **insufficient trained staff** (doctors, physiotherapists, etc.) and **insufficient hospitals** to meet the demands of the population. Also, supply can be limited if the government **chooses** to **reduce** its **spending** on the NHS in favour of something else (e.g. education or defence).
   - The **ageing population** of the UK is also **increasing** the **demands** on the NHS — generally, the older a person is, the greater their use of the NHS.

There are Other Factors to consider when looking at the Health Care Market

1) Consumers **don't** have **perfect information** about health care, i.e. they don't fully understand what treatment is in their best interest to have — this is known as **asymmetric information** (see p.55).

2) Asymmetric information can mean that the **health care professionals**, who **know more** than the **patient** about particular treatments, can provide **unnecessary treatments** for **financial gain** (assuming the treatment is one that's paid for at the point of delivery). In this situation there would be an **excess** of health care treatments being supplied.

3) Consumers can also **fail** to **demand treatments** when they **need them**, which results in a **lower** level of **demand** than there should be. This happens because consumers **don't** have enough information to work out that they're ill and need treatment. This can lead to **higher treatment costs** if the health problem is allowed to get worse and become more expensive to treat.

Demand and Supply — Sport and Leisure

The sports and leisure industry is all about what you do in your spare time. There are lots of different factors that affect the demand and supply of different sports and leisure activities — read on to find out more. **This page is for AQA.**

The **Sports** and **Leisure** industry includes **Travel**, **Sports** and **Entertainment**

1) **Demand** for sports and leisure activities is affected by many factors, such as changes in **income**, the prices of **substitutes** and **complements**, **tastes** and **fashions** and the **structure** of the **population** (i.e. the proportion of people of different ages and gender that make up the population). For example, the demand for use of bowling greens may be high in an area with a high proportion of older people.

2) Other things can affect the demand for sports and leisure activities. For example:

- Work is a substitute for leisure — so **wage rates** can affect the demand for leisure goods and services. As wage rates **increase** people spend **more time** at **work** to increase their **income**. However, when wage rates reach a certain level people begin to **work less** as they earn enough to maintain a good lifestyle and want to have more leisure time.

- If a **sports team** is doing **poorly** then the demand for tickets might **decrease** and the price of tickets could **fall**.

3) Some sports/leisure events have a **fixed supply**. For example, a ticketed sports or entertainment event (such as a football match or rock concert) have a **fixed supply** of **seats** and can be considered with the diagram on the right.

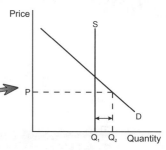

> The **supply of seats** is **fixed** (Q_1), so the supply curve is perfectly **inelastic**. This means that at the **ticket price** (P) there will be **excess demand** for tickets (Q_1 to Q_2). This can lead to **ticket touts** selling tickets to people for **inflated prices** (above P).

Increases in Incomes lead to Increased Demand for Leisure Activities

1) Generally leisure activities are **income elastic** — an increase in incomes leads to a larger increase in demand.
2) The **greater** the **percentage** of **income** spent on a leisure activity the **more income elastic** it is. For example, a snorkelling holiday is **more income elastic** than a swim at the local swimming pool.

Tourism is generally Income Elastic

1) Tourism has varying levels of income elasticities. **Domestic holidays** are **less income elastic** than **international travel** because they're generally cheaper.
2) The **demand** for **foreign holidays** is **very price elastic** in relation to **exchange rates** — for example, a **strong sterling increases demand** in the UK for foreign travel because it makes the holiday **relatively cheaper**.

Practice Questions

Q1 Give two reasons for the growth in demand for health care in the UK.
Q2 Give two non-price influences on the demand for leisure.
Q3 Are leisure activities generally income elastic or inelastic?

Exam Questions

Q1 Explain the problem caused by providing health care that is free at the point of delivery. [6 marks]

Q2 There are a fixed number of tickets available for a football match.
Using a diagram, explain why there can be excess demand for tickets at a given price. [6 marks]

My love of extreme ironing has massively increased my demand for A&E...

Again, two very different markets have been covered on these two pages. Health care provision by the NHS is a good case study to have a think about — the fact that treatments are provided free at the point of delivery means that the price mechanism isn't involved. The sports and leisure market can be affected by quite a few different factors — income is a really important one.

Demand and Supply — Stock Market Shares

*The stock market is where securities such as stocks and shares are bought and sold. This page will give you an introduction to the stock market and an idea of how the demand for shares can be affected. **This page is for Edexcel.***

Shares are Bought and Sold in a Stock Market

1) Some **firms** use the stock market to **raise finance**. One way of raising finance is to **sell shares**.

2) People who **own shares** in a firm are known as its **shareholders** and they may receive **dividends** (a share of the firm's profits that are given to shareholders) in exchange for **holding shares** in the firm.

3) Shares on the stock market are **bought** and **sold** by **shareholders**.

4) The **price** of shares is determined by their **demand** and **supply**, and their **prices** can **fluctuate widely** over very short periods of time.

Doris just lost $18m but she wasn't going to let it ruin her day.

There are Lots of Influences on the Demand for Shares

1) **Demand** for shares will depend on **confidence** in both the **economy** and in the **company** whose shares are being bought. For example, if confidence in the economy is **high** (e.g. during a boom), then **demand** for **shares** tends to be **high** because firms are expected to make higher profits and increase dividend payments. However, if a firm is discovered to be involved in **illegal activities** then **confidence** in that firm will tend to be **low** and **demand** for its shares will **fall**.

2) **Speculation** about **share prices** also has a significant impact on demand. If people believe that share prices will **rise** in the **future**, then they'll **buy them** at their **current price** in the hope of **selling them for more** in the **future**. Speculation can affect demand for shares in a number of ways:

   - Demand for shares in general is likely to be **high** if there's an **expected economic upturn** (e.g. if a boom is coming).
   - Demand for a company's shares can **increase** if the company releases **good news** or if analysts give **favourable reports** on the company — for example, the expectation of high future profits or increased sales.
   - **Rising share prices** for a company can also create **increased demand** for shares in the company. If it seems like the company is doing well then this **increases confidence** in it and **encourages** the buying of its shares.
   - Speculation also includes people **selling** shares because they **expect** the price of the shares to **fall** in the future. This might be because there's an **expected economic downturn**, or due to **negative reports** on a firm, or **falling** share prices. The **selling** of shares will tend to lead to a **fall** in **demand**, which will further **reduce** the price of the shares.

3) Companies can **issue additional shares** to **raise finance**. They might do this when they want to **expand** — the funds they make from selling shares could pay for things like new machinery. Increasing the **supply** of shares is likely to result in a **fall** in **price**, which could lead to an **increase** in **demand**.

Remember, there's a **fixed number** of shares at any one time, so **increases** in demand **significantly increase** the price of shares.

If the **demand curve shifts** from D to D_1 then the **price will rise** to P_1. Because the supply of shares is fixed the supply curve is **perfectly elastic**, so an **increase in demand** is likely to result in a relatively **large increase** in **price**.

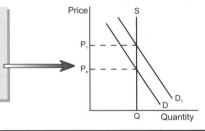

Practice Questions

Q1 What are shareholders?

Q2 Describe two factors which influence the demand for shares.

Exam Question

Q1 The latest sales figures from Gasoil plc show a 10% increase in sales over the last 6 months. Discuss how these sales figures might affect demand for shares in Gasoil plc. [4 marks]

The stock market — I wouldn't mind getting off before it crashes, thanks...

The stock market is all about the prices of different shares. When you buy shares in a company you become a shareholder and it's good news if the company does well because the value of your shares will increase. Demand for shares is affected by the confidence in the economy or in the company whose shares are being demanded. If confidence is high, demand for shares will be too.

Market Failure: Externalities

The price mechanism isn't perfect — this section shows you how markets fail and what governments do to try and stop this happening. Externalities are an important cause of market failure, so you need to learn about them really well. **For all boards.**

Market Failure *occurs when a market* Allocates Resources Inefficiently

1) A market **fails** when the **price mechanism** (i.e. the forces of supply and demand) **fails** to allocate scarce resources **efficiently** and **society suffers** as a result.

2) Market failure is a **common problem** and **governments** often **intervene** to prevent it (see p.58-66).

(see p.58-66)

Market failure can be *Complete* or *Partial*

1) When there's **complete** market failure, **no market exists** — this is called a '**missing market**'.

2) **National defence** is an example of a **missing market** as there's **no market** which allocates national defence. This means that **governments** need to intervene and provide it.

3) When the market functions, but either the **price** or **quantity supplied** of the good/service is **wrong**, then there's **partial failure**.

4) The provision of **health care**, if left completely to market forces, is an example of **partial failure**. If health care was left to market forces, then some people **wouldn't** be able to **afford** the treatment they needed. As a result, **governments** might **intervene** and provide **free** health care.

Externalities *affect* Third Parties

1) **Externalities** are the effects that producing or consuming a good/service has on people who **aren't** involved in the making, buying/selling and consumption of the good/service. These people are often called '**third parties**'.

2) Externalities can either be **positive** or **negative**. **Positive externalities** are the **external benefits** to a third party and **negative externalities** are the **external costs** to a third party.

3) Externalities can occur in **production** or **consumption**. For example:

- A **negative externality** of producing steel could be **pollution** that harms the local environment.
- A **positive externality** of producing military equipment could be an **improvement** in **technology** that benefits society.

- A **negative externality** of consuming a chocolate bar could be **litter** that's dropped on the street.
- A **positive externality** of consumption could be the **benefit** to **society** of someone training to become a **doctor**.

Externalities *can be either* External Costs *or* External Benefits

1) A **private cost** is the **cost of doing something** to either a consumer or a firm. For example, the cost a firm pays to make a good is its private cost and the price a consumer pays to buy the good is their private cost.

2) **External costs** are caused by **externalities**, e.g. if you dropped an empty crisp packet then that creates an **external cost** to the council who have to employ someone to sweep it up.

3) **Adding** the **private cost** to the **external cost** gives the **social cost**. The social cost is the **full cost** borne by **society** of a good or service.

4) A **private benefit** is the **benefit gained** by a consumer or a firm by doing something. For example, the private benefit a consumer might get from purchasing a skiing holiday is their enjoyment of the experience.

5) **External benefits** are also caused by **externalities**, e.g. a factory that **invests** in new equipment may create the **external benefit** of needing less electricity.

6) **Adding** the **private benefit** to the **external benefit** gives the **social benefit**. The social benefit is the **full benefit** received by **society** from a good or service.

7) **Market failure** occurs because in a free market the price mechanism will only take into account the **private costs** and **benefits**, but **not** the **external costs** and **benefits**.

AQA ONLY

Market Failure: Externalities

Externalities can be shown using Diagrams

1) Here's an example of **negative externalities** from **production**.

2) The **marginal private cost** (**MPC**) is the cost of **producing** the **last unit** of a good.

3) The **marginal social cost** (**MSC**) = the **marginal private cost** + the **external cost**.

4) So, the **difference** between the **MPC** and the **MSC** curves is the **external cost** of production — the **negative externalities**.

5) If the **MPC** and **MSC curves** are **parallel** then external costs per unit produced are **constant**. If the curves **diverge** then external costs per unit increase with output.

6) An example of why the curves might diverge is **pollution** — the **external costs** per unit created by pollution can **increase** as output increases.

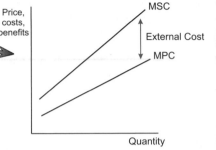

7) Here's an example of **positive externalities** from **consumption**.

8) The **marginal private benefit** (**MPB**) is the benefit to someone of **consuming** the **last unit** of a good.

9) The **marginal social benefit** (**MSB**) = the **marginal private benefit** + the **external benefit**.

10) The **difference** between the **MPB** and the **MSB** curves are the **external benefits** — the **positive externalities**.

11) Again, if the **MPB** and **MSB curves** are **parallel** then external benefits per unit are **constant**. If they **diverge** then external benefits per unit increase with output.

12) An example of when the curves might diverge is **vaccination** — the more people that are vaccinated, the **greater** the **protection** for **unvaccinated** people.

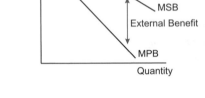

The Equilibrium Point may be Different to the Socially Optimal Point

1) When **supply** and **demand** are equal there's **equilibrium** in the free market.

2) In a free market consumers and producers only consider their **private costs** and **private benefits** — they **ignore** any **social costs** or **benefits**. As a result, the **MPC** curve can be seen as the **supply curve** of a good or service and the **MPB** curve can be seen as the **demand curve**.

3) So, **equilibrium** occurs when **MPC = MPB**. On the diagram this is where output is Q_e and price is P_e.

4) However, the **socially optimum level** of output is where **MSC = MSB**, because this includes the **external costs** and **benefits** to society.

5) This means that the **socially optimum level** of output is Q_1 and the **socially optimal price** is P_1. This level of output and price will give society the **maximum** benefit of any **positive externalities** and still cover the cost of any **negative externalities**.

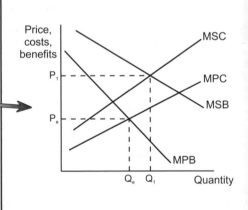

Ignoring Negative Production Externalities leads to Overproduction

1) In this diagram the **optimal output level** of this good is Q_1 and the **optimal price** is P_1. As there are no positive externalities, MPB = MSB.

2) However, in the **free market** only private costs are considered. So **output** would be Q_e and the **price** would be P_e.

3) This would cause **overproduction** and **underpricing** of this good — **more** is produced and sold at a **lower** price than is **desirable** for society. For each unit of this good produced between Q_1 and Q_e the **marginal social cost** is **greater** than the **marginal social benefit**.

4) The **area** between the **marginal social cost** and **marginal social benefit** is shown by the yellow triangle **ABC**. This is the area of **welfare loss** — the loss to society caused by **ignoring externalities**.

For an example see p.46.

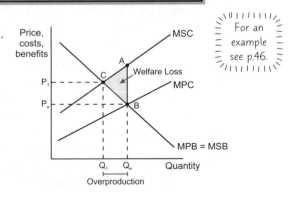

Market Failure: Externalities

Ignoring **Positive Consumption Externalities** leads to **Underconsumption**

1) In this diagram the **optimal level** of **output** for this good is **Q₁** and the **optimal price** is **P₁**. As there are no negative externalities, MPC = MSC.

2) In the free market only **private benefits** are considered. So **output** would be **Qₑ** and **price** would be **Pₑ**.

3) This would cause **underconsumption** and **underpricing** of this good — **less** is consumed and sold at a **lower** price than is **desirable** for society. For each unit of this good consumed between Qₑ and Q₁ the **marginal social benefit** is **greater** than the **marginal social cost**.

4) The **area** between the **marginal social benefit** and **marginal social cost** is shown by the green triangle **DEF**. This is the area of potential **welfare gain** — the gain to society **lost** by **ignoring externalities**.

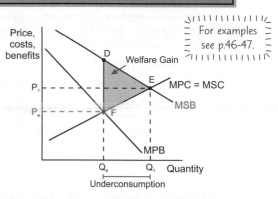

For examples see p.46-47.

Ignoring **Negative Consumption Externalities** leads to **Overconsumption**

1) In this diagram the **optimal level** of **output** for this good is **Q₁** and the **optimal price** is **P₁** (assuming MPC = MSC). The marginal private benefit is **larger** than the marginal social benefit.

2) In the free market only **private benefits** are considered. So **output** would be **Qₑ** and **price** would be **Pₑ**.

3) This would cause **overconsumption** and **overpricing** of this good — **more** is consumed and sold at a **higher** price than is **desirable** for society. For each unit of this good consumed between Q₁ and Qₑ the **marginal social cost** is **greater** than the **marginal social benefit**.

4) The **area** between the **marginal social cost** and **marginal social benefit** is shown by the yellow triangle **KLM**. This is the area of **welfare loss** — the loss to society caused by **ignoring externalities**.

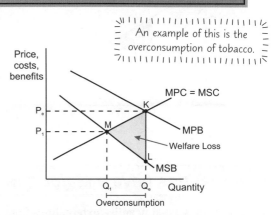

An example of this is the overconsumption of tobacco.

Ignoring **Positive Production Externalities** leads to **Underproduction**

1) In this diagram the **optimal level** of **output** for this good is **Q₁** and the **optimal price** is **P₁** (assuming MPB = MSB). The marginal private cost is larger than the marginal social cost.

2) In the free market only **private costs** are considered. So **output** would be **Qₑ** and **price** would be **Pₑ**.

3) This would cause **underproduction** and **overpricing** of this good — **less** is produced and sold at a **higher** price than is **desirable** for society. For each unit of this good consumed between Qₑ and Q₁ the **marginal social cost** is **lower** than the **marginal social benefit**.

4) The **area** between the **marginal private cost** and **marginal social benefit** is shown by the green triangle **PQR**. This is the area of potential **welfare gain** — the gain to society lost by **ignoring externalities**.

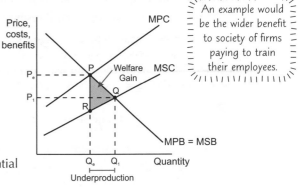

An example would be the wider benefit to society of firms paying to train their employees.

Practice Questions

Q1 What are externalities?

Q2 What are private costs?

Q3 On an externality diagram, where is the socially optimal level of output?

Exam Question

Q1 Explain how overproduction can occur in a free market if negative production externalities are ignored. [8 marks]

Socially optimal point — when all your friends think you're cool...

You've got to learn these diagrams for negative and positive externalities — it's very likely that they'll come up in the exam and you may even need to draw one. So it's worth spending a bit of time practising how to make one. Don't forget to label it properly.

Market Failure: The Impacts of Externalities

These pages look at specific examples of the impacts of externalities.
These pages are for Edexcel — but they're useful examples to learn for AQA and OCR too.

The *Underuse* of *Public Transport* is an example of market failure

1) In a free market, **public transport** (e.g. trains, buses) will be **underconsumed**.

2) This is because commuters will compare **private costs** (e.g. lack of comfort or convenience) with **private benefits** (e.g. value for money) when **deciding** whether to travel by public transport. They'll **ignore** the **positive** externalities of public transport, such as **reduced congestion** and **reduced greenhouse gas emissions** (the emissions per passenger a bus or train produces can be much lower than those produced by a car).

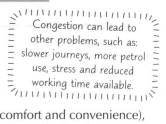

3) Commuters will choose the mode of transport that gives them the **most private benefits** (e.g. comfort and convenience), such as **cars**, so long as the **private costs** are **affordable** (e.g. the cost of buying a car, road tax and petrol).

4) If the **supply** of public transport was **increased** and the **price reduced** (by using subsidies — see p.60), then **demand** may **increase**. This would **reduce** the negative externalities caused by the **overuse** of cars.

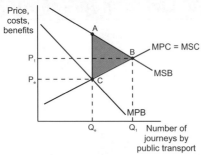

- If only private costs and benefits are considered then Q_e journeys would be made, which is **below** the **socially optimal level** of Q_1.
- If the number of **journeys by public transport** were **increased** to Q_1, then there would be a **welfare gain** of ABC.

Externalities have a Major Impact on the Environment

1) There are several **negative externalities** from production and consumption that have an **impact** on the **environment**:
   - **Pollution** from factories, cars, and so on, has **negative effects** on **air quality** and **people's health**.
   - The **burning** of **fossil fuels** contributes to **global warming**.
   - **Dropped litter** can lead to **bad smells**, and a **rise** in **vermin**, **disease** and **untidiness**.
   - The methods of obtaining **natural resources** (e.g. mining, logging) cause **destruction** to **habitats**.

2) For example, a **chemical factory** may **ignore** the **externalities** it produces, such as the release of waste gases into the atmosphere. If this happens there will be pollution **above** the point where MSC = MSB (the social optimum point).

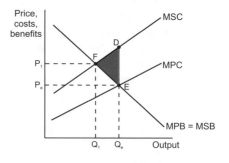

- If only private costs and benefits are considered then Q_e output would be made, which is **higher** than the **socially optimal level** of Q_1.
- The **higher** output of chemicals, Q_e, and **lower** price, P_e, lead to a **welfare loss** of **DEF**.

Waste Disposal and Recycling Externalities are Ignored

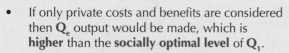

1) **Production** and **consumption** lead to **waste**, which needs disposing of.

2) When waste is disposed of, through **landfill** or by **fly-tipping**, it produces **negative externalities** — such as smells, unpleasant views, and so on. These externalities are **ignored** by the **free market**, so there will be an **overproduction of waste**.

3) One way to reduce waste is to **recycle**, but the free market would also **ignore** the **positive externalities** of recycling — such as reducing the need to use scarce resources. This would lead to a **lower** level of **recycling** than the **socially optimal level**.

Market Failure: The Impacts of Externalities

Education creates Positive Externalities which are often Ignored

1) In a **free market** the **positive externalities** of education will be **ignored** by suppliers of education. Their choices are based on **profit maximisation**.

2) The positive externalities will also be ignored by **students/parents** who will **only** consider the **benefits** to **themselves/their children** — e.g. that a good education will help someone get a better/higher-paid job.

3) There are many positive externalities of education — for example, the better educated the workforce the **more productive** they are, which in turn **increases** a **country's output**. Furthermore, increasing education levels has other **social benefits** such as reduced crime levels and a happier population.

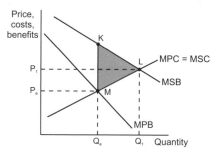

Stylish uniforms — another positive externality of education.

- If the **external benefits** of education are **ignored**, then the **output** would be at Q_e, which is **below** the **socially optimal level** of Q_1.

- If **output** were **increased** to Q_1, then there would be a **welfare gain** of **KLM**.

Health Care generates lots of Positive Externalities

1) In the **free market**, **providers** and **consumers** of **health care** will only consider the **private costs** and **benefits**. The decisions they make will **ignore** any positive **externalities**.

2) There are many **positive externalities** of health care — for example, a healthier workforce will be **more productive** and take less time off work, which will in turn increase a country's **economic output**. There are also **social benefits** to receiving health care, such as improved personal well-being and increased life expectancy.

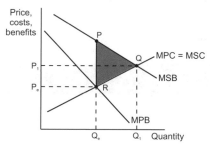

- If the **external benefits** of **health care** are **ignored**, then the **output** would be at Q_e — below the **socially optimal level** of Q_1.

- If **output** were **increased** to Q_1, respectively, then there would be a **welfare gain** of **PQR**.

Practice Questions

Q1 List three externalities connected with transport.

Q2 Describe two negative externalities that impact the environment.

Q3 Name a market which generates positive externalities.

Q4 Draw a diagram that could be used to explain a market where there are positive externalities.

Exam Questions

Q1 Negative production externalities, such as pollution, are of particular concern to governments at present because of their impact on the environment.
What would be the economic impact of these externalities if a government chose to do nothing? [8 marks]

Q2 Use a diagram to show the negative externalities that result from deforestation caused by logging activities. [12 marks]

Positive recycling externalities — the joy of recycling your exam notes...

... just make sure you don't do it before the exam. These are some good examples of market failure due to externalities — so even if you're not doing Edexcel, it's useful to learn them for the exam. The main thing you need to remember is that the free market ignores externalities, which of course leads to market failure as not all costs and benefits are being accounted for. Pretty deep stuff.

Market Failure: Merit and Demerit Goods

Classifying merit and demerit goods involves looking at the social and private benefits and costs. Some things are pretty universally agreed on, but a lot of it comes down to judgement. **These pages are for AQA and OCR only.**

Merit Goods *benefit society but* Demerit Goods *do the opposite*

Merit goods have greater social benefits than private benefits

- The **social benefits** of consuming a merit good are **greater** than the **private benefits** that an individual receives from consuming it. Due to this, merit goods can be thought of as having a **positive** contribution to society — they have **positive consumption externalities** (see p.45).

- However, merit goods tend to be **underconsumed** because consumers **don't realise** the **full benefits** they have. They also tend to be **underprovided**, because suppliers are only interested in their private costs and benefits, so they **ignore** any **positive externalities**.

- **Examples** of merit goods include **health care** and **education**. An example of a positive externality produced by a merit good is the increased benefit to society of someone being treated for an illness. Not all merit goods are welcomed by all potential consumers — for example, the offer of free vaccinations may be rejected.

Demerit goods have greater social costs than private costs

- The **social costs** of consuming a demerit good are **greater** than its **private costs**. Due to this, demerit goods can be thought of as having a **negative** impact on society — they have **negative consumption externalities** (see p.45).

- Demerit goods tend to be **overconsumed** because consumers **don't realise** the **harm** that they cause to themselves. They're also **overprovided**, because suppliers **ignore** the **negative externalities** that they create.

- **Examples** of demerit goods are **cigarettes** and **heroin**. An example of a negative externality produced by a demerit good is the cost of treating a disease that a smoker develops due to smoking cigarettes.

1) Sometimes it's **hard to say** which goods should be classified as merit or demerit goods. Whether a good fits into one of these classifications is usually a **value judgement** — based on people's **opinions** and not on **economic theory** or **facts**.

2) For example, some people consider **contraception** to be a **merit** good, but **others** don't.

The market *Underprovides* merit goods and *Overprovides* demerit goods

Merit *goods generate* Positive Externalities

1) If it's left to the free market then price and quantity demanded of a merit good will be at P_e and Q_e respectively, where the MPB curve **crosses** the MPC/MSC curve. The **market equilibrium** is below the **socially optimal** level of consumption (Q_1) — where MSC = MSB.

2) The area **ABC** is the potential welfare gain **lost** by underconsuming/underproducing the merit good.

3) To increase consumption to the socially optimal level of Q_1 the government could introduce a **subsidy** (see p.60) to bring the price down to P_2.

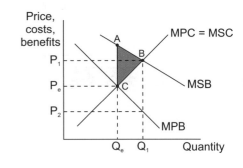

Demerit *goods generate* Negative Externalities

1) Again, if it's left to the free market then the price and quantity demanded of a demerit good will be at P_e and Q_e respectively, where the MPC/MSC and the MPB curves cross. The **market equilibrium** is above the **socially optimal** level of consumption at Q_1 — where MSC = MSB.

2) The area **DEF** is the **welfare loss** caused by overconsuming/overproducing the demerit good.

3) To decrease consumption to the socially optimal level of Q_1 the government could introduce a **tax** (see p.58-59) to bring the price up to P_2.

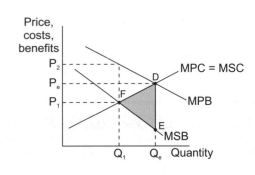

Market Failure: Merit and Demerit Goods

Short-term *decision-making can affect the* Consumption *of goods*

When individuals take a **short-term** approach to decision-making, it can lead to the **underconsumption** of **merit** goods and the **overconsumption** of **demerit** goods.

1) People **often** only consider the **short-term benefits** or **costs**. Individuals can **fail** to see the need to make **provision** for the **future** and for **potential changes** in their circumstances. A good example of this is paying into an old-age pension.

2) The **long-term** private benefits of **merit goods** are **greater** than their **short-term** private benefits and the **long-term** private costs of **demerit goods** are **greater** than their **short-term** private costs.

3) The **short-term benefits** of paying towards a pension (knowledge that you are saving for your old age) are **less** than the benefits of **receiving** that pension when you retire.

4) The **short-term costs** of buying cigarettes are much **less** than the **long-term** costs, e.g. serious smoking-related illness.

Imperfect Information *can affect the* Provision *of goods and services*

Imperfect information may lead to the **underprovision** of **merit** goods and the **overprovision** of **demerit** goods.

1) Imperfect information may mean demand for **merit** goods will be **lower** than it should be, so they'd be **underprovided**. For example, people might not have enough information on how serious their **health problems** might be, so their **demand** for health care isn't as high as it should be and health care is **underprovided**.

2) Imperfect information can also mean that demand for demerit goods will be **higher** than it should be, so they'd be **overprovided**. For example, when people aren't made fully aware of the health problems linked to **high alcohol consumption** this might mean that their demand for alcohol is higher than it should be and it's **overconsumed**.

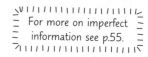
For more on imperfect information see p.55.

Governments *can* Intervene *in markets for merit and demerit goods*

1) The **failure** of the free market to supply the **socially optimal levels** of merit and demerit goods is the **main reason** why governments **intervene** to affect their supply. Governments can **directly provide** certain goods or services (see p.63) or they can uses **taxes** and **subsidies** (see p.58-60) to decrease or increase consumption of certain goods or services to the **socially optimal level**.

2) Governments have **a lot of information** regarding the **costs** and **benefits** of goods/services to both individuals and society as a whole, and can **use** this information to make decisions that benefit the whole of society.

Practice Questions

Q1 What is a merit good and why do merit goods involve value judgements?

Q2 How can imperfect information affect the supply of demerit goods?

Exam Question

Q1 Explain why a free market will underprovide merit goods. [6 marks]

The optimal level of fake tan consumption is 'just' before orange...

It can be tricky to get your head around these concepts, so make sure you take the time to do so. The key thing to remember is that for merit goods social benefits exceed private benefits and for demerit goods the private costs are less than the social costs.

Market Failure: Public Goods

The under-provision of public goods is an important example of market failure and it's one of the main reasons for government intervention to correct market failure. **This page is for all boards.**

Public Goods *are goods that are consumed* Collectively

1) An example of a **public good** could be a flood defence scheme or street lighting.

2) Public goods have **two main characteristics**:

- **Non-excludability** — people **cannot** be **stopped** from consuming the good even if they **haven't** paid for it, e.g. you couldn't stop an individual benefiting from the services of the armed forces.
- **Non-rivalry** — **one person** benefiting from the good **doesn't** stop **others** also benefiting, e.g. more people benefiting from flood defences doesn't reduce the benefit to the first person to benefit.

Private Goods *are the* Opposite *of public goods*

1) **Private goods** are **excludable** (you can stop someone consuming them) and they **exhibit rivalry**.

2) For example, biscuits are a private good — if you eat a biscuit you **stop** anyone else from eating it.

3) Unlike public goods, people have a **choice** as to whether to consume private goods — biscuits can be rejected.

Public Goods *are* Under-provided *by the market*

1) The **non-excludability** of public goods leads to what's called the **free rider problem**.

2) The free rider problem means that once a public good is provided it's **impossible** to **stop** someone from **benefiting** from it, even if they **haven't** paid towards it. For example, a firm providing street cleaning **cannot** stop a free rider, who has **refused** to pay for street cleaning, **benefiting** from a clean street.

3) The **price mechanism cannot** work if there are free riders. Consumers **won't** choose to pay for a public good that they can get for free because other consumers have paid for it.

4) If everyone decides to **wait and see** who will provide and pay for a public good, then it **won't** be provided.

5) It's also **difficult** to set a **price** for public goods because it's **difficult** to **work out** their **value** to consumers.

6) **Producers** will tend to **overvalue** the benefits of a public good in order to **increase** the **price** that they charge. **Consumers** will **undervalue** their benefits to try to get a **lower price**.

7) These problems mean that firms are **reluctant** to supply public goods, and the problems will cause **market failure**.

Some Public Goods *can take on the* Characteristics *of Private Goods*

1) Some goods are **pure public goods**, e.g. lighthouses, but others can be **turned into** private goods. For example, **road tolls** turn a public good into a private good by **excluding** those who **don't** pay to use the road.

2) For some public goods the characteristic of **non-rivalry** can be **restricted** if there's a **limited supply** of the good and **demand** for it is **high**. For example, **public parks** are public goods, but there's a **limit** to the number of people who can benefit from them at any one time. The number of visitors to a park could **increase** to a level where it **stops** others benefiting from it and **reduces** the enjoyment of those who are using it.

3) **Externalities** are a form of public good. They're consumed by those who **don't** pay for them, so they're an example of the **free rider problem**.

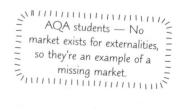
AQA students — No market exists for externalities, so they're an example of a missing market.

Market Failure: Cost Benefit Analysis

Cost benefit analysis is used to decide whether projects that require major investment should go ahead. However, the difficulties in calculating the costs and benefits, and the existence of political factors, can lead to market failure. **Edexcel only.**

Governments use **Cost Benefit Analysis** to **Evaluate** major investment projects

1) **Cost benefit analysis** (**CBA**) involves considering the **total costs** and **benefits** of a **major project**, such as building a new **motorway** or hosting an important **sporting event** (e.g. the London 2012 Olympics), over a fixed period of time.

2) When **politicians** (or other decision-makers) analyse the costs and benefits of a project, they have to look at their **impact** on **everyone** who's affected. For example, for a major sporting event the **gains** to the **host nation**, such as **improved facilities** or **increased tourism**, need to be evaluated **alongside** the **losses**, such as the **diversion** of **public funding** from other projects to pay for the event.

3) All of the costs and benefits are given **monetary values**. However, **externalities** can be **very difficult** to value — such as putting a value on the 'feel-good factor' that a successful sporting event can bring to a country.

4) The **difficulty** of putting monetary value on costs and benefits can lead to **disagreements** between those who are in favour of a project and those who are against it. There can be **big variations** in the **estimated** value of any **costs** and **benefits** and this can lead to **market failure**.

There are **Various Stages** in **CBA**

1) Firstly, the **direct** and **external costs** and benefits are **identified** as accurately as possible. However, **minor costs** or **benefits** are sometimes **missed**, leading to **market failure**.

2) **Monetary values** are then given to the **costs** and **benefits**. One way this is done is by working out **how much** individuals affected by the externalities of a project would **charge** for the **costs** or **pay** for the **benefits**.

3) At the end the **net cost** or benefit is **calculated**. Any **uncertainties** in the **estimates** of **costs** and **benefits** are assessed and factored into the final calculation. If the **costs outweigh** the benefits, then the project **won't** go ahead, but if the **benefits outweigh** the costs, then it **will**.

4) **Political factors** can affect a decision, causing **market failure**. For example, if a project is considered to be a **vote-winner** then the government might fund it, even if the costs outweigh the benefits. This is called **rent-seeking behaviour**.

After a careful CBA the Johnson family decided to use a cheaper alternative to the car for their summer holiday.

Practice Questions

Q1 What does non-excludability mean?

Q2 What does non-rivalry mean?

Q3 Briefly explain what is meant by the free rider problem.

Q4 Give an example of a project that might use CBA.

Exam Questions

Q1 Which of the following reasons explains why is it unlikely that there will be a market-provided flood defence system for an area prone to flooding? Explain your answer.
A) There is insufficient knowledge to build an adequate flood defence system.
B) Flooding is important for farming.
C) Individuals may be charged for their usage of the flood defence system.
D) The existence of the free rider problem. [4 marks]

Q2 Briefly discuss how a government might determine whether to invest in a new rail link between two major cities in its country. [6 marks]

Free riders — a big problem for waves in Australia, California, Newquay...

The difference between public goods and private goods is pretty straightforward and it's easy to see why market failure is caused by people not paying for public goods. If it's left to the market, no one would bother to put up street lamps or provide flood defences. CBA is straightforward too — remember, when political factors affect the outcome of the CBA, this can lead to market failure.

Market Failure: Monopolies

Phew, there certainly are lots of reasons for market failure. Here's another — monopolies. They have lots of factors which can lead to positive or negative impacts on an economy. See if you can get to grips with these two pages. **For AQA only.**

If there's **One Firm** in a market then it has a **Monopoly**

1) A **pure monopoly** is a market with only **one supplier**. However, markets with **more than one** supplier will **also** be referred to as a **monopoly** if **one** supplier **dominates** the market.

2) **Monopoly power** is the ability of a firm to **influence** the price of a particular good in a market. For example, a firm with monopoly power can **control** the **supply** of a good to **influence** its **price** — the firm is able to be a '**price maker**'. This can happen when there's a pure monopoly but also in markets where there's more than one firm — in this circumstance less powerful firms must be '**price takers**' as they're unable to influence the price of the good.

3) Firms often have some monopoly power **regardless** of the competitiveness of the market — for example, by using advertising to **differentiate** their product from similar ones (e.g. differing car models).

4) Firms providing **essential** goods or services with no substitutes have the **greatest** monopoly power.

5) The more **inelastic** the **demand** for a product is, the **greater** the monopoly power tends to be.

There are **Several Reasons** for the **Formation** of a **Monopoly**

Reasons for monopolies forming include:

- Firms can use their **control** of resources or markets to **create** a monopoly by **preventing** competitors from getting access to raw materials or customers — e.g. oil companies often have their own petrol stations.
- Firms can **expand** either through **internal growth** or **mergers** with other firms to exploit **economies of scale** (see p.14-15) and **dominate** a market.
- **Ownership of resources** — for example, if a firm controls the supply of a particular resource it can choose the price it charges for the product/s that the resource is used to make.
- **Geography** — a single petrol station serving an island would have a monopoly.
- **Governments** can create monopolies, e.g. a state-owned national railway.
- **Patents** and **licensing** — if a firm holds a **patent** for a particular product or process then they're the **only firm** that can exploit it. A firm can also **pay a fee** to use a patent held by someone else — this is called **licensing**. Having exclusive use of a patent (or several) may allow a firm to maintain a monopoly in a particular market — for example, a firm may hold the patent for a new pesticide.

Barriers to **Entry** can be used to **Create** and **Maintain** monopolies

1) A **barrier to entry** is any obstacle that makes it **impossible** or **unattractive** for a **new** firm to enter into a market.

2) If entry into the market is **possible**, a **barrier** to entry can make it **more expensive** for a **new** firm to supply the market than an **existing** firm. For example, a large existing firm could cut its prices, losing some **short-term** profits, to **force** a new entrant **out** of the market and ensure its **market dominance** in the **long term**.

3) Other examples of barriers to entry include:

- **Lower costs** — a large firm could use **economies of scale** to **force out** new entrants to a market.
- **High start-up costs** which are **non-recoverable** if a firm leaves the industry — it can be **very expensive** for a new firm to **start up** in a market, e.g. it might need to buy expensive machinery. The **risk** involved might **put off** a new firm as it might not be able to recover its start-up costs if it **fails**.
- **Patents and copyrights** — if the existing monopoly power/s hold important patents and copyright (e.g. the patents for a new invention) linked to a market, this might **prevent** a new firm from supplying **competitive products** in that market.
- **Brand loyalty** — firms can **differentiate** their products from **substitutes** made by competitors using **advertising and branding**. This can create consumers that are loyal to a firm's products and make **entry** for **new firms** (that don't have an established brand) more **difficult**.
- **Legislation** can be used to create and maintain monopolies. For example, a government can **maintain** a monopoly, using the **law to protect** a firm from **competition** — this might happen with a state-owned company.

Market Failure: Monopolies

Some markets are **Natural Monopolies**

1) **Natural monopolies** occur when a market can sustain only **one supplier** that can take advantage of **full economies of scale**.

2) This situation can occur in industries that have **large operations** with **high fixed costs**, such as firms that supply utilities (e.g. gas, water and electricity). For example, an electricity distributor has **high fixed costs** related to its **distribution network** (cables and other infrastructure).

Monopolies cause **Market Failure** and the **Misallocation of Resources**

1) The diagram shows the supply and demand curves of a market. The **market equilibrium** would be at **point M**, where supply is Q_c and price P_c.

2) However, in a **monopoly** situation there's only one firm in the market, so it could misallocate resources by **restricting supply** to Q_m and force the **price** up to P_m.

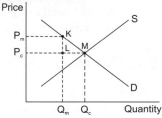

3) This is a **market failure** which causes a **welfare loss** of **KLM** — there are fewer units available for consumers to buy (Q_m to Q_c are no longer available). The area of P_cP_mKL, which would've been part of the consumer surplus, is **added** to the **firm's profits**.

4) By **restricting output** monopolies can **fail** to exploit some **economies of scale**. This means that **productive efficiency** is **not achieved** and the firm is not producing output at the lowest point on its average cost curve (see below).

5) Monopoly firms can also experience **higher costs of production** than firms that exist in a **competitive market** — this can be because **monopolies** have less of an **incentive** to make production methods as efficient (and cost-effective) as possible.

The existence of monopolies has several **Disadvantages**

1) Monopolies **restrict consumer choice** as there are **fewer products** to choose from.

2) Monopolies may have **fewer incentives** to **innovate** because they don't have to **improve** their products to make them better than their competitors' products.

3) Monopolies may have **no incentive** to **cut** costs as they're **price makers** (due to a lack of competition in the market).

4) A monopoly may use its powers to **exploit** its **suppliers** or **buyers**. For example, a monopoly could demand a **low price** from its suppliers — which they might agree to if the monopoly threatens to use another supplier.

Monopolies can bring **Benefits** to an **Economy**

1) In some markets the most **efficient** way of allocating resources is to have **one** producer who's able to exploit **economies of scale** and achieve productive efficiency. If the market consisted of lots of **small producers** they wouldn't be able to **collectively** achieve the **same level** of economies of scale or **productive efficiency**.

2) Monopolies can use their **profits** for research into **new** production methods and products. This could lead to **innovation** and **better products** being made available for customers.

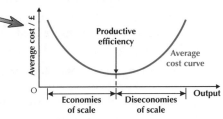

3) **Large firms** can exploit **large economies of scale** and pass on these cost savings to their customers, who are able to take advantage of **low prices**. This will also help their **international competitiveness**.

Practice Questions

Q1 Give four reasons for the formation of a monopoly.

Q2 Give three disadvantages of monopolies.

Exam Question

Q1 Explain why it can be difficult for a new firm to enter into a market where an existing firm has a monopoly.   [8 marks]

My barrier to entry is the moat I built around my house...

And you thought it was just a game. So, monopolies can bring both benefits AND disadvantages to an economy — make sure you learn a couple of examples of each. Oh, and don't skim over the diagrams — you need to understand what they're showing you.

Market Failure: Immobile Factors of Production

Hang in there — just a few more pages on market failure to go. Immobile factors aren't just things which can't physically move — they also include things such as an individual with little training or education. **This page is for AQA and Edexcel only.**

Factors of Production can be Immobile

1) **Land** is an immobile factor of production — it cannot be moved from one location to another. **Land** can also be immobile because, for example, it may only be good for **one type** of agriculture (e.g. land on which rice is grown may not be suitable for growing wheat).

2) A lot of **capital** is **mobile** (e.g. computers) — it can be moved from one location to another, but some is **immobile** because of its **size** (e.g. a steel foundry) or its **specialist nature** (e.g. a nuclear reactor).

3) Land and capital can become immobile by **human action** — e.g. a farmer may **choose** not to change the crops he grows on his land **despite** changes in climate.

Labour Immobility can be Geographical or Occupational

Labour is mobile if workers are able to move from one job to another — this movement could be between **occupations** or between **geographical areas**. However, there are several reasons why labour can be immobile:

Reasons for geographical immobility:

- **Large** house-price, rent and cost-of-living differences **between** areas can make it **very difficult** for workers to **move location** to obtain work.
- There may also be **high costs** involved in **moving** houses.
- A **reluctance** to leave family and friends.
- A **dislike** of change.
- **Imperfect information** about the jobs **available** in different areas.

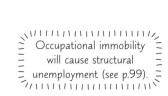
The most significant factor in the UK affecting geographical mobility is the high house prices in the South-East — the area of highest employment opportunities.

Reasons for occupational immobility:

- Lack of **training, education** and **skills** required to do a **different job**.
- Lack of **required** qualifications or **required** membership of a professional body (e.g. doctors have to be **registered** with the General Medical Council).
- Lack of **work experience**.

Occupational immobility will cause structural unemployment (see p.99).

Immobile Factors of Production cause Market Failure

1) Immobile factors of production mean there's often **inefficient** use of **resources** — resources are often **unused** or **underused**. This **inefficiency** in the **allocation** of resources means there's **market failure**.

2) There's a limit to how much a **government** can tackle immobile factors of production. Governments can't **move land** and most of them can't **force workers** to **relocate**.

3) However, governments can take some action to **improve labour mobility**. For example:
- To improve **geographical** mobility governments could offer **relocation subsidies** or **mortgage relief** to make moving to a particular area **more affordable** for workers. Governments could also offer incentives to **encourage** the **construction** of housing in areas where it's needed to provide homes for workers.
- To improve **occupational** mobility governments could provide more **training programmes** to increase people's skills.

Practice Questions

Q1 Give three examples of immobile factors of production.

Q2 What are the two types of labour immobility?

Exam Question

Q1 How can immobile factors of production lead to market failure? [4 marks]

A traffic light — a good example of a geographically immobile worker...

The stuff on this page isn't too complicated — some things that are needed for production can't be moved, whether that's land, labour or capital. This means that these resources might not be used to their full potential, causing market failure.

Market Failure: Imperfect Information

Perfect information will hardly ever actually exist. Unsurprisingly, this leads to another example of market failure. ***For all boards.***

Symmetric Information means Everyone has Equal and Perfect Knowledge

1) In a **competitive market** it's assumed that there's **perfect information**. That means that **buyers** and **sellers** are assumed to have **full** knowledge regarding **prices**, **costs**, **benefits** and **availability** of products.

2) **Perfect** information which is **equally** available to **all** participants in a market is known as **symmetric information**.

3) Assuming that buyers and sellers are **rational** in their behaviour, this symmetric information will allow the **efficient allocation** of resources in and between markets.

4) Symmetric information **rarely** exists — for example, **buyers** often don't have the **time** or **resources** to obtain full information on prices before **buying** a product.

Asymmetric Information involves a Lack of Perfect Information in a market

1) Usually **sellers** have **more** information on a product than **buyers**. For example, a used car salesman will have more information about the history of a car they're selling than a prospective buyer.

2) Sometimes **buyers** may have more information than **sellers**. For example, an antiques collector (buyer) may know more about the value of an antique than the person selling it.

3) When **buyers** or **sellers** have **more information** this is known as **asymmetric information**, or **information failure**.

4) **Providers** of **some** services have a lack of information because the thing they provide a service for is **unpredictable**, e.g. health service providers don't know **when** someone will become ill and with **what** health problem.

Information Failure causes Market Failure

1) **Imperfect information** means that **merit** goods (e.g. education, health care and pensions) are **underconsumed** and **demerit** goods (e.g. tobacco and alcohol) are **overconsumed** (for more on merit and demerit goods see p.48-49). There are many reasons why **imperfect information** affects the **consumption** of merit and demerit goods, for example:

   - Consumers may not know the **full personal benefit** of a merit good. They may not realise that a good education could lead to improved future earnings, or that a regular medical check-up might improve their lifespan.
   - Consumers may **lack** the **information** to decide which university course, pension scheme or medical treatment is right for them.
   - Consumers may not have the information on how **harmful** a demerit good, such as alcohol, can be.
   - **Advertising** for a demerit good may withhold or 'gloss over' any health dangers.

2) Due to **information failure**, merit goods tend to be **underprovided** and demerit goods are **overprovided**. This causes a **misallocation of resources** and **market failure**. There are many reasons why **imperfect information** affects the **provision** of merit and demerit goods, for example:

   - Pension providers have a **greater knowledge** of the **pension schemes available** than their clients — this can lead to them selling **unnecessary** schemes or **more expensive** schemes than may be needed.
   - Doctors have a **greater knowledge** of medicine — they may persuade their **clients** to purchase more expensive care than is **required**.
   - Information on a good/service may be **too complex** to understand. For example, the technical differences between computers may be confusing to a consumer, so they might find it difficult to work out which is best for their needs.

Practice Questions

Q1   What is symmetric information?

Q2   What is asymmetric information?

Exam Question

Q1   Describe how imperfect information can lead to the overprovision of a demerit good.   [4 marks]

You won't find imperfect information in this book...

Don't get confused by all the different names on this page. Make sure you get your head around what perfect information is — when it exists there's symmetric information in a market and when it doesn't this means there's asymmetric information in a market.

Market Failure: Unstable Commodity Markets

Commodities are basic goods that can be bought and sold. Many different factors affect their market prices. **For Edexcel only.**

Commodities of the *Same Type* are *Equivalent* no matter where they're produced

1) A **commodity** is a good which could be **swapped** with any other good of the **same type** without any noticeable difference.

2) For example, you could **exchange** wheat for some different wheat of the same type. It **doesn't matter** if that wheat is from a **different** harvest or was grown in a **different** place — the goods are **similar enough** to each other that it **doesn't matter** which one is used. Other examples of commodities include oil, sugar and tea.

Commodity Markets are often *Unstable*

1) A market for a good is **unstable** if the **price** of the good can change **rapidly** and by **large amounts**. This is caused by factors that affect **supply** and **demand** in the market.

2) Prices in commodity markets can be unstable for many reasons:

- The **supply** of commodities can be price **inelastic** in the **short run** due to the **high costs** involved in obtaining some commodities and the **time** it takes to **increase** their supply. As supply is inelastic this means that changes to supply (or demand) can have a big impact on **price**.

- The **supply** of a commodity can **fluctuate** due to factors that **producers** have little or no control over — e.g. for agricultural commodities, the **weather** can have a major impact on the supply of crops.

- The **demand** for many commodities is price **inelastic** because they're **necessities**, e.g. commodities are often raw materials for other goods, and manufacturers need them **regardless** of the price. As a result, changes in demand (or supply) can have a big impact on prices.

- The **demand** for some commodities can **suddenly** and **dramatically** change, e.g. a **disease** in cows might cause a scare amongst consumers and **dramatically reduce** the demand for **beef**. This **decrease** in demand would **greatly** affect the **price** of beef.

- **Speculation** and **stockpiling** can affect the **supply** and **demand** of commodities. **Speculation** is when traders buy a commodity in the hope of selling it at a higher price later on. This can make the price of commodities **fluctuate** a lot. **Stockpiling** also affects commodity markets (e.g. it can **reduce** the supply of a particular commodity) and can be used to **stabilise prices** (see p.62).

3) The markets for many **agricultural products** (see p.34-35) are **good examples** of **unstable commodity markets**.

The *Price Instability* of commodity markets causes *Market Failure*

1) The **price instability** of commodity markets creates **uncertainty** which leads to **inefficiency** and **market failure**. Uncertainty means that it's difficult for **producers** to **predict their income**, which in turn can **prevent** or **reduce** investment due to the uncertainties of the **returns** they will generate — so resources are used inefficiently. For example, a firm might choose not to invest in more efficient machinery because of uncertain returns.

2) **Price inelastic demand** and **supply** for commodities mean that there can be big rises (and falls) in the price of commodities when levels of demand and supply change. An increase in prices (particularly of necessities) can impact **consumers** heavily — especially those on **low incomes**.

3) Some commodities, especially necessities like basic food products, are **income inelastic** in **demand** because people have a **limit** to the amount of the commodity they need — so as income rises, they **won't** buy more of that product.

Practice Questions

Q1 Give one factor that can have an effect on supply in commodity markets.
Q2 Give one factor that can have an effect on demand in commodity markets.

Exam Question

Q1 In recent years the price of cocoa has demonstrated frequent fluctuations, some of which have been considerable. Explain how unstable commodity prices can lead to market failure. [8 marks]

The market for five-inch high heels — now that's what I call unstable...

You need to learn how changes to supply and demand can lead to large fluctuations in the price of some commodities, and the significance these have for producers and consumers. Remember, instability causes inefficiency and therefore market failure.

Market Failure: A Lack of Equity

Equity is another word for fairness. Some people think that big differences in the amount of income and wealth that different people have is unfair (i.e. there's a lack of equity) and that this is an example of a market failure. **This page is for AQA only.**

Consumption by an Individual depends on Wealth and Income

1) **Income** is the amount of money received over a **set** period of time, e.g. per week or per year.
2) Income can come from **many sources** — e.g. **wages**, **interest** on bank accounts, **dividends** from shares and **rents** from properties.
3) Wealth is the **value** in money of **assets** held — **assets** can **include** property, land, money and shares.
4) The **greater** an individual's income and wealth, the **more** goods and services they're **able** to purchase.

Income and Wealth are not distributed Equally in a market economy

1) Many people view **differences** in income and wealth as **unfair**, especially if they're **significant**.
2) In economies with **high** levels of **inequality** of income and wealth distribution (e.g. Sierra Leone), there can be people who are **starving** whilst others have **very high** levels of income and wealth.
3) Some economists argue this **inequitable** (unfair) distribution of income and wealth is a **market failure**. As a result, they say that **redistribution** of income and wealth would lead to an **allocation** of **resources** that would **increase** the benefit to society, and society's **overall** 'happiness'.
4) The argument for this is that the **benefit** to a poor person from an **additional** £1 of income would be **greater** than the **loss** to a rich person who paid £1 extra in tax.

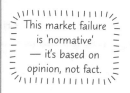
This market failure is 'normative' — it's based on opinion, not fact.

Governments might try to Distribute income and wealth more Equally

1) Governments might try to **redistribute** income and wealth through **taxation** and the payment of **benefits** and other subsidies to the poor, unemployed, elderly and sick.
2) The **free provision** of services (e.g. education, health care, museums) is another way of redistributing income, as the money to **pay** for these services comes primarily from **taxing** the **rich**.
3) The level of redistribution undertaken by governments is a **political decision** based on **value judgements** — it's up to them how much they redistribute income and wealth.
4) Some people argue that redistributing income **reduces** the **incentive** for individuals and firms to work hard. These incentives are needed to encourage **efficiency** within the market, and not having them may cause **greater market failure**.

Georgia had never been very good at value judgements — she'd just traded her car for a new hat.

Practice Questions

Q1 What is income?
Q2 What is wealth?
Q3 Why might the redistribution of income and wealth be considered as undesirable?

Exam Question

Q1 Discuss the ways in which a government may address an unequal distribution of income.   [6 marks]

I'd love it if the government would distribute some more income my way...

This market failure is more opinion-based than the others — not everyone agrees that inequality of income and wealth is a market failure. Whether you agree or not, you need to know why a government may (or may not) act to redistribute income and wealth.

Government Intervention: Taxation

Governments use taxes to offset or reduce negative externalities caused by certain goods/services. **For all boards.**

Governments use Indirect Taxes to affect the Supply of certain goods/services

1) **Indirect taxes** can be imposed on the purchase of **goods or services**.
   There are **two types** of indirect tax: **specific** and *ad valorem*:

> **Specific** taxes — these are a **fixed amount** that's charged per unit of a particular good, no matter what the price of that good is. For example, a set amount of tax could be put on bottles of wine regardless of their price.

> *Ad valorem* taxes — these are charged as a **proportion of the price** of a good. For example, a 20% tax on the price of a good would mean that for a £10 product it's £2 and for a £100 product it's £20.

There are also direct taxes. These are imposed onto individuals or organisations. For example, income tax is paid by people who earn an income.

2) Indirect taxes **increase costs** for **producers** so they cause the **supply curve** to **shift** to the **left**.
   The two types of indirect taxes **affect supply curves in different ways**, as shown in the diagrams below:

A **specific** tax causes a **parallel shift** of the supply curve. The tax is the **same fixed amount** at a **low price** (P_1) and a **high price** (P_2).

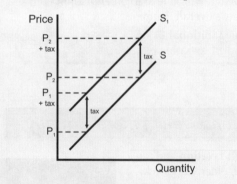

An *ad valorem* tax causes a **non-parallel shift** of the supply curve, with the biggest impact being on higher price goods. The tax is a **smaller amount** at a **low price** (P_1) compared to a high price (P_2).

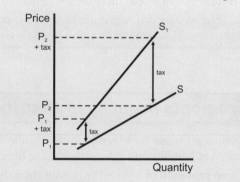

Governments Tax goods with Negative Externalities

1) Governments often put extra **indirect taxes** on goods that have **negative externalities**, such as petrol, alcohol and tobacco.

2) Governments may use **multiple** indirect taxes on **one** item, e.g. in the UK **cigarettes** have a **specific tax** (called **excise duty**) and an *ad valorem* tax on their **retail** price.

3) The aim of this taxation is to **internalise the externality** that the good produces, i.e. make the producer and/or consumer of the product **cover the cost** of its **externalities**. The taxes make **revenue** for the government which can be used to **offset** the effects of the **externalities** — e.g. the revenue generated from a tax on alcohol could be used to pay for the additional police time needed to deal with alcohol-related crime.

4) Another example of a specific tax used by the UK government is **landfill tax**. The tax aims to **reduce** the **impacts** of **market failure** linked to disposing of waste at landfill sites.

James desperately wanted to see where all the non-recyclable rubbish went.

- Local authorities or firms that **dispose** of waste into **landfill** sites are charged an **environmental tax**. The tax is set at an amount which attempts to **reflect** the **full social costs** of using landfill — i.e. the external cost linked to the burying of waste in landfill, such as pollution released from landfill sites.

- The tax should **encourage recycling**, which in turn will **reduce** the **negative externalities** caused by landfill.

- However, the tax has led to an **increase** in fly-tipping by firms to **avoid** having to **pay** the tax.

Government Intervention: Taxation

The **Total Amount** of **Tax Paid** can be shown on a diagram

1) The diagram shows the effect of an *ad valorem* tax — the **supply** curve moves **up** from S to S_1.

2) In the diagram, the **total tax paid** is ACP_1P_2. This is made up of the total tax paid by the **consumer** (BCP_1P) **plus** the total tax paid by the **producer** ($ABPP_2$). The part of the tax paid by the **consumer** is equal to the rise in price from **P** to **P_1**. The part of the tax paid by the **producer** is equal to the difference between **P_2** and **P**.

3) The **amount** of tax passed on to the **consumer** will depend on the **price elasticity** of demand — if demand for a good is **price inelastic**, most or all of the extra **cost** is likely to be **passed on** to the consumer. If demand for a good is **price elastic**, then the **producer** is much **more likely** to take on most of the **extra cost**.

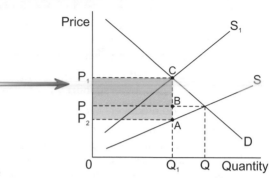

There are **Advantages** and **Disadvantages** to this kind of tax

Advantages

1) The **cost** of the negative externalities is **internalised** in the **price** of the good — this **may reduce** demand for the good and the level of its production, **reducing** the **effects** of the negative externalities.

2) If demand **isn't** reduced, there's still the benefit that the revenue gained from the **tax** can be **used** by the government to **offset** the externalities — e.g. tax on **cigarettes** could be used for funding government services to help people to **stop smoking**.

Disadvantages

1) It can be **difficult** to put a **monetary value** on the 'cost' of the **negative externalities**.

2) For goods where **demand** is **price inelastic**, the demand **isn't reduced** by the **extra cost** of the tax.

3) Indirect taxes usually **increase** the cost of **production**, which **reduces** a product's international competitiveness.

4) Firms may choose to **relocate** and sell their goods abroad to **avoid** the indirect taxation. This would **remove** their contributions to the economy, such as the **payment** of **tax** and the **provision** of **employment**.

5) The money raised by taxes on demerit goods **may** not be spent on **reducing** the effects of their externalities.

Practice Questions

Q1 Describe the difference between a specific tax and an *ad valorem* tax.

Q2 Sketch a diagram to show how the supply curve shifts when an *ad valorem* tax is introduced on a good or service.

Q3 Give one advantage and one disadvantage of indirect taxes on goods with negative externalities.

Exam Question

Q1 The diagram shows the impact of an indirect tax imposed on a demerit good. The revenue received by the government would equal:
A) £2000
B) £800
C) £1600
D) £400
Explain your answer.   [4 marks]

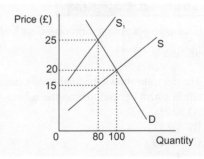

I think it's time for a government intervention — they really need help...

So there are two types of indirect tax that you need to know about. Remember that they both cause the supply curve to shift, but in a slightly different way. On the diagram at the top of this page make sure you understand that the cost of the tax can be split into the parts paid by the consumer and producer. If you're doing Edexcel there's a bit more detail you need to know (see p.30-31).

Government Intervention: Subsidies

The government can intervene in a positive way — by giving subsidies to producers or consumers. **This page is for all boards.**

Subsidies are paid to Producers by the government

1) The government may pay subsidies with the aim of **encouraging** the **production** and **consumption** of goods and services with **positive** externalities — e.g. merit goods. A subsidy **increases** the **supply** of a good/service, so the **supply curve** shifts to the **right**.

2) Subsidies can also be used to **encourage** the purchase and use of goods and services which **reduce** negative externalities, such as public transport, or as **support** for companies to help them become more **internationally competitive**.

3) Both consumers and producers can **gain** from a subsidy.

4) In the diagram, the **total cost** of the subsidy to the government is VTP_2P_1. This is made up of the total **consumer** gain ($VUPP_1$) **plus** the total **producer** gain (UTP_2P). The **consumer** gain is equal to the fall in price from **P** to P_1. The **producer** gain is equal to the difference between **P** and P_2.

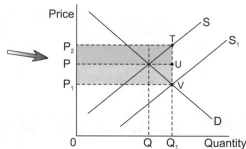

5) The **subsidy** results in the price of the good/service **falling** from **P** to P_1, and the **quantity** demanded **increasing** from **Q** to Q_1.

6) The **proportion** of the subsidy producers and consumers benefit from depends on the **elasticity** of the **supply** and **demand** curves.

7) Sometimes **subsidies** might be given **directly** to **consumers** instead.

There are Advantages and Disadvantages to Subsidies

Advantages

1) The **benefit** of goods with positive externalities is **internalised**, i.e. the cost of these externalities is covered by the government subsidy, so the **price** of the goods is **reduced** from what it would be in the absence of the subsidy.

2) Subsidies can **change preferences** — producers will supply goods with positive externalities and consumers will consume them and receive the benefits from them. Also, making a merit good **cheaper** by the presence of a subsidy makes it **more affordable** and **increases demand** for it.

3) The **positive externalities** are **still** present. For example, if a subsidy is paid for **wind farms**, the wind farms will still **reduce pollution** levels.

Disadvantages

1) It can be **difficult** to put a **monetary value** on the 'benefit' of the **positive externalities**.

2) Any subsidy has an **opportunity cost** — the money spent on it might be better spent on something else.

3) Subsidies may make producers **inefficient** and **reliant** on subsidies. The subsidy means that producers have **less incentive** to reduce costs or innovate.

4) The **effectiveness** of subsidies depends on the **elasticity** of demand — subsidies **wouldn't** significantly **increase** demand for **inelastic** goods.

5) The **subsidised** goods and services **may not** be as good as those they're **aiming** to **replace**. For example, it can be **more expensive** to produce a unit of electricity using wind power than fossil fuels.

Practice Questions

Q1 Give one advantage and one disadvantage of subsidies for goods with positive externalities.

Exam Question

Q1 The diagram shows the impact of a subsidy on a merit good. Government expenditure on the subsidy would equal:
   A) GFJ
   B) OLFC
   C) ACFJ
   D) EFG
   Explain your answer.   [4 marks]

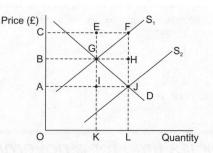

Subsidise your heating bills — move in with your next-door neighbour...

Subsidies can act as an incentive to producers or consumers, or they can help a company to be internationally competitive.

Government Intervention: Price Controls

Setting minimum and maximum prices can have a big effect on supply and demand. **For AQA and Edexcel only.**

Governments can set a Maximum Price for a good or service

1) A maximum price (or price ceiling) may be set to **increase consumption** of a merit good or to make a **necessity** more **affordable**. For example, a government may set a maximum rent price to keep the cost of renting a property affordable.

2) If a maximum price is set **above** the market equilibrium price, it will have **no impact**.

3) If it's set **below** the market equilibrium, it will lead to **excess demand** and a **shortage** in **supply** of Q_1 to Q_2. The excess demand cannot be cleared by market forces, so to prevent shortages the product needs to be rationed out, e.g. by a ballot.

4) A good's price elasticity of **supply** and price elasticity of **demand** will have a **big** effect on the **amount** of excess demand.

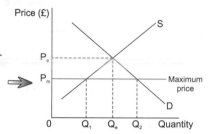

Governments can set a Minimum Price for a good or service

1) **Minimum** prices (or price floors) are often set to make sure that **suppliers** get a **fair** price. The European Union's Common Agricultural Policy (CAP) involves the use of a **guaranteed minimum price** for many **agricultural** products.

2) If a minimum price is set **below** the market equilibrium price, it will have **no impact**.

3) If it's set **above** the market equilibrium price, it will **reduce** demand to Q_1 and **increase** supply to Q_2, leading to an **excess supply** of Q_1 to Q_2.

4) To make a minimum price for a good work the government must **purchase** the excess supply at the **guaranteed** minimum price. The goods bought by the government will either be **stockpiled** or **destroyed**.

5) Government **expenditure** would then be ABQ_2Q_1.

6) A good's price elasticity of supply and price elasticity of demand will have a **big** effect on the **amount** of excess supply.

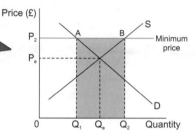

Maximum Prices

Advantages:
- Maximum prices can help to **increase fairness**, by allowing **more** people the **ability** to purchase certain goods and services.
- They can also be used to **prevent** monopolies from **exploiting** consumers.

Disadvantages:
- Since demand is **higher** than supply, some people who **want** to buy the product **aren't** able to.
- Governments **may** need to introduce a **rationing** scheme to **allocate** the good, e.g. through a ballot.
- Excess demand can lead to the creation of a **black market** for a good.

Minimum Prices

Advantages:
- Producers have a guaranteed **minimum income** which will encourage **investment**.
- **Stockpiles** can be used when supply is **reduced** (e.g. due to bad weather) or as **overseas aid**.

Disadvantages:
- Consumers will be paying a **higher** price than the market equilibrium.
- Resources used to produce the **excess** supply could be used **elsewhere** — there's an **inefficient** allocation of resources.
- **Government spending** on a minimum price scheme could be used in **other areas** — schemes may have a **high opportunity cost**.
- **Destroying** excess goods is a **waste** of **resources**.

Practice Questions

Q1 Give two disadvantages of guaranteed maximum prices and two disadvantages of minimum prices.

Exam Question

Q1 Use a diagram to show how the setting of a maximum price for a good can result in excess demand. [8 marks]

The government egg stockpile is huge — I think it's time for a crackdown...

What a terrible yolk... anyway, moving on... setting a maximum or minimum price for something means that the market forces can't determine the price of a good or service — minimum and maximum pricing acts to restrict the price that can be charged.

Government Intervention: Buffer Stocks

Governments might use buffer stocks to reduce market failure in agriculture. **This page is for AQA and Edexcel only.**

Buffer Stocks are used to try to Stabilise commodity prices

1) **Prices** in **commodity markets**, especially for agricultural products, can be **very unstable** (see p.56).
2) **Buffer stock** schemes aim to **stabilise** prices and **prevent** shortages in supply.
   They can **only** work for **storable** commodities — e.g. wheat.
3) A **maximum** price (price ceiling) and **minimum** price (price floor) for a commodity are set by a government.
4) When the market price for a product goes **below** the price **floor**, the government **buys** it and stores it in stockpiles. **Demand** is **increased** and the price is brought up to an **acceptable** level.
5) When the market price goes **above** the price **ceiling**, the government **sells** the product from its stockpiles. Supply is **increased** and the price is **brought down** to an **acceptable** level.

- For example, the **quantity supplied** (Q_1) in a **good** year (when levels of production have been high) is shown by the supply curve S_1, so its **market price** would be P_1.
- This price is **below** the **minimum** price, so to **prevent** this price fall, the government would **purchase** a quantity of Q_3 to Q_1 of the good at the set **minimum price**. Supply would be **reduced** and the market price would **rise** to the set **minimum** price.
- The goods **bought** by the government would be **added** to its stockpile.
- The **quantity supplied** (Q_2) in a **poor** year is shown by the supply curve S_2. The **market price** would be P_2.
- The government would **sell** Q_2 to Q_4 from its stockpile, at the set **maximum** price. Supply is **increased** and the market price would **fall** to the set **maximum** price.
- If the market price is **between** the set minimum and maximum, no action is taken.

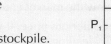

Buffer Stocks often Aren't Successful

In theory, the **income** from **selling** the product at the set **maximum** price should pay for **purchases** at the set **minimum** price and the **running** of the scheme. However, buffer schemes often don't work for a number of reasons:

- If the **minimum** price is set at **too high** a level, the scheme will **spend excessively** purchasing stocks to **maintain** this minimum price.
- If there's a **run** of **good** or **bad** harvests, then the scheme may **buy excessively** or **run out** of stock.
- **Storage** and **security** of the stockpiles can be **expensive**.
- Some commodities will **deteriorate** and go to waste over time, causing **losses** for the scheme.
- Producers may **overproduce** because they will get a **guaranteed minimum price**. This can lead to massive **stockpiles** and a **waste** of **resources**.

Practice Question

Q1 Give three reasons why buffer stock schemes might not be successful.

Exam Question

Q1 A buffer stock scheme for wheat production is being used. In a year when supply is shown by the supply curve S_1 the price per bushel received by farmers will be:
   A) P_1
   B) P_2
   C) P_3
   D) P_4
   Explain your answer.   [4 marks]

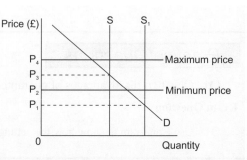

I tried to stabilise prices with butter stocks — it was a tasty, tasty mess...

Buffer stocks involve maximum and minimum prices at the same time (wowser) — make sure you know how they work.

Government Intervention: State Provision

State provision is costly for a government — they have to judge whether something's worth its cost. **For AQA and Edexcel only.**

Governments **Directly Provide** some goods and services

1) Governments use **tax revenue** to pay for **certain** goods and services so that they're **free**, or **largely free**, when consumed. Examples in the UK **include** the NHS, state education, and the fire and police services.

2) **Public goods**, such as **defence** and **street lighting**, are also **provided** by the state.

3) State provision can come **directly** from the government, e.g. state schools and the army, or alternatively, governments can **purchase** the good or service from the **private sector** and provide it to the **public** for free, e.g. in some areas **community health services** are **purchased** from private companies and then **provided free** to NHS patients.

The state provided Viv with all the latest medical equipment — unfortunately, she was a chef.

State Provision is a way to **Overcome** market failure

1) Governments might provide certain things to **increase** the **consumption** of merit goods, such as **education** and **health**.

2) **Free provision** of services can help to **reduce inequalities** in access, e.g. due to **wealth**.

3) Free provision also **redistributes** income — most of the money to **pay** for the services comes from taxing **wealthier** citizens.

4) The **level** of state provision is a **value judgement** made by the government — it's up to the government to decide the **amount** of a good/service that they **provide**. This decision is likely to be based on **how important** they think it is for **society** for them to provide the good/service.

State Provision has several **Disadvantages**

1) State provision may mean there's **less incentive** to operate efficiently due to the absence of the **price mechanism**.

2) State provision may **fail** to respond to **consumer demands**, as it lacks the motive of **profit** to determine **what's supplied**.

3) The **opportunity cost** of state provision of a good or service is that **other** goods or services **can't be supplied**.

4) State provision can **reduce** individuals' **self-reliance** — they know the good or service is there for them if they need it.

Health Care is a **Merit Good** that's sometimes **Provided** by Governments

1) The government funds the NHS so that **society benefits** from the **positive externalities** of **health care**. For example, the consumption of health care can contribute to a healthier, happier population and reduce the number of days people take off work due to sickness.

2) However, there are **drawbacks** to the **state provision** of health care by the NHS. These include:

   - Demand for health care in the UK has increased dramatically since the NHS was introduced. Because the NHS is **free at the point of delivery**, this has led to **excess demand** (see p.40) and problems like long waiting lists.

   - Hospitals and clinics can be **wasteful** of **resources**, such as money wasted on unused prescriptions.

   - The NHS may not always respond to the **wants** and **needs of patients** — e.g. local NHS officials might relocate medical services against the wishes of the population in their area for cost-saving reasons.

   - The NHS can **reduce patients' self-reliance**. For example, it can remove the incentive for patients to deal with medical issues themselves — patients might visit their doctor or hospital with problems which could be treated at home with medicines they could buy in a shop (e.g. colds or sore throats).

Practice Questions

Q1 Give two advantages of state provision of goods.

Q2 Give one example of state provision in the UK.

Exam Question

Q1 Describe the possible disadvantages of state provision of health care. [6 marks]

My bedroom is a state — it'll take some serious intervention to sort it out...

There are different reasons for state provision of goods and services. For example, the government might want to encourage the consumption of a merit good, or make a certain good or service accessible to everyone no matter how much they earn.

Government Intervention: Regulation

Regulation is another way governments can intervene and try to reduce market failure. **This page is for all boards.**

Government Regulation comes in Various forms

1) **Regulations** are rules that are enforced by an authority (e.g. a government). They can be used to **control** the activities of producers and consumers and try to **change** their **undesirable behaviour**.

2) Regulations are used to try to **reduce** market failure and its impacts.
They can **help** with a number of areas of **market failure**:

- **Reducing** the use of **demerit** goods and services — e.g. by **banning** or **limiting** the sale of such products.
- **Reducing** the power of **monopolies** — e.g. using a regulating body to set rules such as **price caps**.
- Providing some **protection** for consumers and producers from **problems** arising from **asymmetric information** — e.g. the Sale of Goods Act **protects consumers** against firms supplying **substandard** goods.

3) Firms or individuals who **don't** follow the regulations can be **punished**, e.g. with **fines**, **closure** of factories, etc.

Regulations can be Difficult to Set

1) It can be difficult for a government to work out what is 'correct'. For example, it might be **difficult** to set the '**correct**' minimum age for the purchase of alcohol — medical groups might want the legal age **increased**, alcohol producers might want it **reduced**. Or, a government might set the level of acceptable pollution by firms **too low** or **too high**.

2) There's a need for regulation in **some** areas to be **worldwide** rather than in just one country. For example, regulations to **control** greenhouse gas **emissions** might be **more effective** if they were enforced worldwide — regulations in **one country** may reduce its emissions, but this could be **offset** by an increase in emissions **elsewhere** in the world (not covered by this regulation).

3) Following excessive regulations can be **expensive** and may force firms to **close** or to **move** to a different country.

4) **Monitoring** compliance with regulations can be **expensive** for a government.

5) If the **punishment** for **breaking** regulations isn't harsh enough, then they may **not** be a **deterrent** and **change behaviours**.

Some regulations are set to Encourage the use of Renewable Energy

1) The UK government has introduced **Renewables Obligation Certificates** (ROCs) to **encourage** the use of power generated from **renewable** energy sources (e.g. wind and hydroelectric power).

2) Electricity **suppliers** are given a set **minimum percentage** of power that must come from **renewable** sources.

3) Companies who **generate** the renewable energy are issued with ROCs which link to the **amount** of renewable energy they've **generated**. They then **sell** these certificates on to **suppliers**.

4) **Suppliers** that **fall short** of the **target percentage** of **power from renewable sources** have to pay a **financial penalty**.

5) The money **raised** from these penalties is **distributed** between the suppliers who **did** reach the **target**.

AQA ONLY

Privatised Utility Companies in the UK are regulated

1) Regulating bodies, such as Ofcom (the regulator for the **telecommunications** and **media** industries), can set **rules** and impose **price controls**.

2) Regulating bodies may **use** these rules and price controls to try to **increase competition** in markets where there's a **monopoly** power. For example, Ofcom **increased competition** in the **UK broadband market** by allowing other companies to use telephone lines owned by BT to offer broadband services.

Practice Questions

Q1 Describe a market failure that regulation can be used to help solve.

Q2 Give one difficulty involved in the setting of regulations.

Exam Question

Q1 Assess how effective regulations would be for tackling the market failure caused by firms that pollute excessively. [4 marks]

Ban the sale of pink cars — reduce childhood embarrassment now...

Regulations are just rules. There are loads of different ways they can be used — this page should give you an idea of some of them.

Government Intervention: Pollution Permits

Pollution permits are a way of making firms pay for the negative externalities linked to pollution. **For all boards**.

The EU has a Scheme for Trading Pollution Permits

1) The **EU emissions trading system** (**ETS**) is an example of a tradable pollution permit scheme. In the ETS these permits are called **emission allowances** — they grant the holder the permission to **emit** a **certain amount** of **greenhouse gases**.

2) The EU allocates a given level of **greenhouse gas emissions** to its **member governments**. Governments then **allocate** their **share** of allowances to national firms involved in the scheme — firms get a new set of allowances each year.

3) Firms are **fined** if they **exceed** their allowances, but if a firm doesn't use up all of its allowances in a year (i.e. they emit a lower amount of greenhouse gases than their allowances set out) they can **sell** any **remaining allowances** to other firms. Firms might receive some allowances for **free** — to cover any remaining emissions they might have to **buy extra allowances** or use **unused allowances** from previous years.

4) Each year the number of allowances available is being **reduced**. This gives firms an **incentive** to **lower their emissions** (e.g. by investing in technology to cut emissions) — if they don't they might get to a point where they don't have enough allowances to cover their emissions and have to buy more.

5) To **offset** some of their emissions firms can also **invest** in **emission-saving schemes** outside of the EU. The emission reduction that a scheme generates is taken off the firm's EU emissions total. For example, a UK firm could invest in low-carbon power production in India to offset some of its emissions in the UK with emission reduction in India.

6) The aim of the scheme is that high-polluting firms, by buying extra permits or investing in emission-saving schemes outside of the EU, will **internalise** some of the costs of pollution.

7) As well as acting as an **incentive** for firms to **cut emissions** the ETS has other advantages. These include:

- **Governments** can use the **revenue** they make from **selling allowances** to **offset** the effects of **pollution** — e.g. by investing in emission-saving technology research.
- **Low-polluting firms** will **gain revenue** and should expand at the expense of **high-polluting firms** — they can sell their spare allowances to high-polluting firms.
- Pollution targets (and allowances) can be **reduced over time** to reduce the total emissions of a country and the EU as a whole.

Pollution allowances (permits) are often called 'carbon allowances'. This is because carbon dioxide is a major greenhouse gas that the allowances cover. However, the ETS allowances also cover other greenhouse gases, such as nitrous oxide.

The ETS has had Problems since it started in 2005

1) **Too many permits** (emission allowances) were **issued** in the first phase of the scheme (2005-2007). This meant there was **no incentive** to **cut emissions** and the **market** for permits **collapsed**.

2) Some firms have taken **legal action**, arguing their allocation was **too low**. If too few permits are issued to a firm this increases their costs, which might make them less competitive and encourage them to **relocate** outside the EU.

3) It may be **cheaper** for firms to invest in **emission-saving schemes overseas**, and/or **buy permits**, rather than invest in the technology to reduce their own emissions. This avoids tackling the problem where the emissions are being created.

Carbon Offsetting Schemes allow individuals to Offset their Carbon Emissions ◄

EDEXCEL ONLY

1) Individuals and firms can pay for schemes aimed at **reducing carbon emissions** — e.g. tree planting. The amount paid is set to match the cost of carbon-reduction measures to remove the same amount of carbon emissions as their activities produce. For example, some airlines allow consumers to **pay to offset** the calculated **carbon emissions** of their flight.

2) The **disadvantages** of carbon offsetting schemes are:
- **Regulation** is **difficult** and **fraud** (i.e. companies not actually offsetting carbon) is **common**.
- There are **difficulties** in **measuring** the emissions to be **offset** and those that are **saved** by the schemes.

Practice Questions

Q1 Explain briefly how the ETS acts as an incentive for firms to cut their emissions.
Q2 Give one disadvantage of carbon offsetting schemes.

'That's right Sir, without a permit I can't allow you to pollute that... or that...'

Tradable pollution permits are a pretty clever idea. It's just a shame that there are a few problems associated with them...

Government Intervention: Other Methods

Extending property rights and overcoming asymmetric information are other interventions. **For Edexcel and OCR only.**

A lack of **Property Rights** can cause **Negative Externalities**

1) If **property rights** aren't extended over a **resource** (e.g. a river), **negative externalities** can arise because **no one owns** the **resource** and takes **responsibility** for it. For example, a factory that emits waste water into a nearby river wouldn't be held accountable for this pollution if no one had property rights over the river.

2) If property rights over resources are extended to organisations, then it allows an organisation **control** over the **usage** of a resource. For example, a water company with property rights over a river can allow, charge for, or refuse permission for others to pollute the river.

The **Extension** of **Property Rights** uses the **Market Mechanism**

1) **Negative externalities** are **internalised** by the extension of property rights.

2) Owners of the rights can **charge** consumers and producers for using the property and **sue** if permission hasn't been granted.

3) The **money raised** can be used to **reduce** the **effects** of any **negative externalities**.

4) An extension of property rights could **improve management** of **resources** so they'll **last longer**. It could also mean negative externalities are **more carefully monitored** and **regulated**.

There are several **Problems** associated with **Extending Property Rights**

1) It can be **difficult** for a **government** to **extend property rights**. For example, EU rules allow boats from other EU countries to fish in UK waters, stopping the allocation of property rights over these waters.

2) **Externalities** can affect **more than one country**. For example, deforestation in Malaysia could have impacts for the whole world by contributing to climate change, but the UK can't extend property rights to Malaysia.

3) The **high costs** of **suing** an individual or company that infringes property rights can put off organisations from taking action to uphold those rights.

4) The **use** of a **property right** can be **difficult** to put a **value** on.

5) There are often difficulties in **tracing** the **source** of **environmental damage**. For example, a chemical leak into a river could kill fish in a fish farm a great distance from the source of the leak — the property rights holder for the fish farm may not have the information available to demand compensation from the firm responsible.

Governments can **Intervene** to help consumers make **Well-Informed Decisions**

1) Governments try to provide **information** on the **full costs** and **benefits** of goods and services. This information is given to try to help consumers make **rational choices** and prevent market failure caused by consumers and producers having **asymmetric information**. **Examples** of government-provided information include:

- School and hospital performance league tables.
- Advertising campaigns encouraging healthy eating.
- Compulsory food labelling for most foods.
- Health warnings on cigarette packets.

2) The **provision** of information will impact on the **demand** for the goods.

3) The **effectiveness** of government information provision is often questioned. For example, the **growing obesity problem** in the **UK** suggests that government **healthy eating campaigns** aren't having a significant impact on the public.

Practice Questions

Q1 Describe two problems linked to extending property rights.

Exam Question

Q1 Explain how governments can address the problem of asymmetric information to correct the market failure associated with the consumption of cigarettes. [6 marks]

That's it, I reckon I should get compensation every time I hear a bad song...

The extension of property rights is a good example of a method by which negative externalities are internalised. Getting this right can be hard though — just imagine trying to put a value on some air pollution... Governments can intervene in a market simply by trying to make sure consumers have enough information to make the best possible decisions, and hopefully solve the market failure.

Government Failure

Government failure is when government intervention causes a misallocation of resources in a market. **For all boards.**

Government Intervention can cause the Misallocation of Resources

1) Government intervention can lead to **resources** being **misallocated** — this is **government failure**.

2) When looking at government failure in a market you should consider it in relation to the market failure it was attempting to correct. For example:

- Local authorities can **charge** for some forms of non-household **waste disposal**, e.g. some county councils charge for the disposal of DIY waste. This is an attempt to force waste producers to **internalise** the **externalities of waste disposal**.
- However, there's evidence that this has led to an **increase** in **fly-tipping**. This fly-tipping produces **negative externalities** for local residents (e.g. the visual pollution caused by discarded items) and requires **resources** to be allocated to **clear up** the **fly-tipping**.
- In this instance the **intervention** that aimed to **reduce** the **negative externalities** linked to **waste disposal** has resulted in the production of **other unintended negative externalities**.

Government Intervention may cause Market Distortions

Government interventions can **cause** market distortions rather than **removing them**. There are several examples of this:

- **Income taxes** can act as a **disincentive** to working hard — if you increase your earnings by working hard then you'll have to pay more income tax.
- **Governmental price fixing** can lead to **surpluses**. This can happen when governments promise a **minimum price** for a certain product to help producers, such as farmers, increase their incomes.
- **Subsidies** may encourage firms to be **inefficient** by removing the **incentive** to be efficient.

Government Bureaucracy can Interfere with the way markets work

1) Governments have lots of **rules and regulations** — often referred to as **'red tape'**. These usually exist in order to **prevent market failure**.

2) The enforcement of these rules and regulations by government officials is known as **bureaucracy**. Excessive bureaucracy (e.g. too many regulations slowing down a process unreasonably) is seen as a form of **government failure**.

3) Red tape can interfere with the forces of **supply and demand** — it can prevent markets from working **efficiently**. For example, **planning controls** can create **long delays** in construction projects. If these delays affect housing developments then this could restrict supply for the housing market.

4) In general, lots of red tape could mean that there are **time lags** so governments can't respond quickly to the **needs** of **producers** and/or **consumers**. This might result in a country having a **competitive disadvantage** to countries that are able to respond more quickly.

5) Bureaucracy can lead to a **lack of investment** and **prevent** an economy from operating at **full capacity**.

Conflicting Policy Objectives are a source of Government Failure

1) A government's effort to achieve a certain **policy objective** may have a **negative impact** on another. For example, if a government introduces **stricter emission controls** for industry this would contribute towards its **environmental objectives**. However, this could **increase costs** for firms and **reduce their output** — causing unemployment and a fall in economic growth.

2) Politicians are also constrained by what is **politically acceptable**. For example, it's unlikely that the UK government would ban the use of private cars to reduce greenhouse gases because of the idea's **political unpopularity**.

3) Governments often favour **short-term solutions** because they're under pressure to solve issues **quickly**. For example, increasing the capacity of the UK road network will help with short-term congestion, but may increase road usage (and congestion) in the long term.

Government Failure

Government Failure can be caused by Inadequate Information

1) It can be **difficult** to **assess** the extent of a **market failure**, and that makes it difficult to put a **value** on the **government intervention** that's **needed** to correct the failure. For example, an incorrect valuation of a market failure might lead to taxes or subsidies being set at an inefficient level.

2) Governments may not know how the population **want resources** to be **allocated**. Some economists would argue that the **price mechanism** is a better way of allocating resources than government intervention.

3) Governments don't always know how **consumers** will **react**. For example, campaigns to **discourage under-18s drinking alcohol** may lead to alcohol being viewed as desirable and **increase drinking** by this age group.

Administrative Costs can also be a cause of Government Failure

1) Government measures to correct market failure, such as policies and regulations, can use a **large amount of resources** — this can result in **high costs**. For example, the maintenance costs of a scheme to offer farmers a minimum price for a product can be substantial.

2) Some government interventions require **policing**, which can also be **expensive**. For example, for pollution permit schemes the emissions of the firms included in the scheme must be monitored to check they aren't exceeding their allowances.

Pollution permits are discussed on p.65.

There are some other causes of Government Failure

Some other reasons for government failure are:

- **Regulatory capture** — firms covered by **regulatory bodies**, such as utility companies, can sometimes **influence** the decisions of the regulator to ensure that the outcomes **favour** the **companies** and not the consumers. For example, a regulated industry might pressurise their regulatory body into making decisions that benefit them.

- It takes **time** for governments to work out where there's market failure, and then devise and implement a policy to correct it — meanwhile, the problem may have changed.

- Government policies can be affected by issues outside of its control known as '**external shocks**' — e.g. a major oil leak would impact on the effectiveness of anti-pollution policies.

Practice Questions

Q1 What is government failure?

Q2 Give an example of how a government intervention can lead to a market distortion.

Q3 List three causes of government failure.

Exam Questions

Q1 A government banned the sale of a legal substance which has effects similar to some illegal drugs and can be hazardous to health. Which one of the following situations would be considered a government failure? Explain your answer.
A) Public opinion of the government improved as the ban demonstrated a strong concern for public health.
B) Consumption of the substance fell dramatically and there were fewer hospital admissions due to its use.
C) The cost of imposing the ban was greater than the net benefit generated by it.
D) The public became more aware of the dangers of the substance. [4 marks]

Q2 A government has increased the level of tax on cigarettes. A neighbouring country has a lower rate of tax on cigarettes. Explain how this intervention could lead to a government failure. [6 marks]

It's taken time for me to develop my policy on blue cheese — I'm not a fan...

There are quite a few potential causes of government failure. This gives you an insight into how tricky it can be for governments to implement something that effectively sorts out a market failure. Maybe we should all be a bit kinder to governments when they get it a bit wrong... Anyway, conflicting policy objectives, inadequate information and administrative costs are key causes to remember.

Examples of Government Failure

These pages cover a selection of examples of government failure. **This is for Edexcel but is useful for other boards too.**

The **Common Agricultural Policy (CAP)** *was set up to help farmers*

1) The main aim of the CAP is to **correct market failure** caused by **fluctuating prices** for agricultural products. By correcting these fluctuations it aims to provide a **reasonable**, **stable income** for farmers.

2) To achieve its aim the CAP uses measures such as subsidies and buffer stocks (see p.62 for buffer stocks). Another measure is import restrictions on goods from outside the EU — for example, **tariffs** are placed on **imported goods** to allow the guaranteed minimum price level to be maintained.

3) The CAP has had **some success** in stabilising prices and farmer incomes, but it has also caused several **problems**:

- The CAP **encourages increased output** as farmers are guaranteed a **minimum price** for all that they produce. Increased output can lead to **environmental damage** from a greater use of intensive farming methods and chemical fertilisers.

- The **minimum prices** have also led to an **oversupply** of agricultural products, which have to be **bought** and **stored** by government agencies at **great expense**. Governments have **sold these stocks** at a low price **outside of the EU** — negatively affecting farmers outside the EU who **cannot compete** with such **low prices**.

- There are large amounts of **wasted food products** when perishable goods have to be **destroyed**.

- The increased food prices caused by the CAP are particularly **unfair** on **poorer households** who spend a larger proportion of their income on food. It can be argued that the **welfare gains to farmers** brought about by the CAP are **smaller** than the size of the **welfare loss to consumers**.

- There's a **cost to the taxpayer** of getting rid of excess agricultural produce (either by destroying it or by selling it for a very low price). This is because the produce disposed of in this way achieves a **lower price** than was paid to the producer for it by the EU.

- The CAP can cause **conflicts** with **other countries** as it can make exports from non-EU countries **less competitive**, e.g. as products from non-EU countries can be subject to import tariffs. Also, there's **conflict between countries** within the EU about how much of the CAP budget they should each receive.

4) The CAP has resulted in **distortions** in agricultural markets — it has encouraged **oversupply**, leading to a **misallocation of resources**. This misallocation of resources causes a **net welfare loss to society**, as does the high opportunity cost of running the policy.

5) In recent years prices have **moved closer** to the **market price** as part of the EU's reforms of the CAP, but there are still problems with the policy.

Fishing Quotas *were introduced to help make fishing more* **Sustainable**

1) Fishing quotas were introduced by the EU in an attempt to make sure **fish stocks** remain **stable** in European waters. They aim to **prevent overfishing**, which can have severe negative impacts on fish populations, by setting **limits** on the amount of fish that can be caught.

2) The system of fishing quotas has been **heavily criticised** and has a few key problems:

- Fish stocks are **depleting** even with quotas in place. This could indicate that the quotas have been **set too high** and **overfishing** is still taking place.

- Fishing boats that exceed their quotas often throw large amounts of dead fish back into the sea — these dumped fish are known as **discards**. As well as damaging fish stocks, these discards are also wasteful.

- There has been **poor monitoring** of fish catches. This could mean that fishing boats have been overfishing and it hasn't been detected.

3) Problems with EU fishing quotas have led to a need for **reform**. One proposed change is called a **landing obligation**. This means that everything fishermen catch must be kept on board and be counted against their quotas — they aren't allowed to discard any fish. This landing obligation is likely to be difficult to police — it would be a huge task to check that every fishing boat hasn't discarded any fish at sea.

Examples of Government Failure

Governments may provide Subsidies to Public Transport

1) Bus and train journeys may be **subsidised** to **reduce car usage** and **pollution levels**.

2) Subsidies **don't always** lead to **increases** in **passenger numbers** — bus transport is often viewed as an **inferior good** so even if it's cheaper, demand might not increase. Individuals may also find travelling by car **preferable** for reasons of privacy or convenience.

3) The allocation of resources to public transport services that don't increase their usage and don't cause a reduction in pollution can be seen as a **misallocation of resources** and will lead to a **net welfare loss**. Underused public transport services may actually contribute to higher overall emissions as people aren't using their cars less.

As incomes rise, demand for inferior goods fall — see p.21.

Road Congestion Schemes aim to Reduce Externalities linked with Traffic

1) Road congestion schemes are a method of **reducing** the **external costs** linked to **road congestion** and the **pollution** (air and noise) that it creates. These schemes are also called **road pricing**.

2) The schemes work by **charging users** to travel on roads in areas where **congestion** is a **problem**.

3) Ideally the charge needs to be set at a level that will result in the **socially optimal level of traffic**. However, working out what this charge is could be very difficult.

4) Getting the charge wrong has impacts on the effectiveness of road congestion schemes:

   • If the price is set **too low** then it will have a limited impact on traffic levels.

   • If the price is set **too high** then too few cars will use the area covered by the charge. This will result in **reduced trade** for businesses within the congestion charge area, an **under-utilisation** of the road space in the congestion charge area, and may also cause congestion in **other areas**.

5) Road congestion charges may **unfairly** impact on **poorer motorists** and put them off using their cars to travel to an area within a scheme.

Jeremy took extreme measures to avoid road congestion schemes.

Governments may intervene in Housing Markets by setting Maximum Rents

1) Price controls, such as maximum rents, are used by governments to **protect tenants** from **excessive rental charges**.

2) The downside of the control of rent prices is that they can cause **shortages** of rental properties. This can be shown using a diagram:

   • Introducing a maximum rent would **decrease** the **rent price** from P_e to **MR**. This would cause the demand for rental properties to increase from Q_e to Q_d and supply to fall from Q_e to Q_s.

   • This could cause a shortage of rental properties of Q_s to Q_d because there's an **excess demand** for them — only some individuals demanding a rental property will get one (Q_s).

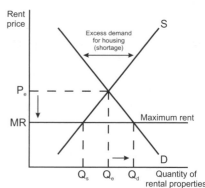

3) The problems caused by maximum rents are an example of government failure:

   • The **excess demand** for rental properties could lead to a **shortage** of available properties and cause a **black market** to develop. In a black market people are likely to end up paying more than the maximum rent level, so they won't gain any benefit from the government's maximum rent level. Also, landlords operating illegally on the black market may not offer a good service to their tenants.

   • A **shortage** of rental properties can also impact the supply of **workers**. People might not be able to find somewhere to rent near to where they work — this could affect the ability of firms to attract new staff in areas where shortages are particularly bad.

Examples of Government Failure

The National Minimum Wage (NMW) aims to make wages fairer

1) The NMW was introduced in the UK to stop firms setting wages so low that their employees could not afford a decent standard of living. It aims to **prevent** the **exploitation** of workers due to the payment of **unfairly low wages**.

2) The NMW acts to address problems that can exist in the market for labour, such as:

> National minimum wage was talked about on p.37. Have a look back to see how it affects the supply of, and demand for, labour.

- Workers in low-paid jobs could be discriminated against and paid a **different rate** for the same amount of work (an hour).

- Many **migrants** are willing to accept very **low wages** because they're still higher than those in their home country, which can lead to them being **exploited**.

3) **Increasing** the NMW could have some **advantages**:

- Increasing the NMW may help those on **very low incomes** and **reduce** the level of **poverty** in the country.

- An increase may also **boost** the **morale** of workers as they'll receive better wages. Happier workers tend to be **more productive**, so output may increase as a result.

- A higher NMW means there's **greater reward** for doing a job that pays the NMW. It gives people more **incentive** to get a job rather than be unemployed.

- The government's **tax revenue** is likely to be **greater** if the NMW is increased.

4) However, there are also arguments **against** increasing the NMW as it can be a cause of **government failure**:

- Increasing the NMW can **increase wage costs** for firms. This might mean they have to **cut jobs**, resulting in increased **unemployment**.

- An increase to the NMW could decrease the **competitiveness** of **UK firms** compared to firms in other countries that have lower wage costs. UK firms may have to pass on increased wage costs to consumers by **increasing** their **prices** and this could contribute to **inflation**.

- There are **doubts** about whether increasing the NMW really **decreases poverty**. This is because many of the poorest members of society, such as the elderly and disabled, are **not in work** (so aren't able to benefit from an increased wage rate).

Practice Questions

Q1 Give two measures used by the CAP to correct market failure in agricultural markets.

Q2 Describe one problem linked with fishing quotas.

Q3 Give two reasons for subsidising public transport.

Q4 What happens if the pricing of a road congestion scheme is set too low?

Q5 Use a diagram to show how setting maximum rent prices can lead to a shortage of rental properties.

Q6 Give two reasons why a national minimum wage can lead to government failure.

Exam Questions

Q1 Which of the following is a government failure linked to the introduction of a maximum rent for tenants that is set below the market equilibrium rent price? Explain your answer.
A) Excess supply of rental properties.
B) The protection of tenants from excessive rental charges.
C) A black market for tenants willing to pay more than the maximum rent can develop.
D) An increased level of poverty in tenants. [4 marks]

Q2 It has been decided that the level of funding available for farm subsidies is to be reduced over the next 5 years. Explain two advantages of reducing the subsidies paid to farmers. [4 marks]

Q3 Evaluate the arguments for and against a nationwide system of road pricing in major cities. [10 marks]

I reckon my washing-up quota is set too high — I wish I had a dishwasher...

Wow, so there are quite a few examples of government failure then too. Thankfully most governments will be trying to correct these failures, although doing this is easier said than done — it's not straightforward to iron out problems with big policies like the CAP.

Measuring Economic Growth

*Instead of looking at individual markets, firms or people, macroeconomics looks at the economy as a whole — so that includes the government, all firms, all individuals, other countries etc. **These pages are for all boards.***

There are **Four** main **Macroeconomic** indicators

These four **main** macroeconomic indicators can be used to measure a country's **economic performance**:

1) The rate of **economic growth**.
2) The rate of **inflation**.
3) The level of **unemployment**.
4) The state of the **balance of payments**.

Governments **use** these indicators to **monitor** how the economy is doing.

Alex was thrilled by the high level of inflation.

GDP is a measure of *Economic Growth*

1) Economic growth can be measured by the change in **national output** over a period of time. The national output is **all** the **goods** and **services** produced by a country.

2) Output can be measured in **two** ways:

Volume
Adding up the **quantity** of goods and services produced in one year.

Value
Calculating the value (£billions) of all the goods and services produced in one year.

National output is **usually** measured by **value** — this is called the **Gross Domestic Product (GDP)**.

3) GDP can also be calculated by adding up the total amount of national **expenditure** (aggregate demand, see p.82) in a year or by adding up the total amount of national **income** earned in a year. This means that, in theory, national output = national expenditure = national income (see p.80-81 for more on the **circular flow** of income).

Economic Growth is usually measured as a *Percentage*

1) The **rate** of economic growth is the **speed** at which the **national output** grows over a period of time.

2) Over the course of **several** years, the speed of this growth is **not** usually constant. Here are a few useful terms:

- Long periods of high economic growth rates are often called **booms**.
- If there's **negative** economic growth for **two consecutive quarters** (a 'quarter' is just a 3 month period of time — a quarter of a year), this is called a **recession**. A **long** recession is often referred to as a **slump**.
- An **economic depression** is worse than a recession — it's a **sustained** economic downturn which lasts for a **long** period of time (e.g. several years).

> Remember — a slowdown in the rate of economic growth means growth is still rising, but more slowly. It doesn't mean economic growth is negative — output isn't falling.

3) Over one year, a country's GDP may **increase** or **decrease**. This simply measures the **change** in the amount of goods and services produced between one year and the next. The change in GDP can be shown in **two** ways — as a **value** (£billions), or as a **percentage**.

4) To **measure** the rate of economic growth over time as a percentage, use the formula:

$$\frac{\text{Change in GDP (£billions)}}{\text{Original GDP (£billions)}} \times 100 = \text{Percentage change}$$

5) Some GDP growth may be due to **prices rising** (inflation, see p.74). **Nominal GDP** is the name given to a GDP figure that **hasn't** been adjusted for inflation. This figure is **misleading**, as it will give the impression that GDP is **higher** than it is.

6) Economists **remove** the effect of inflation to find what's called **real GDP**. For example, a 4% increase in the **nominal GDP** during a period when **inflation** was 3% means that **real GDP** only rose by about 1%. The other 3% was due to rising prices.

Measuring Economic Growth

GDP Per Capita can indicate the Standard of Living in a country

1) GDP can be used to give an indication of a country's **standard of living**. This is done by **dividing** the total **national output** by the country's population to get the national output **per person** — GDP per capita. Here's the formula:

$$\frac{\text{Total GDP}}{\text{Population }size} = \text{GDP per capita}$$

'Per capita' just means 'per head' or 'per person'.

2) In theory, the **higher** the **GDP per capita**, the **higher** the **standard of living** in a country.

3) Economists also use **Gross National Income (GNI) per capita** to compare living standards between different countries. (The GNI is the GDP **plus** net income from abroad — this **net** income is any income earned by a country on investments and other assets **owned abroad**, **minus** any income earned by foreigners on investments **domestically**.)

4) GNI per capita is calculated in a **similar** way to GDP per capita — by **dividing** the **total** GNI by the country's population.

Using GDP to make Comparisons has Limitations

The more different the two countries are, e.g. a rich developed nation and a poor underdeveloped economy, the greater the comparison problems.

1) **GDP** and **GDP per capita** are used to **compare** the economic performance and the standards of living in **different** countries:
   - A **high GDP** would suggest a country's **economic performance** is **strong**.
   - A **high GDP per capita** suggests that a country's **standard of living** is **high**.

2) Using the GDP and the GDP per capita to make comparisons between countries has its **limitations**. There are **several** things that GDP and GDP per capita figures might **not** take into **account**:

   - The extent of the **hidden economy** — economic activity that **doesn't** appear in official figures.
   - **Public spending** — some governments provide **more benefits**, such as unemployment benefits or free health care, than others. For example, two countries might have **similar** GDP per capita figures, but one country might **spend** much more money **per person** on providing benefits that improve the standard of living.
   - The **extent** of income inequality. Two countries may have **similar** GDP per capita, but the distribution of that income between rich and poor **may** be very different.
   - **Other** differences in the standard of living between countries, such as the number of hours workers have to work per week, working conditions, the level of damage to the environment, different spending needs (e.g. cold countries spend **more income** on heating to achieve the **same level** of comfort that exists in warm countries).

Index Numbers represent percentage changes

Index numbers are useful for **making comparisons** over a period of time. The first year is called the **base year** — the index number for this year is set at **100**. Changes up **or** down are expressed as numbers above or below 100. For example:
- A 3% **rise** in real GDP over one year would mean the index rose to **103** in year 2.
- A 2% **fall** in real GDP over one year would mean the index fell to **98** in year 2.
- An index number of **108** in year 4 means an 8% rise from the **base year**.

Practice Questions

Q1 What are the four main macroeconomic indicators?
Q2 What is the difference between nominal and real national output figures? Why is this important?
Q3 What can index numbers be used to show?

Exam Question

Q1 Why might comparing the GDP per capita of two countries fail to provide an accurate comparison of their standards of living? [8 marks]

I thought GDP wrote revision guides? No? GCP? PCG? Oh, forget it...

There are two key facts on these pages — GDP is the value of all the goods and services produced in a country in a year. Economic growth is measured as the percentage change in GDP over time. You'll need to learn the rest of this stuff too though. Sorry.

Measuring Inflation

Inflation is always being mentioned on the news — it's a key figure which is used to help measure how the economy is doing. **These pages are for all boards.**

There are *Two Ways* to *Define Inflation*

1) Inflation is the sustained **rise** in the **average price** of **goods** and **services** over a period of time. Keep in mind that:
   - The prices of some goods may be rising **faster** than the average.
   - Some prices may be rising **more slowly**.
   - Some prices may even be **falling**.

2) Inflation can also be seen as a **fall** in the **value** of money. This means that:
   - A **fixed** amount of money (e.g. £10) buys **less** than before.
   - The **purchasing power** of money has fallen (for more on purchasing power, see p.78).

Inflation can be *Positive* or *Negative (or 0)*

1) **Inflation** (or positive inflation) is when the **average price** of goods and services is **rising**.

2) Sometimes the **average price** will actually be **falling**. This is called **negative inflation**, or **deflation**.

3) Other times, a country may experience **hyperinflation**. This is when prices rise **extremely quickly** and money rapidly **loses** its value.

4) If the rate of inflation is **slowing down**, e.g. from 6% to 4%, this is called **disinflation**. Prices are still rising but at a **slower** speed.

There are *Two* main *Measurements* used for *Inflation*

The *Retail Price Index (RPI)*

1) **Two** surveys are carried out to **calculate** the RPI.

2) The first survey is a survey of around 6000 households, called the **Living Costs and Food Survey**.

3) This is used to find out **what** people spend their money on, e.g. petrol, apples, haircuts. The survey also shows what **proportion** of income is spent on these items. This is used to work out the relative **weighting** of each item (this will be important in a second) — for example, if **20%** is spent on transport, then a 20% **weighting** will be given to transport.

4) The second survey is based on **prices** — it measures the **changes** in price of around **700** of the most **commonly** used **goods** and **services** (these goods and services are often referred to as the 'basket of goods').

5) The items are chosen **based on** the Living Costs and Food Survey. What is in the basket **changes** over time, because technology, trends and tastes change (see the diagram below for some examples). This ensures that the basket always **reflects** what the **average household** might spend its money on.

6) The price **changes** in the second survey are **multiplied** by the **weightings** from the first survey. These are then converted to an **index number** (see p.73 for more on index numbers). So **inflation** is just the **percentage change** to the index number over time — e.g. if the index number **rises** from 100 to 102, then **inflation** is 2%.

> The weightings are important because the larger the proportion of a household's income that's spent on an item, the larger the effect a change in the price of that item will have on average spending.

Goods added to the basket		Goods removed from the basket
Daily disposable contact lenses	Ebooks	Local newspapers
	Honey	Analogue radios
Blueberries		Disposable cameras
		Boiled sweets

The basket of goods

Measuring Inflation

The *Consumer Price Index (CPI)*

The CPI is calculated in a **similar** way to the RPI, but there are **three main** differences:

1) Some items are **excluded** from the CPI, the main ones being:
   - Mortgage interest payments
   - Council tax

2) A slightly **different formula** is used to calculate the CPI.

3) A **larger** sample of the population is used for the CPI.

These differences mean that the CPI **tends** to be a little **lower** than the RPI — the **exception** is when **interest rates** are very low. However, they both tend to follow the same **long-term** trend.

Many other countries collect data on inflation in a **similar** way to the CPI, so it's often used for **international comparisons**.

The *CPI* and *RPI* have *Limitations*

The RPI and CPI can be really **useful**, but they also have their **limitations**:

1) The RPI **excludes** all households in the top 4% of incomes. The CPI covers a **broader range** of the population, but it **doesn't** include mortgage interest payments or council tax.

2) The information given by households in the Living Costs and Food Survey can be **inaccurate**.

3) The basket of goods only changes **once** a year — so it might miss some short-term changes in spending habits.

The *RPI* and *CPI* are important for *Government Policy*

See pages 96-97 for more on inflation.

The RPI and CPI are used to help determine **wages** and **state benefits**.

1) **Employers** and **trade unions** use them as a starting point in wage negotiations.
2) The **government** uses them to decide on increases in **state pensions**, and other welfare **benefits**.
3) Some benefits are **index-linked** — they rise **automatically** each year by the **same** percentage as the chosen index.

They're also used to measure changes in the UK's **international** competitiveness.

1) If the rate of inflation measured by the CPI is **higher** in the UK than in the other countries it trades with, then UK goods become **less** price competitive, as they'll **cost more** for other countries to buy.
2) So — **exports** will **reduce**, and **imports**, which will be made relatively **cheaper** by domestic inflation, will **increase**.

Practice Questions

Q1 In what two ways can inflation be defined?

Q2 What happens to prices during a period of:
   a) Negative inflation
   b) Hyperinflation
   c) Disinflation

Q3 In what ways is the RPI different from the CPI?

Q4 Aside from measuring inflation, give an example of a use of RPI/CPI.

Exam Question

Q1 Explain three limitations of the RPI as a measure of inflation. [6 marks]

Revision can be a bit deflating, but try to stay positive...

And there I was thinking inflation was just blowing up a balloon. The RPI and the CPI are two different measures of inflation — make sure you know what they are, the key differences between the two, and some examples of what else they're used for.

Measuring Unemployment

There are two main ways of measuring unemployment — each has its advantages and disadvantages. **For all boards.**

There are **Two** ways of **Defining Unemployment**

1) The **level** of unemployment is the **number** of people who are looking for a job but cannot find one.

2) The **rate** of unemployment is the number of people out of work as a **percentage** of the **labour force**.

The **rate** of unemployment is used when making **comparisons** between countries, as different countries have different **population sizes**.

> The labour force is all the people who are willing and able to work. This includes those working and those looking for work.

There are **Two** ways of **Measuring Unemployment**

1) The Claimant Count

The claimant count is the **number** of people claiming unemployment-related benefits from the government, known as the Jobseeker's Allowance (JSA). There are **advantages** and **disadvantages** of using the claimant count to measure unemployment:

Advantages:
- This data is **easy** to obtain (you just count the number of people claiming JSA) and there's **no** cost in collecting the data.
- It's updated **monthly**, so it's always **current**.

Disadvantages:
- It can be **manipulated** by the government to make it seem **smaller** — for example, a change in the rules (e.g. **raising** the school leaving age to 19) could reduce the **number** of people who could claim JSA, which would make it **seem** that unemployment was falling.
- It **excludes** those people who **are** looking for work but are **not** eligible to (or choose not to) claim JSA.

2) The Labour Force Survey

The International Labour Organisation (ILO) uses a **sample** of the population. It asks people who **aren't** working if they're **actively seeking** work. The **number** of people who answer 'yes' (whether they're claiming JSA or not) are added up to produce the **ILO unemployment count**. There are **advantages** and **disadvantages** to using this figure:

Advantages:
- It's thought to be **more accurate** than the claimant count.
- It's an **internationally** agreed measure for unemployment, so it's easier to make **comparisons** with other countries.

Disadvantages:
- It's less **up to date** than the claimant count because of the way the data is **collected**.
- It's **expensive** to collect and put together the data.
- The sample may be **unrepresentative** of the population as a whole — making the data **inaccurate**.

The figure from the Labour Force Survey tends to be **higher** than the claimant count because certain groups of people are **excluded** from the claimant count. For example, some people **can't claim** JSA because they have a **high earning** husband/wife, or they might have too much money in **savings**.

Unemployment comes at a **Cost** to the **Whole Economy**

> See p.98-99 for more information on unemployment.

Governments want to keep track of **unemployment figures** for a number of reasons:

1) A **high** rate of unemployment suggests that an economy is doing **badly**.

2) Unemployment will lead to **lower incomes** and **less spending**. This will have an impact on **companies** too — they might sell **fewer goods**, or need to **cut prices** and make **less profit**.

3) Unemployment means there's **unused** labour in the economy, so **fewer** goods and services can be **produced**.

4) It also means the government has **extra costs**, such as **welfare benefits**, and **less revenue** because **less tax** is paid.

Measuring the Balance of Payments

The balance of payments is all about the money coming into and going out of the country. ***This page is for all boards.***

The **Balance of Payments** refers to **International Flows** of money

The balance of payments records:

- The flow of money **out** of a country, e.g. to **pay** for **imported** goods.
- The flow of money **into** a country, e.g. **payments** from **exported** goods.

> If goods are exported, they leave the country and money moves the other way, i.e. into the country to pay for them. For imports, it's the opposite.

It's the **value** of **exports** and **imports** that's calculated in the balance of payments, **not** the **volume**.
So if **prices change**, but **volume** remains the **same**, then the **value** of exports and imports will **change**.

There are **Four** sections to the **Current Account**

The **main** part of the balance of payments you need to know for the AS exam is the **current account**, which records the **international exchange** of goods and services. It consists of **four** sections:

1) **Trade** in **goods**, often called 'visible trade' — so goods will either be **visible imports** or **visible exports**.
   Examples: cars, computers, food.
2) **Trade** in **services**, often called 'invisible trade'. These can be **imported** or **exported** too.
   Examples: tourism, insurance, transport.
3) **International** flows of **income** earned as salaries, interest, profit and dividends.
   Examples: interest on an account held in a foreign country, dividends from a company based abroad.
4) **Transfers** of money from one person or government to another.
   Examples: foreign aid, transfer of money to or from a family member who lives in another country.

The balance of payments **Isn't** always **Balanced**

1) The flows of money coming **into** a country **may not** balance the flows of money **out**.
   - If the money flowing **in** exceeds the money flowing **out**, there's a **surplus**.
   - If the money flowing **out** exceeds the money flowing **in**, there's a **deficit**.
2) In recent years, the UK has had a **deficit** in its balance of payments. Although the UK has usually had a **surplus** in **invisible trade**, it has also had a **large deficit** in **visible trade**.
3) A deficit **isn't** necessarily a bad thing — but it might be a sign that a country is **uncompetitive**.
4) Governments want to **avoid** a large, long-term deficit — this **would** cause bigger problems (see p.101).

Tom had always been good at balancing anything.

Practice Questions

Q1 Give two negative effects unemployment has on an economy.

Q2 For each of the items below, identify where it would appear in the current account of the balance of payments and whether it is a flow into or out of the UK.

Item 1   A British car company increases its sales to the Far East.

Item 2   Dividend from shares in an American company paid to a British shareholder.

Item 3   A British family holidaying in Spain who pay for a taxi in Madrid.

Exam Questions

Q1 Name the two main measures of unemployment, giving one advantage and one disadvantage of each.   [4 marks]

Q2 Explain what a surplus and a deficit are on the current account of the balance of payments.   [4 marks]

Labour Force be with you...

There's a lot on these two pages — definitions, advantages, disadvantages... You'll need to understand it all before you move on.

Measuring Development

No one is perfect — not even economists (shocking, I know). It's impossible to get a truly accurate measure of economic performance, so sometimes economists include development to try to get a better overall impression. There are lots of ways to consider development — take a look at these pages to get an idea of some of them. **These pages are for Edexcel only.**

Looking at *Development* can give a *Fuller* picture

1) Measurements of **growth** or **unemployment** are used to work out the **standard of living** in a country, but often those figures **don't** tell the full story. A **better** way to look at a country's standard of living is to measure its **economic development**.

2) Measuring the economic **development** of a country means trying to work out the **level** of social and human **welfare**, sometimes called the **quality of life**.

3) To **measure** development, economists need **more indicators** than just economic growth, inflation levels and unemployment rates, to be able to get a **fuller picture** of the quality of life in a country.

4) This is especially important when **comparing** the economies of two very **different** countries, e.g. a **rich**, **economically developed** country, such as the UK, and a **poor**, **less economically developed** country, such as Niger.

The *Human Development Index* considers a *Broader* range of *Indicators*

1) The **Human Development Index** (HDI) was developed by the United Nations to measure and rank countries' levels of **social** and **economic** development.

2) The HDI includes **social indicators** to give a fuller picture of the quality of life in a country.

3) The HDI combines indicators in **three** equally weighted sections:

> 1) **Health** (as measured by life expectancy).
> 2) **Education** (as measured by average and expected years in school).
> 3) **Standard of living** (as measured by real GNI per capita).

4) These figures are used because they are:
   - Fairly **standard** around the world.
   - Relatively **easy** to collect.

Richard frequently used the wrong indicator.

The HDI is used in different *Ways*

1) The HDI can be used to **measure** changes in **development levels** over time in a country.

2) It can also be used to **compare** the levels of development **between** countries.

3) Countries are either **ranked** in order with country number 1 being the highest...

4) ...or the HDI is given as an **index** with a range between 1 and 0.
   - Above 0.8 indicates a **high** level of human development.
   - Between 0.8 and 0.5 suggests a **medium** level of human development.
   - Below 0.5 shows a **low** level of human development.

For example, in 2013 the UK's HDI rank was 26 and its index was 0.875.

Purchasing Power Parity is used for the HDI's standard of living indicator

1) When **comparing** GNI per capita between countries that use **different currencies**, the **exchange rate** might not always reflect the **true worth** of the two currencies.

2) To **overcome** this problem, the HDI measures GNI per capita using the principle of **purchasing power parity** (PPP).

3) **Purchasing power** is the **real** value of an amount of money in terms of what you can **actually** buy with it. This can **vary** between countries — for example, in a **less developed** country, e.g. Malawi, $1 will buy **more** goods than in a **more developed** country, e.g. Canada.

4) When the HDI is calculated, the GNI per capita of each country is **adjusted** to take into account the **differences** in purchasing power in different countries — this means that the comparison between countries is **more accurate**.

Measuring Development

The HDI has its Critics

1) **Life expectancy** measured in years does not indicate anything about the **quality** of life during those years (e.g. working hours could be **long** and conditions could be **unpleasant**, air quality might be **very poor**, people might not have much **freedom**, etc.).

2) Measuring the average number of years people spend in school doesn't measure the **quality** of teaching or how well people learn what they're taught.

3) There are **problems** with using GNI per capita figures which can lead to **inaccuracies** — for example, GNI per capita **doesn't** include the hidden economy and this tends to make up a **larger proportion** of the economy in **less developed** countries.

4) The HDI figure alone doesn't measure the extent of **inequality** in a country — a country with a **satisfactory** HDI rank might have a few **very wealthy** people and a **large** number of **very poor** people.

There are Other ways to Measure Development

1) One way of measuring development is finding the **percentage** of adult male labour working in **agriculture**.
   - Agricultural work is very hard and **workers** are often paid **very little**.
   - The **economic output** from agriculture is **generally** quite **low** too.
   - As countries become more developed they tend to use **more machinery** for farming and employ **fewer workers**.
   - As a result, countries with a **high percentage** of the population working in agriculture generally have **low** levels of **economic development**.

2) Another measure of development is the number of **mobile phones** per thousand of the population.
   - Mobile phones improve **communication** and **trading**, which can lead to **greater** economic development.
   - A **large** number of mobile phones in a country indicates that **wages** are **high** enough for people to **afford** to pay for them.

3) Some other indicators to measure a country's development are:
   - Levels of **disease**.
   - Levels of **malnutrition**.
   - **Newspapers** bought per thousand of the population.
   - **Energy consumption** per head (electricity and gas).
   - Levels of political and social **freedom**.
   - Levels of **environmental** impact and sustainability.
   - **Access** to **clean** water.

Practice Questions

Q1 What is economic development?
Q2 What are the three sections to the Human Development Index?
Q3 Give two uses of the Human Development Index.
Q4 List three other ways to measure development.

Exam Question

Q1 Evaluate the likely accuracy of using the Human Development Index as a way of measuring a country's standard of living. [12 marks]

Purchasing power parity — try saying that quickly over and over...

Remember — generally in economics, no single statistic is perfect (this is especially true when sampling is involved). The usefulness of any statistic depends on the circumstances and exactly what you are trying to measure. You'll need to learn the specific uses/limitations of the Human Development Index and be aware of other measures that could be considered as well.

The Circular Flow of Income

Before you learn about the joys of aggregate demand and supply, you'll need to know about the circular flow of income. It explains the link between national output, national income and national expenditure. **These pages are for all boards.**

Income Flows *between* Firms *and* Households

1) In simple terms, an **economy** is made up of **firms** and **households**.

2) Firms **produce** goods and services, and **all** of these **goods** and **services** make up the **national output**.

3) The **households** in a country **provide** the labour, land and capital that **firms** use to produce the national output. The money **paid** to households by firms for these **factors of production** is the **national income**.

4) Households **spend** the money they get from the national income on the goods and services (outputs) that firms create — the **value** of this spending is the **national expenditure**.

5) So, all of this creates a **circular flow of income**, which can be shown by the formula:

> National **output** = National **income** = National **expenditure**

6) This **flow** of income can also be shown as a **diagram**:

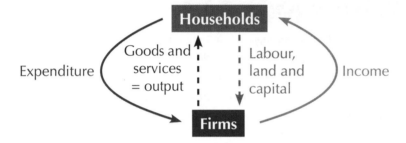

There are **Injections** *into and* **Withdrawals** *from the flow of income*

1) An economy's circular flow of income is **affected** by **injections** and **withdrawals** (or leakages).

2) **Injections into** the circular flow of income come in the form of **exports**, **investment** and **government spending** — these go directly to **firms**.

3) **Withdrawals** come in the form of **imports**, **savings** and **taxes** — these withdrawals can be made by **households** or **firms**.

4) **Injections** and **withdrawals** can be shown in a circular flow like this:

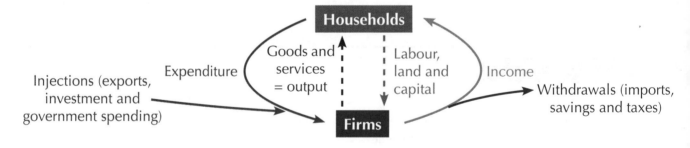

- If **injections** into the circular flow are **greater** than **withdrawals**, this means that **expenditure** is **greater** than **output** — so firms will **increase output**. As a result national output, income and expenditure will all **increase**.

- If **withdrawals** from the circular flow are **greater** than **injections**, this means that **output** is **greater** than **expenditure** — so firms will **reduce output**. As a result national output, income and expenditure will all **decrease**.

- If **injections** and **withdrawals** are **equal**, then the economy is in **equilibrium**.

The Circular Flow of Income

Injections have a Multiplier Effect on the circular flow

1) When an **injection** is made into the circular flow, the **actual change** in the **national income** is much **greater** than the **initial** injection — this is called the **multiplier effect**. Take a look at the following **example**:

- The government gives a firm £50 million to **invest** in new machinery. The money is used to pay households for land, labour and capital, so it's an **injection** of £50 million of **new income** into the circular flow.

- £12 million of this income **leaks** out of the circular flow as withdrawals (savings, tax and imports), but the **remaining £38 million** is **spent** on goods and services, so all £38 million goes to firms as **expenditure** — increasing **output**.

- Another £10 million **leaks** out of the circular flow as withdrawals from firms (savings, tax and imports), but the remaining £28 million is paid by firms as **income** to households.

- The cycle will continue, with households and firms **spending** some of the money and the rest **leaking** out of the circular flow, until there's nothing left of the **initial** investment.

- So the **original** £50 million has gone **round** the circular flow **multiple** times, though some of it has **leaked away** at each stage. This means the **total effect** of the initial investment on national **output**, **income** and **expenditure** is £50m + £38m + £28m + ... etc. — it's actually much **more** than £50 million.

The multiplier effect works on all kinds of things.

2) The **size** of the multiplier effect depends on the **rate** at which money **leaks** from the circular flow — e.g. the **bigger** the leakages, the **quicker** the money will **leave** the circular flow and the **smaller** the multiplier effect will be.

3) So, if **lots** of money is being spent on **imports** (or used as savings or tax), then the **multiplier effect** will actually be quite **small** because the injection will **quickly** leak out of the circular flow.

For AQA students, the accelerator process is covered on p.83.

Wealth is Different to Income

1) Wealth is the total **value** of all the **assets** owned by individuals or firms in an economy.

2) Assets can include **actual money**, e.g. savings, and **physical items**, e.g. houses or cars.

3) Unlike income, which is a **flow** of money, wealth is a **stock** concept — you can think of it as a **stockpile** of **resources**. These resources **aren't** currently being **used** in the circular flow of income, but they **could** be at some point.

4) Although income and wealth are **different** things there's a **correlation** between them. For example, it's likely that an individual with a **high income** will also have **high wealth**, because they'll be able to **purchase** more **expensive** assets and have **more money** to **save**.

EDEXCEL ONLY

Practice Questions

Q1 What are the three injections into the circular flow of income?

Q2 What are the three withdrawals from the circular flow of income?

Q3 Give a definition of wealth.

Exam Question

Q1 Comment on the potential multiplier effect on the circular flow of income of a large increase in government spending on the NHS.

[6 marks]

My assets include good looks, charm and modesty...

If there are no injections or withdrawals, or if injections = withdrawals, then national output, national income and national expenditure are all equal. If injections and withdrawals aren't balanced, this will lead to a change in the national income. It can be a bit tricky to get your head around, but you should be able to use the diagrams to help you figure out what's going on.

Aggregate Demand

Here's another delightful economics term — aggregate demand. 'Aggregate' is basically just a fancy economics way of saying 'total' — so aggregate demand means the 'total demand' in an economy. **These pages are for all boards.**

Aggregate Demand *is the* Total Spending *on goods and services*

1) **Aggregate demand** (AD) is the **total demand**, or the **total spending**, in an economy over a given period of time.
2) So aggregate demand is made up of all the **components** that **contribute** to spending/demand in an economy.
3) It's calculated using the **formula**:

> **AD = Consumption (C) + Investment (I) + Government spending (G) + (Exports (X) – Imports (M))**

Consumption *and* Saving *are affected by a number of factors*

1) Consumption (sometimes referred to as consumer spending or consumer expenditure) is the **total** amount spent by **households** on goods and services. It **doesn't** include spending by **firms**.
2) An **increase** in **consumption** will mean an **increase** in **AD** — a **reduction** in **consumption** will mean a **reduction** in **AD**.
3) Consumption is the **largest** component of aggregate demand — it makes up about **65%** of AD in the UK.
4) This means that **changes** in the level of **consumption** will tend to have a **big impact** on aggregate demand.
5) Savings are made **instead of** consumption — so income can be consumed **or** saved.
6) When consumption is **high**, saving tends to be **low**, and **vice versa**.
7) Here are some of the **main factors** affecting consumption and saving:

- **Income** — generally, as income **increases** consumption will **rise**. The **rate** at which **consumption** rises is usually **lower** than the **rate** at which **income** increases because households tend to **save** more as well.

- **Interest rates** — **higher** interest rates lead to **less** consumer spending. Consumers **save** more to take **advantage** of the higher rates and they're **less likely** to **borrow** money or **buy** things on **credit** because it's more expensive. Consumers may also have **less money** to spend if interest rates on **existing** loans and mortgages increase.

- **Consumer confidence** — when consumers feel **more confident** about the **economy** and their own financial situation, they **spend more** and **save less**. Confidence is **affected** by a **number** of factors. For example, in a **recession** consumers are usually **reluctant** to spend because their **confidence** in the economy is **low** — they might, for example, be worried about **losing** their jobs. This reluctance can **continue** even after a **recession**.

- **Wealth effects** — a **rise** in household **wealth**, e.g. due to a rise in **share** prices or **house** prices, will often lead to a **rise** in **consumer spending** and a **reduction** in **saving**. This is because of consumer **confidence** — if house prices rise **faster** than **inflation**, home owners will feel more **confident** in their own finances.

- **Taxes** — **direct tax increases** lead to a **fall** in consumers' disposable income, so they spend **less**. **Indirect tax increases**, e.g. an increase in VAT, **increase** the cost of spending, so consumers tend to **reduce** their consumption. A **reduction** in direct or indirect taxes will lead to an **increase** in consumer spending.

- **Unemployment** — when unemployment **rises**, consumers tend to spend **less** and save **more**. People tend to become more worried about **losing** their jobs and **save more**. A **fall** in unemployment means **more** people have money to **spend**, and consumers are **less** worried about losing their jobs, so consumer spending **increases**.

Don't confuse *Saving and Investment*

1) It's important to realise that **investment** and **saving** are **different** things.
2) **Savings** tend to be made by **households**, whereas **investments** tend to be made by **firms**.
3) For example, **savings** made by a household might be money put into a **savings bank account** each month. An **investment** made by a firm could be money paid to **build** a new office.

Aggregate Demand

Investment *is made by* Firms

1) **Investment** is money spent by **firms** on **assets** which they'll use to **produce** goods or services — this includes things such as **machinery**, **computers** and **offices**.

2) Firms **invest** with the **intention** of making **profit** in the future.

3) There are **several** factors that **affect** investment:

Risk

1) The **level** of **risk** involved will affect the **amount** of investment by firms.

2) If there's a **high risk** that a firm **won't** benefit from its investment then it's unlikely that the firm will invest. For example, when there's **economic instability** (see p.103 for more on this), **less investment** will be made.

Business confidence

The more **confident** a business is in its **ability** to make **profits**, the **more** money it's likely to **invest**.

Government incentives and regulation

1) **Government incentives** such as subsidies or reductions in tax can affect the **level** of **investment**. For example, a **reduction** in corporation tax might **encourage** firms to invest, because they'll have **more funds** available to do so.

2) A **relaxing** of **government regulations** will **reduce** a firm's costs and make it **more likely** to invest.

Interest rates

1) When **interest** rates are **high**, **investment** tends to be **lower**.

2) Firms often **borrow** the money they want to **invest**, so **high** interest rates would **reduce** how **profitable** an investment would be.

3) High interest rates will also mean there's a **greater** opportunity cost of investing **existing** funds instead of putting them into a **bank account** with a high interest rate.

Technical advances

1) Firms need to **invest** in **new technology** to stay competitive.

2) Investment will **rise** when **significant technological advances** are made.

AQA ONLY

A rise in demand Beyond *capacity might cause a* Bigger *increase in investment*

1) Sometimes **demand** for certain products is so **high** that firms need to expand **beyond** their **capacity** to meet it.

2) If firms expect that the **increased** demand will last for a **long** period of time, they're much more likely to **increase** their **capacity**. To do this, firms will need to **invest** in **new capital**, e.g. machinery.

3) For any **given change** in demand for goods/services beyond capacity, there will be a **greater percentage increase** in the demand for the capital goods that firms need to produce those extra goods/services. This is known as the **accelerator process** — firms will make 'accelerated' investment in **capital goods**, expecting to make **profit** in the future.

Practice Questions

Q1 What is the formula for aggregate demand?
Q2 What is the difference between saving and investment?
Q3 What is 'business confidence' and how does it affect investment?

Exam Questions

Q1 How might high taxes and high interest rates affect the level of consumption? [6 marks]

Q2 Describe three factors which might affect the level of investment in an economy. [6 marks]

Take it from me — Investment gets SO annoyed if he's mistaken for Saving...

Each component of aggregate demand is affected by multiple factors. These pages have described the things that affect consumption (the biggest component) and investment. You'll see similar ideas popping up on the next couple of pages too.

Aggregate Demand

You've seen the things that affect two of the components of aggregate demand (consumption and investment) — here are a couple of pages on the factors affecting the other two components (government spending and net exports). **For all boards.**

Government Spending *doesn't include* Transfers *of* Money

1) The **government spending** component of aggregate demand is the money spent by the government on **public** goods and services, e.g. education, health care, defence and so on.

2) Only money that **contributes** to the **output** of the economy is included — this means that **transfers** of money such as **benefits** (like the Jobseeker's Allowance) or **pensions** are **not** included.

3) Government spending is quite a **large** component of aggregate demand, so changes in government spending can have a big **influence** on aggregate demand.

Government Spending *doesn't have to be* Equal *to* Revenue

1) A government **budget outlines** a government's **planned** spending and revenue for the next year. Governments will usually have either a budget **deficit** or a budget **surplus**.

- If government spending is **greater than** its revenue, there will be a **budget deficit**.
- If government spending is **less than** its revenue, there will be a **budget surplus**.

Most of a government's revenue comes from taxation.

2) Governments use **fiscal policy** (see p.110-113) to alter their **spending** and **taxation** to **influence** aggregate demand.

- If aggregate demand is **low** and economic growth is **slow**, or even negative, then a government may **overspend** (causing a budget **deficit**) in order to **increase** aggregate demand and **boost** economic growth.
- If aggregate demand is **high** and the economy is experiencing a **boom**, a government might **increase taxes** and **spend less** (causing a budget **surplus**) to try to **reduce** aggregate demand and **slow down** economic growth.

The government budgetigar's planned spending on seeds would cause another deficit.

3) An **imbalance** in the budget will affect the **circular flow of income** — a **budget surplus** will indicate an **overall withdrawal** from the circular flow, but a **budget deficit** will indicate an **overall injection** into the circular flow.

4) An imbalance in the budget is fine in the **short run**, but in the **long run** governments will try to **balance** out any **surpluses** and **deficits**. A long-term **surplus** might mean the government is **harming** economic growth by choosing **not** to spend, or by keeping taxes **too high**. A long-term **deficit** is likely to mean a country has a large national **debt**.

5) Sometimes governments will **balance** the **budget** so that government spending will be **equal** to revenue. This should have little **effect** on aggregate demand.

An Export *from one country is* Always *an* Import *to another*

1) **Exports** are **goods** or **services** that are produced in one country, then sold in another. Imports are the opposite — they're goods and services that are brought **into** a country after being **produced elsewhere**.

2) Exports are an **inflow** of money to a country, and imports are an **outflow** — so exports are an **injection** into the circular flow of income and imports are a **withdrawal**.

3) Exports minus imports (X – M) make up the **net exports** component of aggregate demand.

4) If the amount spent on imports **exceeds** the amount received from exports (as it does in the UK), **net exports** will be a **negative** number.

Aggregate Demand

There are many Factors that will Affect Imports and Exports

Several factors will affect the **net exports** component of aggregate demand:

There's more on exchange rates on p.104-105.

The exchange rate

A change in the **value** of a currency will affect net exports in **different ways** in the **long** and **short run**:

- In the **long run** — if the **value** of a currency **increases**, **imports** become relatively **cheaper** and **exports** become relatively **more expensive** for foreigners. As a result, **demand** for **imports** (**M**) rises and **demand** for **exports** (**X**) **falls**. So a **strong** currency (i.e. a currency with a high value) will **worsen** net exports (**X – M**) in the **long run** and reduce aggregate demand, but a **weak** currency will have the **opposite effect** and **improve** net exports.

- In the **short run** — demand for imports and exports tends to be quite price **inelastic**. For example, some goods **don't** have close substitutes, e.g. oil, while others might **have substitutes**, but there's a **time lag** before countries will **switch** to them — so in the short run demand **won't change** much. This means that **initially** when the value of a currency **increases**, net exports will actually **improve** (increase) because the **overall value** of exports **increases** and the **overall value** of imports **decreases**.

Changes in the state of the world economy

The state of the **world economy** will affect exports and imports. For example, the USA exports lots of goods to Canada. If Canada goes through a period of **low** (or negative) **growth** then **exports** from the USA to Canada will **decrease**. Assuming imports are unaffected, this means a **worsening** in the USA's net exports. Similarly, if Canada was experiencing **high growth rates**, exports from the USA are likely to **increase** — **improving** net exports.

Non-price factors

These include things such as the **quality** of goods. For example, advancements in technology in a country that lead to the production of **higher quality** goods would be likely to cause an **increase** in exports from that country, because people are willing to **pay more** for something if it's really good. This would mean an **improvement** in **net exports**.

Net exports tend to make up a **small percentage** of aggregate demand, so changes in net exports have a **minor impact** on AD.

Practice Questions

Q1   What does the government spending component of aggregate demand consist of?

Q2   What will cause a budget deficit?

Q3   Define 'imports' and 'exports'.

Q4   What 'non-price factors' may lead to an improvement in net exports?

Exam Questions

Q1   Which of the following pairs of government policies is most likely to lead to an increase in aggregate demand in an economy?
A)   Increase government spending and increase taxes.
B)   Decrease government spending and increase taxes.
C)   Increase government spending and decrease taxes.
D)   Decrease government spending and decrease taxes.
Explain your answer.   [4 marks]

Q2   Explain two factors which could increase the demand for a country's exports.   [10 marks]

Apparently net exports have nothing to do with fishing...

So there it is — that's all the components of aggregate demand. It's really important that you know what the components of aggregate demand are, what affects them and how important each component is to the overall aggregate demand. But that's not all you need to know about aggregate demand, not by a long shot — turn the page and be wowed by the majestic aggregate demand curve.

Aggregate Demand Analysis

Aggregate demand is the total demand in an economy — so the AD curve is similar to the normal demand curve. Sometimes a change in AD will cause a movement along the AD curve, other times the curve will shift. **These pages are for all boards.**

The **Aggregate Demand Curve** is similar to the normal **Demand Curve**

1) The aggregate demand curve uses **different** axes to the normal demand curve (p.16) — along the x-axis is **national output**, and up the y-axis is **price level**.

2) The price level represents the **average** level of prices in an economy — in the UK this price level is likely to be the **Consumer Price Index** (see p.75).

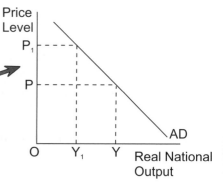

3) The aggregate demand (AD) curve slopes **downwards** — the **lower** the price level, the **more** output is demanded. **Lower** prices mean consumers can buy **more** goods/services with their money.

4) A **change** in the **price level** will cause a **movement along** the AD curve — for example, if the price level **rose** from P to P_1, the total (aggregate) demand would **fall** from Y to Y_1.

5) A rise in the price level will cause output to fall because:

- Domestic **consumption** will be **reduced** — things become **more expensive**, so people can purchase **fewer** goods and services.

- The **demand** for **exports** will be **reduced** — domestically produced products become **less competitive**.

- The **demand** for **imports** will **increase** — if prices **haven't** risen abroad, imports will become **cheaper** in comparison.

The **AD Curve** can **Shift**

Aggregate demand can **increase** or **decrease**, causing the AD curve to shift **right** or **left**.

The **AD Curve** might **Shift** to the **Right**

1) The AD curve will **shift** to the **right** if there's a **rise** in consumption, investment, government spending or net exports that **hasn't** been caused by a change in the price level. For example:

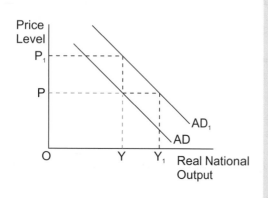

- A **reduction** in income tax will cause an **increase** in consumers' disposable income. This tends to lead to an **increase** in consumption, so there will be an **increase** in aggregate demand and a **shift** of the AD curve to the right from **AD** to $\mathbf{AD_1}$ (see the diagram to the left).

- If a government changes its fiscal policy (see p.110) and decides to **increase** its spending **above** any increase in its revenue, then this is an **injection** into the circular flow of income. It will cause an **increase** in aggregate demand and a **shift** of the AD curve to the **right**, e.g. from AD to AD_1.

- A **weak** currency will make **exports cheaper** and **imports more expensive**. This will lead to a **rise** in **net exports**, so there will be an **increase** in **aggregate demand** and a **shift** of the AD curve to the **right**, e.g. from AD to AD_1.

2) The outward shift of the curve means that at a **given price level**, **more output** can be produced — but also, a **given** amount of **output** will have a **higher** price level. For example, if there's an increase in aggregate demand from AD to AD_1 — at price level P, there's an increase in output from Y to Y_1, and at output Y, the price level increases from P to P_1.

3) Labour is a **derived demand** — an **increase** in AD means **output increases**, so the **demand** for labour **increases**. **More** jobs are created so that the **extra** output can be **produced**, and there will be an **increase** in **employment** levels.

Aggregate Demand Analysis

*The **AD Curve** might **Shift** to the **Left***

1) The AD curve will **shift** to the **left** if there's a **fall** in consumption, investment, government spending or net exports that **hasn't** been caused by a change in the price level. For example:

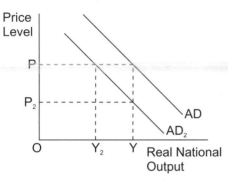

- A **rise** in **interest rates** will lead to a **reduction** in **consumer spending** because people will choose to **save** more. Higher interest rates also lead to a **reduction** in **investment** because borrowing the money to invest becomes **more expensive**. Both of these factors lead to a **reduction** in **aggregate demand**, and a **shift** of the AD curve to the **left**, e.g. from AD to AD_2 (see the diagram to the left).

- A **strong** currency will make **exports more expensive** and **imports cheaper**, so there will be a **fall** in **net exports**. This will lead to a **reduction** in **aggregate demand** and a **shift** of the AD curve to the left, e.g. from AD to AD_2.

2) The inward shift of the curve means that at a **given price level** (P), **less output** (Y_2) can be produced — but also, a **given** amount of output (Y) will have a **lower** price level (P_2). There will also be a decrease in **employment** levels.

The **Multiplier Effect** leads to a **Larger Increase** in aggregate demand

1) Page 81 introduced the **multiplier effect** — when money is **injected** into the circular flow of income, the **value** of the **initial** injection is **multiplied**. One person's **expenditure** becomes someone else's **income**, so the money goes round the circular flow **multiple** times until it's all **leaked** out.

2) One **injection** into the circular flow is the **government spending** component of aggregate demand. An **increase** in **government spending** will have a **multiplier** effect on the circular flow of income, and on aggregate demand.

3) For example, if a government **injects** money into **health care**, the money might be used for **wages**. Some of this money would then be spent by **consumers** — **increasing consumption**. This would create a **second** increase in AD, and the cycle will continue until all the money from the initial injection has **leaked out**.

4) The overall **size** of the **multiplier** will depend on the **size** of the **leakages** from the circular flow of income, but it's **very difficult** to measure in practice. This is partly because the multiplier effect of government spending can take **years** to show up in the economy (i.e. there are **time lags**) — e.g. the benefits to the economy of government spending on improving transport links may take **years** to come into full effect. Measuring the size of the multiplier is also made difficult because, like everything else in the economy, it's **changing all the time**.

*The **Marginal Propensity to Consume** effects the size of the **Multiplier***

1) The **marginal propensity to consume** (MPC) is the **proportion** of an **increase** in income that people will **spend** (instead of saving).

2) This affects the **size** of the multiplier — for example, in a country where the MPC is **low**, the multiplier will be **small**, because an increase in income will only lead to a **small increase** in **consumption**. The rest of the increase in income will be **saved**.

3) The MPC tends to be **higher** in **less developed** countries, so the multiplier will be **bigger**.

Practice Questions

Q1 Give one example of a cause of movement along the AD curve.

Q2 What might determine the size of the multiplier in a country?

Exam Question

Q1 Discuss the effect of an increase in government spending on aggregate demand. Refer to the multiplier effect in your answer.

[10 marks]

I guess your propensity to consume biscuits and tea is currently pretty high...

There can be movements along the aggregate demand curve, and shifts of the curve itself. Make sure you understand the difference between the two — there will be a movement along the curve if there's a change in the price level, but the actual curve will only move when it's AD that changes. You also need to know the effect the multiplier will have on AD.

Aggregate Supply

Aggregate supply is just the total output which can be supplied in an economy. **These pages are for all boards.**

Aggregate Supply *varies with the* Price Level

1) **Aggregate supply** (AS) is the **total** amount of goods and services which can be **supplied** in an economy at different **price levels** over a given period of **time**.

2) Here's an example of an **AS curve**:

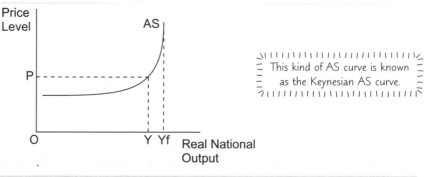

> This kind of AS curve is known as the Keynesian AS curve.

- At **low** levels of output aggregate supply is **completely elastic** (where the curve is horizontal) — this means there's **spare capacity** in the economy, so **output** can **increase** without a rise in the **price level**. For example, if there's a lot of **unemployment** in an economy, firms will be able to employ **more** workers and **increase** output, **without** increasing price levels.

- When the curve begins to **slope upwards** this shows that the economy is experiencing **problems** with supply (known as supply bottlenecks), which are causing **increases** in **costs**. For example, this might be due to a **shortage** of **labour**, or a **shortage** of certain **raw materials**.

- The curve becomes **vertical** when the economy is at **full capacity** (Yf) — here, aggregate supply is **completely inelastic**. All resources are being used to their **maximum potential** and output **can't** increase any more.

Changes *in the* Factors of Production *will cause a* Shift *of the AS curve*

1) An **improvement** in the factors of production will cause the AS curve to shift to the **right**, e.g. from AS to AS₁.

2) If the AS curve shifts to the right there will be a **decrease** in the **price level**, i.e. the **same amount** of goods/services can be supplied at a **lower** price level.

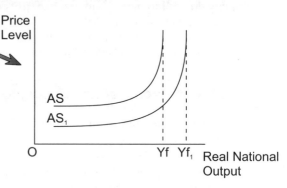

3) There's also an **increase** in the **capacity** of the economy, i.e. the **maximum** possible output **increases**.

4) For example, **investment** that leads to **advancements** in **technology**, and **more efficient** production, will mean a **reduction** of production costs for firms and an **increase** in their **maximum** possible output.

5) Other examples of **improvements** in the factors of production which might **shift** the AS curve to the **right** are:

- An **improvement** in education and skills — better education and training should lead to **more productive** individuals, i.e. the **output** per person will **increase**. This means firms' **costs** are **reduced** (they can create the **same** output using **fewer** 'worker hours') and their **maximum** output is increased.

- A **supply** of **new** resources — new resources will mean **new** output can be produced, so the **maximum** output of the economy is increased. Also, an **increase** in the **supply** of a **raw material** will bring its price **down** and **increase output** because costs of production are **reduced**.

- An **increase** in health care spending — if an increase in spending leads to an **improvement** in health care then the **overall** health of workers will **improve**. They're likely to have **less** time off work and retire at an **older** age. This means the **productivity** and **size** of the economy's labour force **increases**, which increases the **capacity** of the economy.

- An **increase** in competition — greater competition in an economy will cause a **fall** in prices. Inefficient firms which **can't compete** will **close** and be **replaced** by more efficient firms — **increasing** an economy's **capacity**.

6) A **deterioration** in the factors of production that **reduces** an economy's capacity will cause the AS curve to shift to the **left**, e.g. if there's a massive **reduction** in the **supply** of oil then the **maximum** possible output will be **reduced**.

7) A sudden **decrease** in aggregate supply could be caused by supply-side shocks, such as **natural disaster** or **war**.

Aggregate Supply

Shifts of the **AD** and **AS** curves **Affect** the macroeconomic policy indicators

1) **Macroeconomic equilibrium** occurs where the AD and AS curves **cross**, e.g. at price level P and output Y.

2) A **shift** of either curve will **move** this equilibrium to a **different** point.

3) Shifts of AD and AS curves **affect** the four main macroeconomic indicators (see Section 4) in **different ways**.

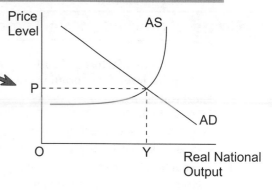

A shift in aggregate demand

- For example, when there's an **increase** in aggregate demand and the AD curve shifts from AD to AD_1, the **new** equilibrium point will be at price level P_1 and output Y_1.

- This means there's an increase in output, so there's **economic growth**. Because of an increase in **derived demand**, more **jobs** are created and therefore unemployment is **reduced**.

- However, the **rise** in price level means there's a **rise** in **inflation**. Higher prices may also lead to a **lack** of **competitiveness** internationally, meaning a **decrease** in exports, a **rise** in imports and therefore a **worsening** in the current account of the balance of payments.

- A **decrease** in AD will have the **opposite** effect — **output** will be **reduced** and there will be an **increase** in **unemployment**. Price levels will be **reduced**, which will lead to an **improvement** in the current account of the balance of payments.

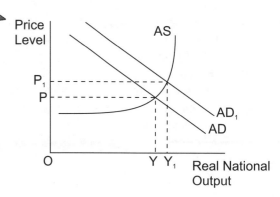

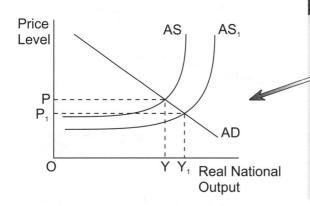

A shift in aggregate supply

- A shift of the AS curve will either improve or worsen **all four** indicators at the **same time**.

- For example, an **increase** in AS, shown by a shift to the right from AS to AS_1, will lead to an **increase** in the **capacity** of the economy. This will result in an **increase** in output — so there's **increased** economic growth. There will be **more jobs**, reducing **unemployment**. The **price level** will tend to **fall** and the economy will become **more competitive** internationally, **improving** the balance of payments.

- On the other hand, a **decrease** in AS would **worsen** the state of all four macroeconomic indicators.

Practice Questions

Q1 As an economy approaches full productive capacity, what happens to the elasticity of supply?

Q2 Give an example of an improvement in the factors of production which would shift the AS curve to the right.

Q3 Give an example of a deterioration in the factors of production which would shift the AS curve to the left.

Exam Question

Q1 Describe the possible effects on an economy of a shift to the right of the aggregate supply curve. [8 marks]

All the curves on these pages are making me blush...

Remember — a deterioration in the factors of production will shift the AS curve to the left, but an improvement in the factors of production will shift it to the right. You should know and understand some of the changes which would cause these shifts.

SECTION FIVE — AGGREGATE DEMAND AND AGGREGATE SUPPLY

Short Run and Long Run Aggregate Supply

AQA looks at aggregate supply in the short and long run. If you're taking AQA you need to know the Keynesian view of AS from the previous two pages, but you'll also need to know about the separate SRAS and LRAS curves too. **For AQA only.**

Costs of production are Fixed in the Short Run

1) In the short run, **factors** and **costs** of production are **fixed**. So if there's an increase in the **price level**, firms' **profit** per unit of output also **increases**.

2) **Short run** aggregate supply (SRAS) curves slope up from left to right — they show that with an **increase** in the **price level**, there's an **increase** in the amount of **output** firms are willing to supply.

3) The SRAS curve will **shift** if there's a **change** in the **costs** of production.

4) A **reduction** in the **costs** of production means that at the **same** price level, **more output** can be **produced**, so the SRAS curve will shift to the **right**.

5) For example, a **reduction** in the price of oil might shift the curve from SRAS to $SRAS_1$ — so at price level P, **output** would **increase** from Y to Y_1.

6) **Changes** in things such as wage rates, the taxes firms pay and productivity will cause **shifts** of the SRAS curve.

7) For example, an **increase** in wages means an **increase** in the costs of production, so the SRAS curve will shift to the **left**.

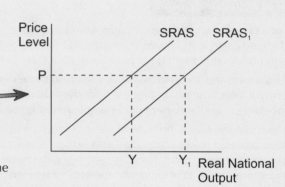

Factors of production change in the Long Run

1) In the **long run** it's assumed that, because factors and costs of production can **change**, an economy will move towards an equilibrium where **all resources** are being used to **full capacity** (so the economy is running at its full **productive potential**). This is known as **long run aggregate supply** (LRAS).

2) This means that the LRAS curve is **vertical** (perfectly inelastic). An increase in the price level (e.g. to P_1) **won't** cause an increase in output because the economy is running at full capacity, so it **can't** create any more output.

3) Long run aggregate supply is **determined** by the **factors of production** — the LRAS curve will **shift** if there's a **change** in the factors of production which affects the **capacity** of the economy.

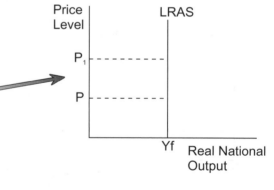

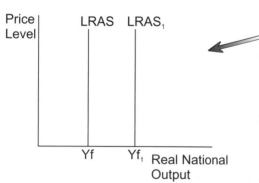

4) A change in the factors of production which **increases** the **capacity** of the economy will shift the LRAS curve to the **right**, e.g. from LRAS to $LRAS_1$. This **increases** output (in other words, there's economic growth) from Yf to Yf_1 — the **same** price level now corresponds to a **higher** level of output.

5) A change in the **capacity** of the economy has an effect on the **costs** of production, so it will also **shift** the **SRAS** curve. For example, an **increase** in an economy's capacity will **reduce** the costs of production and shift the SRAS curve to the **right**.

6) The **capacity** of an economy (and therefore LRAS and SRAS) will be affected by things such as the level of **enterprise** in the economy, the **attitude** of workers (e.g. if they're hard-working), the level of **productivity**, **technological advances**, and the **mobility** of factors of production.

7) For example, if productivity **increases**, **more** output can be produced **per unit** of input, so the capacity of the economy will **increase** (and the LRAS and SRAS curves will shift to the right).

Short Run and Long Run Aggregate Supply

An *Increase* in AD alone won't increase *Output* in the *Long Run*

In the **short run**, an **increase** in **aggregate demand**, e.g. from AD to AD₁, will cause an **increase** in output, i.e. economic growth, and a **reduction** in unemployment. Prices will rise, causing **inflation**, and there will possibly be a **worsening** of the balance of payments.

However, in the **long run**, an increase in AD **won't** lead to an increase in output or a reduction in unemployment, because the economy is already at **full** capacity — there will only be a **rise** in prices, i.e. **inflation**, and potentially a **worsening** of the balance of payments.

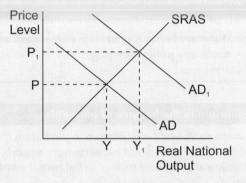

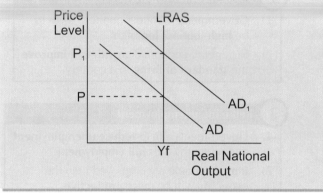

- In general, to improve **all four** macroeconomic policy indicators at the **same time**, there needs to be an **increase** in **LRAS**.

- For example, if long run aggregate supply shifts from LRAS to LRAS₁, then in the long run **output** is **increased**, **unemployment** remains at zero, the **price level falls** and the balance of payments will potentially **improve**.

- So a **shift** of the LRAS curve will tend to cause **all four** macroeconomic policy indicators to **improve** or **worsen** at the **same time**.

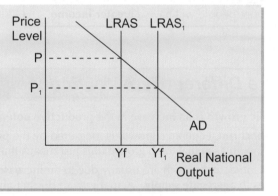

Banks can play a part in determining the Position of the LRAS curve

1) Firms often **borrow** money from **banks** to **invest**, usually so that they can **increase** their output — e.g. a firm might borrow money to invest in **new machinery**.

2) If a country has a **strong** banking system then this will help its economy to **grow**. It will mean there's **more money** available for investment in the economy, and this should lead to an **increase** in the **productive potential** (capacity) of the economy.

In the exam it might refer to the 'institutional structure of the economy' — the banking system is part of this.

3) So **improvements** in a country's banking system will **shift** the LRAS (and the SRAS) curve to the **right**.

Practice Questions

Q1 What effect will a shift of the LRAS curve to the right have on the four main macroeconomic policy indicators?

Exam Question

Q1 A shift of the LRAS curve to the right might be caused by:
    A) a reduction in wages.   B) the discovery of a new raw material.
    C) a reduction in taxes.   D) a drop in interest rates.
    Explain your answer.   [4 marks]

NB: if you aren't an economy, running at full capacity isn't a good idea...

In general, long and short run aggregate supply curves are shifted by the same things that cause shifts of the Keynesian AS curve on p.88. The long run aggregate supply curve will be shifted by anything that alters the capacity of the economy. The SRAS curve will be shifted by anything that shifts the LRAS curve, and also by any changes in the costs of production.

Economic Growth

Governments have certain objectives they want to achieve for the benefit of their country's economy and society. This page gives a bit of an introduction to the main objectives before looking at economic growth. **This page is for all boards.**

There are **Four Main Objectives** of Government Macroeconomic Policy

Governments have several objectives, but there are **four main macroeconomic objectives** they're trying to achieve:

1 Strong economic growth

1) Governments want economic growth to be **high** (but not **too** high).

2) In general, economic growth will **improve** the **standard of living** in a country.

2 Keeping inflation low

1) In the UK, the government aims for **inflation** of **2%**.

2) The **Monetary Policy Committee of the Bank of England** uses **monetary policy** (see pages 114-117) to achieve this target rate.

3 Reducing unemployment

1) Governments aim to **reduce unemployment** and move towards **full employment**.

2) If **more** people are employed then the economy will be **more productive**. **Aggregate demand** will also **increase** as more people will have a **greater income**.

4 Equilibrium in the balance of payments

1) Governments want **equilibrium** in the balance of payments, i.e. they want **earnings** from **exports** and other **inward flows** of money to **balance** the **spending** on **imports** and other **outward** flows of money.

2) This is **more desirable** than a **long-term deficit** or **surplus** in the balance of payments — which can cause problems.

There are **Different Types** of Economic Growth

1) **Economic growth** is an **increase** in the **productive potential** of an economy.

2) In the **short run**, economic growth is measured by the **percentage change** in real national output (real GDP — see p.72). This is known as **actual** (real) growth (this just means that the **effect** of **inflation** has been **removed** from the growth figure).

3) Increases in actual growth are usually due to an **increase** in **aggregate demand**, but they can also be caused by **increases** in **aggregate supply**. Actual growth doesn't always increase — it tends to **fluctuate up** and **down**.

4) **Long run** growth (also known as **potential** growth) is caused by an **increase** in the **capacity**, or **productive potential**, of the economy. This usually happens due to a **rise** in the **quality** or **quantity** of **inputs** (the **factors of production**). For example, more **advanced** machinery or a more **highly skilled** labour force.

5) Long run growth is shown by an **increase** in the **trend rate** of growth. The **trend rate** of growth is the **average rate** of economic growth over a period of both economic **booms** and **slumps**. It **rises smoothly** rather than fluctuating like actual economic growth, so the **actual rate** of growth often doesn't **match** the **trend rate**.

6) **Increases** in long run growth are caused by an increase in **aggregate supply**.

A **Production Possibility Frontier (PPF)** can show **Economic Growth**

1) **Short run** and **long run** economic growth can be shown with a **PPF** (see p.8).

2) Short run growth **occurs** when there's **spare** capacity (unused or underused resources). Therefore short run growth can be shown by a **movement** from point A (**within** the PPF, where there's **spare** capacity) to point B (**on** the PPF, where all **resources** are **fully** used).

3) Long run growth **occurs** if there's an **increase** in the **capacity** of the economy — this would make the PPF shift **outwards** to PPF₁ (shown by a movement from point B to point C).

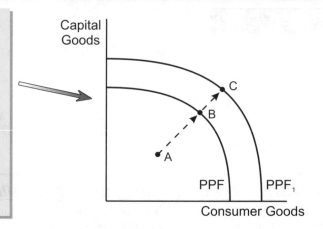

Economic Growth

Economies go through Cycles of Different Rates of Growth

Economies tend to **grow steadily** over time — so **trend growth** is usually shown as a line that's **rising smoothly**. However, **actual growth** goes through periods of **positive** and **negative** growth — it's usually shown as a line fluctuating up and down. The **slope** of the line shows the **rate** of growth, e.g. when the line slopes **upwards**, this indicates a period of **positive** growth. The fluctuations are known as the **economic cycle**. There are **different stages** to the cycle — booms, recessions and recoveries.

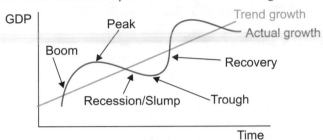

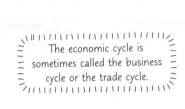

The economic cycle is sometimes called the business cycle or the trade cycle.

Boom

- In a boom, GDP is **growing quickly**, so the actual rate of growth is likely to be **above** the trend rate of growth.
- Aggregate demand will **rise**, causing a **reduction** in unemployment and a **rise** in inflation.
- There will also be an **increase** of **investment** by firms in an attempt to keep up with **demand**.

Recession/Slump

- A **recession** occurs when there's **negative** economic growth for at least **two consecutive quarters** (a 'quarter' is just a quarter of a year). A **slump** is a long period of recession.
- Aggregate demand will **fall**, causing a **rise** in unemployment and a **fall** in prices.
- There will also be **less** investment by firms.

Recovery

- A **recovery** comes **after** a trough, at the **end** of a recession/slump.
- In a recovery the economy begins to **grow** again — it'll go from negative economic growth to positive economic growth.
- There will be more **spending** in the economy, so aggregate demand will **increase**. This will **reduce** unemployment, cause inflation to **rise** and lead to an **increase** in investment.

Large fluctuations in actual economic growth will be caused by demand-side or supply-side **shocks**.

Demand-side shocks are shocks to **aggregate demand**. They can either increase or decrease aggregate demand (and therefore economic growth). For example:

- If a country's **major trading partners** go into a **recession**, this may significantly reduce demand for the country's **exports**.
- If consumer confidence is **boosted**, e.g. due to **house prices rising**, this will **increase consumer spending**.

Supply-side shocks are shocks to **aggregate supply**. They can either increase or decrease aggregate supply (affecting economic growth). For example:

- The discovery of a major **new source** of a raw material will greatly reduce its price and increase its supply — **increasing** the **capacity** of the economy.
- A **poor harvest** reduces the supply of food, increases its price, and **reduces** the economy's **capacity**.

The Difference between actual output and trend output creates Output Gaps

1) The **difference** between an economy's **actual** level of output and its **trend** level of output (the estimated long-term trend value of output) is known as the **output gap**.

2) A negative output gap occurs when **actual output** is **below** the **trend** level of **output** (between points 1 and 2 on the diagram). This happens in an **under-performing** economy where some resources are **unused** or **underused** (e.g. there might be high unemployment).

3) A positive output gap occurs when **actual output** is **above** the **trend** level of **output** (between points 3 and 4). This happens in an **overheating** economy where resources are being **fully used** or **overused**.

4) A **negative** output gap is **potentially deflationary** (i.e. it might cause deflation) as the economy is **under-performing**.

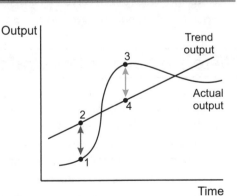

5) A **positive** output gap is **potentially inflationary** (i.e. it might increase inflation) because the economy is **overheating**.

Economic Growth

The *Ways* of *Creating Short Run Economic Growth*

1) **Short run** economic growth can be the result of **rising aggregate demand** (**AD**). The factors which cause this increase in AD are sometimes called **demand-side factors** — here are some examples:

> - **Lowering interest rates** would **encourage** investment and **increase** consumer spending.
> - **Raising welfare benefits** would **increase** government and consumer spending.

Aggregate Demand is made up of C + I + G + (X − M) (see p.82 for more).

2) A **rise** in **short run aggregate supply** (SRAS) can also create short run economic growth. Any factor which **reduces production costs** will cause an **increase** in SRAS.

3) **AD** and **AS** (aggregate supply) curves can be used to show what happens when there's **short run** economic growth:

When **AD increases**, e.g. from AD to AD$_1$, national output grows from Y to Y$_1$.

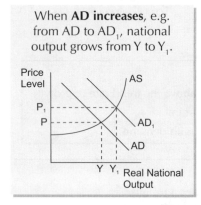

When **SRAS increases**, e.g. from SRAS to SRAS$_1$, national output grows from Y to Y$_1$.

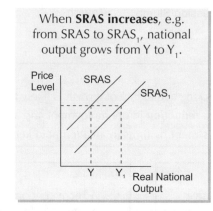

However, if AD is on the **vertical** part of the AS curve (or on the LRAS curve), then an **increase** in AD **won't increase** national output (but **prices** will **rise**).

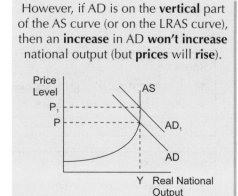

The *Ways* of *Creating Long Run Economic Growth*

1) **Long run** economic growth is the result of **supply-side factors** that increase the **potential** for **economic growth**.

2) The **productive potential** of a country can be **increased** by **raising** the **quantity** or **quality** of the **factors of production**, for example:

> - **Raising** agricultural **output** by using genetically modified (GM) crops.
> - **Investing** in more **modern** machinery.
> - Setting up **training schemes** to **improve labour productivity** (see p.12)
> - Through **innovation** — e.g. new technology.

Don't confuse the potential for growth with actual economic growth. The potential for growth may exist but no growth happens.

3) A **government** can also help to create long run economic growth by **creating** stability in a country (e.g. by enforcing laws) and through encouraging **economic stability** (e.g. so that there are no big changes in inflation).

4) If the **population** of a country **grows**, so will its **productive potential** — so governments could **encourage** immigration in order to **increase** the **size** of its population.

5) An **increase** in a country's productive potential **shifts** the AS (or LRAS) curve to the right.

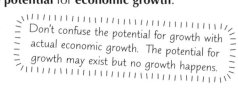

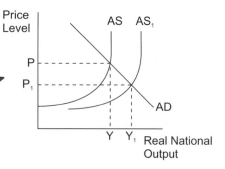

6) So national output **increases** from Y to Y$_1$ and the price level **drops** from P to P$_1$.

There are *Several Constraints* on *Economic Growth*

1) In many countries, economic growth can be **held back** because of an **absence of capital markets**. For example, in many countries in Africa it's either **not possible** to **borrow** money, or the rates of interest are **extremely high**. If it's **difficult** to **borrow** money, it's **harder** to get **investment** and **create** economic growth.

2) If a government **lacks control** over its country, or is seen to be **corrupt** or **incompetent**, it may make the country seem **unstable** — this tends to lead to a **lack** of **investment** from other countries.

3) A **small** population, or a **reduction** in the size of a population (e.g. due to people **emigrating**), would **constrain** growth.

4) Other factors such as **poor infrastructure** (e.g. if transport and communication networks are underdeveloped) may also **constrain** economic growth.

Economic Growth

Economic Growth has Benefits for Employees, Firms and Governments

1) **Economic growth** will lead to **higher wages** for **employees**. It will also produce a **rise** in the **standard** of **living**, as long as prices **don't** rise more than the increase in wages.

2) **Firms** usually earn **greater profits** during a period of economic growth — consumers tend to spend more (due to their increased wages), so firms sell more. Firms will use that profit to **invest** in better machinery, make **technological advances** and **hire** more employees.

3) **Economic growth** causes wages and employment to **rise**, which will **increase** the **government's tax revenue** and **reduce** the amount it pays in **unemployment benefits**. The government can use this **extra revenue** to **improve** public services or the country's infrastructure **without** having to **raise taxes**.

All of these benefits will help to **increase** the chances of **future growth**, so the growth can continue in the long run.

The Costs of economic growth can be Economic, Environmental and Social

1) Economic growth can create **income inequality**, where **low-skilled workers** may find it hard to get the **higher wages** that other workers are benefiting from.

2) If economic growth causes **demand** to **increase faster** than **supply**, this will cause **demand-pull inflation** (see p.96) and prices will rise.

3) **Higher wages** for employees are often linked to an **increase** in their **responsibilities** at work (e.g. if they've been promoted). This can **increase stress** and **reduce productivity**.

4) A **deficit** in the **balance of payments** can be created by **higher incomes** because people buy **more imports**.

5) **Industrial expansion** created by economic growth may bring **negative externalities**, such as pollution, which **harm** the **environment** and **reduce** the quality of life.

6) **Beautiful scenery** and **habitats** can be **destroyed** when **resources** are **overexploited**.

7) **Finite resources** may be **used up** in the creation of economic growth, which will **constrain** growth in the **future**.

EDEXCEL & OCR ONLY

Sustainable Growth is Difficult to Achieve

Sustainable economic growth means making sure the economy **keeps growing** in the future, **without** causing **problems** for future generations. Sustainable growth relies on a country's ability to:

- **Expand output** every year.
- Find a **continuous supply** of raw materials, land, labour and so on, to continue production.
- Find **growing markets** for the increased output, so it's always being bought.
- **Reduce negative externalities**, e.g. pollution, to an acceptable level so they don't hamper production.
- Do all of the above things at the **same time** as many **other** countries who are pursuing the **same objectives**.

It's very difficult for a country to do these things, and if it fails then growth **cannot** be **sustained**. However, **sustainable** growth provides **long-term** benefits to society and makes it easier to **plan ahead**.

Practice Questions

Q1 What is meant by the actual rate of economic growth?
Q2 Give an example of a demand-side shock that might lead to economic growth.
Q3 List three examples of costs of economic growth.

Exam Questions

Q1 Define the term economic cycle. [5 marks]
Q2 Evaluate to what extent high rates of economic growth are desirable. [12 marks]

How to make long run economic growth — chase after it dressed as a bear...

There's lots to learn on these four pages — make sure you understand the difference between long and short run growth. Also, economic growth might sound like a good thing, but in the exam you might be asked to write about its costs — so learn 'em.

Inflation

Inflation can rise because of higher costs and increased consumer demand. Exciting inflation-related information like this is waiting for you on these pages — enjoy. **These pages are for all boards.**

Inflation *can be caused by* Cost-Push Factors

1) **Cost-push inflation** is inflation which is caused by the **rising cost** of **inputs** to production.

2) Rising costs of inputs to production force producers to **pass on** the **higher costs** to **consumers** in the form of **higher prices**, which causes the **aggregate supply curve** to shift to the left (from AS to AS₁).

3) Here are some **examples** of causes of cost-push inflation:

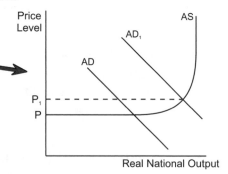

A rise in wages above any increase in productivity
- If wages make up a **large proportion** of a firm's **total costs** then this could lead to a **significant rise** in **prices**.
- Price rises could lead to **further** wage demands, which **in turn** could lead to price increases, and so on (this is a **wage-price spiral**).

A rise in the cost of imported raw materials
- If the **world prices** of inputs **rise** then, in the short run, **producers** will pay the **higher cost** and set **higher prices**.
- Also, if a country's currency **decreases** in **value** then producers will have to **pay more** for the **same imports**.

A rise in indirect taxes
- If the government **raises indirect taxes** (see p.58), this will **increase costs** and, in turn, **prices**.
- If a good is **price inelastic** then **more** of the cost of the **tax** will be passed on to the **consumer**.

Inflation *can* Also *be caused by* Demand-Pull Factors

1) **Demand-pull inflation** is inflation caused by **excessive growth** in **aggregate demand** compared to supply. This growth in demand **shifts** the **aggregate demand curve** to the **right** (from AD to AD₁), which allows sellers to **raise prices**.

2) Here are some **examples** of causes of demand-pull inflation:

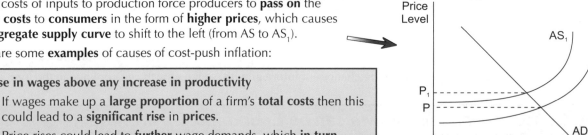

High consumer spending
- High consumer spending could be caused by **high levels** of **confidence** in the **consumers' future employment prospects** (e.g. during a period of low unemployment).
- **Low interest rates** encourage **cheap borrowing** and greater **spending**.

The money supply growing faster than output
- If **interest rates** are **low** then **borrowing** will **increase** and consumers will **spend more**. This could cause **more money** to be in the economy than can be **matched** by the **output** of goods and services (sometimes termed 'too much money chasing too few goods') and lead to a **rise** in **prices**.
- Some economists believe that **excess money** is the **biggest** cause of inflation.

Bottleneck shortages
- If **demand** grows **quickly**, then there are likely to be **shortages** because labour and resources are being **fully used** so that **output** can **keep up** with **demand**. Shortages will cause **prices** to **rise** and **firms' costs** to **increase**.
- Price rises caused by shortages (e.g. a rise in wages for skilled labour) in **one area** of the **market** may be **copied** by other markets (e.g. higher wages for low-skilled labour), which will lead to more **general inflation**.

Inflation

There are several Costs and Consequences of Inflation

1) Inflation will cause the **standard of living** of those on **fixed**, or **near-fixed**, **incomes** to **fall**. This will have the **biggest impact** on those in **low income employment** or on **welfare benefits**.

2) A country's competitiveness will be **reduced** by **inflation** as exports will cost **more** to buy and imports will be **cheaper**. If **exports fall** and **imports rise**, then this could create a **deficit** in the **balance of payments** and **increase unemployment**.

3) Inflation **discourages saving** because the value of savings falls. This makes it **more attractive** to spend (creating demand-pull inflation) **before** prices rise further.

4) A **reluctance** to **save** creates a **shortage** of funds for **borrowing** and **investment**, which means that it's harder for firms to make improvements, e.g. buying new machinery. If **interest rates** go up to reduce inflation, this will also **reduce investment**.

5) Inflation creates **uncertainty** for firms as rising costs will **reduce investment** — harming future growth.

6) Inflation can cause **shoe leather costs**, which are the costs of the **extra time** and **effort** taken by consumers to search for **up-to-date** price information on the goods and services they're using, and **menu costs**, which are the **extra costs** to firms of **altering** the **price information** they provide to consumers.

Deflation Isn't a good thing

1) When the **rate of inflation** falls **below 0%** it's called **deflation**. Although there are many costs and consequences of inflation, deflation **isn't** very good either.

Don't confuse deflation with disinflation. Disinflation is when inflation rates fall, e.g. from 3% to 2%.

2) Deflation is often a sign that the economy is **doing badly**, as it's usually caused by **falling output** and **increased unemployment**.

3) Deflation can cause **big problems**. For example, if consumers think that prices are falling then they may choose **not** to spend in the hope that prices will **fall further**.

4) **Less spending** and **lower prices** will also mean **lower profits** for firms and reduced economic growth.

Inflation of 2% is Acceptable

1) In the UK, the Bank of England and the government consider **low inflation (up to 2%** per year) to be **acceptable**. **Excessive inflation (above 2%)** is undesirable and can cause the problems mentioned above.

2) The government uses a **combination** of **monetary policy**, **fiscal policy** and **supply-side policies** to try to keep the rate of inflation at 2% (see p.110-121). However, to achieve this the government has to make **trade-offs** between their **inflation target** and their **other three** main economic objectives (see p.122-123 for more on the conflicts between objectives).

3) Some economists, called **monetarists**, believe that bringing down inflation in the **short run** will **help** the government in the **long run** to achieve the other main economic objectives.

Practice Questions

Q1 What is cost-push inflation?
Q2 Give two possible causes of demand-pull inflation.
Q3 How might deflation be damaging to an economy?
Q4 What level of inflation does the UK government aim for?

Exam Question

Q1 The UK government aims to keep inflation at 2%. Evaluate the reasons why the UK government might want to keep inflation at this rate. [12 marks]

I inflated by an unacceptable 2% over Christmas...

The diagrams aren't here just to look pretty — they should help you to understand what's going on. You'll need to know reasons for cost-push and demand-pull inflation, and why the UK government wants to keep inflation at around 2%.

Unemployment

Turns out there's a lot more to say about unemployment levels than just 'the number of people who are looking for a job but can't find one.' There are a lot of causes and effects of unemployment. **These pages are for all boards.**

Governments *want* Full Employment

1) **Full employment** is where everybody of working age (excluding students, retirees, etc.), who wants to work, can find employment at the **current** wage rates.

2) Full employment **doesn't mean** everyone has a job — in most economies there will **always** be people between jobs.

3) Governments **want** full employment, as at full employment **production** will be **maximised** and earnings and standards of living will **rise** too.

4) Like economic growth (see p.9), unemployment can be shown with **PPF diagrams**, and **AS** and **AD curves**.

If there's **unemployment** in an economy then it **won't** be operating at **full capacity**, so it'll be represented by a point **within** the PPF curve (e.g. **point A**). At **full employment** the economy **can** operate at **full capacity**, so it can be represented by a point **on** the PPF curve (e.g. **point B**).

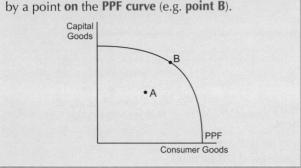

If the economy operates at **full capacity** then **output** would be at **point D**. However, unemployment **reduces aggregate demand** and **output** is **less** than it would be at full capacity (e.g. at **point C**). The difference between **points C** and **D** shows the **lost output** caused by unemployment.

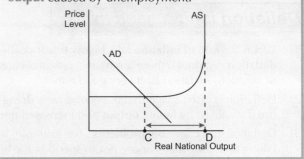

Demand-side Factors *can* Determine *the level of* Unemployment

1) The **demand** for labour by employers is a **derived** demand — an employer's demand for labour is derived from the **consumers'** demand for goods and services (for more see p.36).

2) This means that if demand in the economy is **low**, then unemployment will **rise**.

3) **Cyclical** unemployment (also known as demand deficient unemployment) happens when the economy is in a **slump**. Because aggregate demand is **falling** during a slump, then employment will **fall** too.

Cyclical unemployment is usually referred to as a type of involuntary unemployment. For policies on reducing cyclical unemployment see p.110-121.

Supply-side Factors *can also* Determine *the level of* Unemployment

Supply-side causes of unemployment are the result of **problems** in the labour market. Here are some examples:

Frictional Unemployment

1) **Frictional** unemployment is the unemployment experienced by workers **between** leaving one job and starting another. This **includes** those who have finished education and are looking for a job.

Frictional unemployment is usually referred to as a type of voluntary unemployment. For policies on tackling supply-side causes of unemployment see p.118-119.

2) Employees are often changing jobs **between firms** for several reasons — for example, they might be looking to **improve** their **career prospects**, or their **contract** may have come to an **end**.

3) The **length** of time that employees spend looking for a **new** job will depend on several things:

- In a **boom** the number of job vacancies is much **higher**. So frictional unemployment is likely to be **short-term**.

- In a **slump** frictional unemployment could be much **higher** as there will be a **shortage** of jobs.

- The level of **welfare benefits** can influence the length of time between jobs. If welfare benefits are **generous** then people have **less incentive** to look for a new job, or can afford to take their time to look for a **good** job — so the time spent between jobs **may** increase.

- Labour and geographical immobility will also affect the length of time between jobs. If a region is suffering from **structural** unemployment (see next page) then this length of time can increase.

Unemployment

Structural Unemployment

1) Structural unemployment is caused by a **decline** in a certain **industry** or **occupation** — usually due to a **change** in **consumer preferences, technological advances** or **cheaper alternatives**. It often affects **regions** where there's a decline in **traditional manufacturing** (e.g. shipbuilding or the steel industry) and it's made worse by **labour immobility**:

Structural unemployment is sometimes referred to as a type of involuntary unemployment.

- **Occupational** immobility occurs when some occupations may decline over time, but the workers in these occupations **don't** have the skills required to be able to do the jobs that are available.
- **Geographical** immobility is where workers are unable to **leave** a region which has high unemployment to go to another region where there are jobs. This might be because they can't **afford** to move to a different region, or they have **family ties**.

2) If a **region** is affected by structural unemployment then it could also suffer from the **negative multiplier effect** — unemployment will lead to less **spending**, and so cause **more** unemployment in the region.

3) The **problem** of structural unemployment may become **more common** in the future:
- **Technological change** for both products and production methods is **accelerating quickly**. This will **speed up** the **decline** of out-of-date industries.
- Consumer spending is **more likely** to change as consumers are better **informed** (through the internet and social media) than ever before — making them more likely to **switch** to **lower priced** or **higher quality** goods.

Seasonal Unemployment

1) **Seasonal** unemployment results from **uneven** economic activity during the year — some periods of the year are very **busy**, but in quieter periods there will be unemployment.

2) Several industries employ more workers in **some** periods of the year and fewer in others. For example:
- **Tourism** — an area which has lots of **tourists** during the summer may suffer from unemployment in the winter.
- **Agriculture** — more workers are needed during **harvesting**, which may only be a **few months** a year.
- **Construction** — there may be less work **available** in winter as the weather often prevents construction.

There are several Costs and Consequences of Unemployment

1) Unemployment stops an economy reaching its **maximum potential** — some labour is being unused, which means that some resources will be underused, e.g. **empty** offices and factories, **unexploited** natural resources, or **unused** machinery.

2) The unemployed will have **lower incomes**, which means that they'll spend less and **reduce** the **profits** of firms. This can lead to the **negative multiplier effect**.

3) Unemployment will mean **less** income tax revenue for governments, and **less** consumer spending will reduce their indirect tax revenue. The government will also have to **spend** more on unemployment **benefits**.

4) There **could** be a rise in certain **social problems** if there's high unemployment. Areas with high unemployment often have high **crime** rates, and reduced incomes can cause people to suffer from **health problems** and **stress**.

5) Workers who are unemployed for a **long** period of time may find that the skills and training they have become **outdated**. This will **reduce** their **employability** and make it **more** likely that they'll stay unemployed.

Practice Questions

Q1 Briefly describe: (a) structural unemployment   (b) frictional unemployment   (c) seasonal unemployment

Exam Question

Q1 A rise in the level of unemployment is likely to cause:
A) economic growth.
B) increased consumption in an economy.
C) reduced consumption in an economy.
D) a reduction in tax levels for full-time workers.

Explain your answer. [4 marks]

"These are well fair benefits," said the man at the job centre...

There's quite a lot of information here, but luckily it's nothing too complicated. There are different types of unemployment for you to understand — but whatever the cause, high levels of unemployment are undesirable, so take the time to learn why.

The Balance of Payments

*In Section 4 (p.77), you'll have seen a bit about the balance of payments — I imagine you've been eagerly waiting to find out more, so here are a couple of pages just for you. I know, I'm too good to you. **These pages are for all boards.***

There are **Four** sections of the **Current Account**

The four sections are: trade in **goods**, trade in **services**, **investment income** and **transfers**.

① Trade in goods

1) Trade in goods measures **imports** and **exports** of **visible** goods — e.g. televisions, apples, potatoes, books.

2) The UK's **biggest** goods exports include things such as **machinery**, **mechanical appliances** and **pharmaceuticals**.

3) The UK's **biggest** goods imports also include **machinery** and **mechanical appliances**, along with **mineral fuels** (e.g. coal) and **oils**.

② Trade in services

1) Trade in services measures **imports** and **exports** of **services** such as insurance or tourism.

2) Some of the UK's biggest **exported** services are **banking** and **insurance**.

3) The UK's biggest **imported** services include **tourism** (e.g. holidays abroad).

③ Investment income

Investment income covers flows of money **in** and **out** of a country resulting from **earlier** investment. These flows include **interest payments**, **dividends** and **profits**. For example:

- Deposits in **foreign banks** receive **interest payments**.

- Businesses set up **overseas** by a UK company will earn **profits** for the UK **parent company**.

- Shares bought in **foreign firms** will bring **dividend payments** to the UK shareholder — the shares themselves **won't** appear on the current account.

④ Transfers

1) Transfers are the **movements** of money **between** countries which **aren't** paying for goods or services and aren't the result of investment.

2) Transfers include **payments** made to family members **abroad** and **aid** paid to or received from **foreign countries**.

Recent data on the **UK's balance of payments** shows:

1) A **large deficit** on the balance of **visible** trade — the UK **imports more** goods than it **exports**.

2) A small **surplus** on the balance of **invisible** trade — the UK **exports** a slightly **higher amount** of services than it **imports**.

3) A **surplus** on flows of **investment income** — the UK receives more payments from investment than it pays out.

4) A **deficit** on transfers — the UK **pays** money to the EU and also makes **foreign aid payments**.

As a result, the UK has a **large deficit** on its current account, and it has had a deficit **every year** since 1984. This means that the UK's current **macroeconomic policy** includes having to deal with a balance of payments deficit.

You need to learn some of the **Main Causes** of a balance of payments **Deficit**

There are lots of reasons why a country might have a balance of payments **deficit** — here are a few to start with:

High levels of consumer spending (low savings rate)

- When there's **economic growth**, consumers and firms **buy** more **imports**.

- If the **income elasticity of demand** for imports is **high** then there will be a **greater increase** in imports.

Fall in price competitiveness of goods

When the costs of production in a country rise **faster** than in **competitor** countries — e.g. due to higher labour costs, production inefficiencies etc., then exports will **fall** and imports will **rise**.

A rise in inflation

When inflation **rises** exports will **fall** because they'll become **more expensive** and **less competitive** in **foreign** countries. Imports will **rise** because it'll become **cheaper** for consumers and firms to buy **imports** rather than domestic products.

The Balance of Payments

A fall in labour productivity
- A **fall** in labour productivity in a country will make products **more expensive** to make.
- This will cause an **increase** in the **price** of those products, so **exports** will **fall** and **imports** will **rise**.

Rise in the exchange rate
- A **rise** in the value of a currency will make goods **more expensive** to foreign buyers, so **exports** will **fall**.
- At the same time, foreign goods will be **cheaper** to buy, so **imports** will **rise**.

External shocks
- If there's a **rise** in the world prices of imported **raw materials**, e.g. oil, timber or metals, and the **demand** for these materials is relatively **price inelastic**, then a country will end up **paying more** for these imports — at least in the **short run**.
- An **economic downturn** in countries to which a country **exports** can cause a sudden **reduction** in the amount of **exports** that are demanded.
- The imposition of **trade barriers** (see p.106) on goods by a trading partner could mean a sudden reduction in the number of exports made to that country.

Ellie was suffering from a different kind of external shock.

Increased competition from other countries
- Some countries (especially more developed countries) may not be able to **compete** with **low** costs of **production** in other countries, e.g. **newly industrialised** nations.
- Other countries may **struggle** to **compete** with countries that have access to more **advanced** technology or more **efficient** methods of production, which can **lower** costs and **improve** the **quality** of the products they make.
- Countries that **can't compete** internationally will see a **reduction** in exports.

There are **Consequences** of a **Balance of Payments Deficit**

1) A balance of payments deficit means that a country can enjoy a **higher standard of living** (at least in the short-term), but it will need to **borrow** on world capital markets to **pay** for the deficit. This means there's an opportunity cost to a balance of payments deficit, as the **interest paid** on the money borrowed could be used for something else, e.g. health care.

2) The **selling** of a currency, e.g. sterling, to pay for imports will **exceed** the buying of the currency. This will mean:
   - In the foreign exchange market the **value** of the currency will **fall**.
   - **All** imports will **cost more**, but price inelastic goods will still be imported — at a greater cost.
   - The **rise** in the **cost** of things like imported raw materials or semi-manufactured goods will cause **cost-push** inflation, so a country's goods become **less** competitive.
   - If the cost of **importing** is **rising** and **fewer** goods are being **exported**, the balance of payments will continue to **worsen** in the **short run**. However, in the **long run**, the **lower** exchange rate might make the country's goods and services **more price competitive** and **boost** exports — **reducing** the deficit.

3) A balance of payments deficit may also lead to **job losses** domestically — for example, if **more** goods are being **imported**, that may mean **fewer** goods need to be **produced domestically**, so jobs will be lost.

Practice Questions

Q1 Explain the term 'external shock', with reference to an economy's balance of payments.

Q2 What is the likely impact on the economy of a balance of payments deficit?

Exam Question

Q1 In recent years the UK economy has had a balance of payments deficit. Explain why. [8 marks]

Deficit? No, it can hear perfectly well...

You've got to learn what the four sections of the current account are and how a balance of payments deficit might be caused. You should also keep in mind that a balance of payments deficit can bring some pretty undesirable consequences.

Other Economic Policy Objectives

*Governments have lots of other objectives for the economy. Here are another four objectives they might try to achieve —
but remember that different governments will have different priorities. **These pages are for Edexcel and OCR only.***

Governments try to **Distribute Income** more **Equally**

1) In any economy, there is a wide **range** of **earnings**. Earnings **depend** on a number of things, including:
   - **Labour skill** — training and education raises a person's **labour productivity** and, usually, their **pay rate**.
   - **Market forces** in the **labour** market — **shortages** or **surpluses** of various kinds of labour **influence** the **wage rate**, e.g. a **shortage** of electricians may **increase** an electrician's wage, a **surplus** may **reduce** it.
   - **Geography** — in **less** prosperous parts of the country, **earnings** are **lower**.
   - **Level** of **responsibility** — in general, the greater the **authority** and **responsibility** of a job, then the **higher** the **pay**.

2) Governments may want to **distribute** income more **equally** to **increase** overall **welfare** — they will want to **reduce** poverty so there's a better overall **standard of living**. Governments may also consider **too much** inequality in society to be **unfair**.

3) The redistribution of income can also **benefit** the **economy**. High earners tend to **save** more of their income and **low** earners tend to **spend** most or all of it — so income redistribution will **increase overall** consumer spending, and **raise** aggregate demand, output and employment.

4) The government can redistribute income by **reducing** the **net income** (take-home pay) of **high earners** and **increasing** the **net income** of people with **no** or **low incomes** — this can be done by:
   - **Tax** — especially income tax.
   - **Welfare payments** — paid to those on no, or low, incomes.

5) However, redistributing income carries a **risk** as some income differences are **beneficial**:

   - The **reward** of **higher wages** acts as an **incentive** to hard work, training and risk-taking — so **too little** inequality would mean these **incentives** are **lost** and people will not work as hard.
   - **Wealth creation** can produce **employment** and **income opportunities** for others.
   - **Spending** by people with **high incomes** becomes **earnings** for others.

Governments try to **Protect** the **Environment**

Environmental protection has become **more important** to governments. Two of the **main** factors governments recognise are:

1 Damage/pollution to the environment

The role of the government is to:

1) **Identify** environmental damage caused by firms/individuals, e.g. **carbon emissions** from factories or cars.

2) Measure the **cost** of this damage.

3) Use **financial penalties** or certain **restrictions** or **bans** to **reduce** environmental damage and provide an **incentive** for firms/individuals to **decrease** the damage they cause. These might include:
   - Non-market policies — outright bans or limits on **polluting practices**. For example, **banning** cars which produce **unacceptable** levels of **carbon dioxide**.
   - Market policies — influencing the **cost** of polluting and therefore changing the behaviour of firms/individuals. For example, **tradeable pollution permits** (see p.65) — these put a **restriction** on the **amount** of pollution a firm can produce, but firms are allowed to buy/sell permits between themselves.

2 Depletion of finite resources caused by continued economic growth

1) Some governments feel it's necessary to use **non-renewable resources**, such as oil and copper, more **wisely** to either **avoid** a future without them, or just to make them last for **longer**.

2) For example, governments might want to **encourage** the **development** and **use** of **renewable** energy resources, so that resources such as coal and oil will last for **longer**, and to ensure that there will be new sources of energy to **replace** them when they do **run out**. They might try to achieve this by giving **financial incentives** to firms to develop or use **renewable** energy.

Other Economic Policy Objectives

Governments try to ensure *Economic Stability*

1) Economic growth tends to fluctuate up and down (this is called the economic cycle — see p.93) — this involves periods of **high** growth (booms) followed by periods of **low** or even **negative** growth (slumps, recessions or depressions).

2) If the fluctuations are **frequent** or particularly **big** then there will be economic instability. This will:
   - **Discourage** firms from planning any long-term investment, which **harms** the economy in the **long run**.
   - **Discourage** foreign firms from making **investments**, which means that the country **misses out** on extra **money** being brought **into** the economy and the **creation** of **new jobs**.

3) Governments try to reduce the fluctuations in growth and **avoid** both slumps and booms. They try to do this through a combination of **fiscal** and **monetary** policies (see p.110-117 for more on these).

4) Governments also try to avoid **volatility** in the rate of inflation, unemployment and exchange rates — big **fluctuations** in any of these will also discourage investment and make it hard for governments and firms to plan for the future.

If something is volatile, it tends to vary by large amounts — this means it is unstable.

5) Economic stability will also depend on how **politically stable** a country is. If governments are **corrupt** or **cannot** enforce the **rule of law** on their people then the country's economy will be unstable too.

Governments try to improve *Productivity*

1) Improving a country's **productivity** will help **future economic growth**.

2) Governments don't have much **control** over the **productivity** of **private** companies — but there are ways in which they can encourage improvements. For example, they might offer financial help to firms so they can buy **more efficient** equipment, or they could introduce **regulations** to **increase** competition between firms so that they're **forced** to improve their **productivity**.

3) In the public sector, the government has more **direct control** over productivity. For example, the **UK government** could improve the NHS's productivity by **introducing** procedures that might be **cheaper** and/or more **effective**.

4) Governments can also improve the **productivity** of society in **general**. For example, the government could increase **spending** on **schools** and **improve education**, which will help to develop a **better trained** and more **productive** labour force.

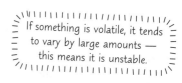

Governments use supply-side policies to improve productivity. See p.118-121 for more.

Practice Questions

Q1 List three factors which might cause one person to earn more than another.

Q2 In what ways could a government redistribute income?

Q3 Why might a government encourage the use of renewable energy resources?

Q4 In what ways could fluctuations in economic growth damage an economy?

Q5 How could a government encourage improvements in productivity of private companies?

Exam Question

Q1 Explain with examples how a government might try to alter the behaviour of firms that damage the environment.

[8 marks]

Financial penalties — a cause for dread for any England fan...

So you've learnt all about the big four macroeconomic objectives — here's another four objectives to have a think about. Not all governments have these objectives, but you should learn the principles behind them. It's also worth remembering that governments might not choose a policy that's best for a country economically — they might choose one that's the most popular with voters.

Exchange Rates

To help countries with different currencies to trade with each other, a system of currency exchange is needed. The price at which one currency buys another is the exchange rate. **These pages are for OCR only, but are useful for AQA and Edexcel students.**

There are **Two** main types of **Exchange Rate**

1) A **fixed** exchange rate is just that — fixed, so it **doesn't change** with changing demand. A country's government or its **central bank**, such as the Bank of England, would **buy** and **sell** the currency to **keep** the exchange rate close to this fixed rate.

2) A **floating** exchange rate is free to **move** with changing demand.

The rest of these two pages are about **floating exchange rates**. These are decided by the changing **supply** and **demand** of **currency**, which are caused by things such as:

- **Changes** in the **amount** of imports and exports.

- **Movement of capital** — this is when capital is **moved** from **one currency** to **another**. There are many reasons for the movement of capital — for example, capital might be moved to take advantage of the **best interest rates**, or moved within a company to be used in a **different** country.

- **Speculation** — where people **buy** and **sell** currency because of changes they **expect** are going to happen in the future.

Neil knew how to raise interest rates.

Supply and Demand determines the Exchange Rate

Just like with any good or service, the **value** (price) of a currency depends on its **supply** and **demand**.

Supply

1) The main **factors** which affect the **supply** of a currency are **imports** of goods and services, **investments** made abroad (i.e. in a foreign currency), and **speculative** selling and **official** selling (by a government or central bank) of the currency.

2) For example, an **increase** in the **supply** of pounds to S_1 will cause a **decrease** in the **value** of the pound to P_1. This increase in supply may be due to things such as an **increase** in **imports** to the UK and **increased selling** of the pound.

3) A **decrease** in the **supply** of pounds to S_2 will result in an **increase** in the **value** of the pound to P_2. This decrease in the supply of the pound may be due to things such as a **decrease** in **imports** to the UK and **decreased selling** of the pound.

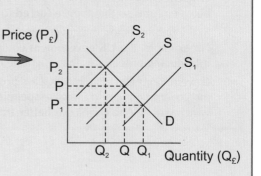

Demand

1) The main **factors** which affect the **demand** for a currency are **exports** of goods and services, **investments** made **from** abroad (i.e. investments made in the domestic currency from a foreign currency), and **speculative** purchasing and **official** purchasing (by a government or central bank) of the currency.

2) An **increase** in the **demand** for pounds to D_2 will cause an **increase** in the **value** of the pound to P_2. This increase in demand may be due to things such as an **increase** in **exports** from the UK and **increased buying** of the pound.

3) A **decrease** in the **demand** for pounds to D_1 will cause a **decrease** in the **value** of the pound to P_1. This decrease in demand may be due to, for example, a **decrease** in **exports** from the UK and **decreased buying** of the pound.

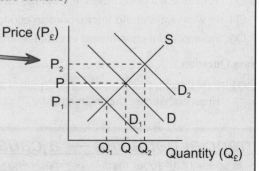

Exchange Rates

The **Exchange Rate** affects the demand for **Imports** and **Exports**

1) As well as imports and exports having an **effect** on the exchange rate, the exchange rate has an **effect** on the **demand** for imports and exports.

2) For example, when the **value** of the pound **decreases**, the demand for **exports increases** because it's **cheaper** for other countries to buy UK goods. The demand for **imports decreases** because it's **more** expensive for the UK to buy from **abroad**.

3) On the other hand, when the **value** of the pound **increases**, the demand for **exports decreases** because it's **more expensive** for other countries to buy goods **from** the UK. The demand for **imports increases** because it's **cheaper** for the UK to **buy** goods from abroad.

4) A **decrease** in the value of the pound will therefore **increase** aggregate demand, because the **net export** part of the aggregate demand formula (X – M, see p.82) will **increase**, with more goods being exported and fewer goods being imported. An **increase** in the value of the pound will lead to a **decrease** in aggregate demand, because net exports will **decrease**, with more goods being imported and fewer goods being exported.

5) However, the **price elasticity of demand** for exports and imports is **important** too. For example, if the **price** of an **import** rose and **demand** for it was **price inelastic**, then the amount of money spent importing it may **increase** (so the **value** of **M increases** rather than **decreases**). This is because even a large increase in price may only **slightly** (if at all) reduce demand.

The **Exchange Rate** affects the **Macroeconomic Policy Objectives**

Changes in the **exchange rate** will affect the **four main macroeconomic policies**.

Economic growth
- The **value** of a currency will have an effect on the rate of **economic growth**.
- For example, a **low** exchange rate can have a **positive** effect on the economy — e.g. if the **value** of the pound is **low**, exports will **increase**, which can lead to **economic growth**.

Unemployment
- The **level** of unemployment can be affected by the exchange rate.
- For example, if the **value** of the pound is **low** and exports **increase**, this can lead to **economic growth**, which in turn might **create** more jobs and **reduce** unemployment.

Inflation
- The level of **inflation** can be affected by the exchange rate.
- For example, an **increase** in the value of the pound can help to **control** inflation. Imports become **cheaper**, so **UK producers** need to keep their prices **down** in order to **compete** — the combination of these two things will **lower** inflation.
- The effect of a **decrease** in the value of the pound on inflation is **less clear**. There will be an **increase** in the price of **imports** — but factors such as **elasticity of demand** and whether producers pass on increases in prices to **consumers** have a **big impact** on whether inflation goes up or not.

The balance of payments
- The value of a currency will help to determine if there's a balance of payments **deficit** or **surplus** — but don't forget that price elasticity of demand will be important too.
- For example, if the pound's value **decreases**, the price of imports **increases** — the demand for **non-essential** imports decreases, but the demand for some imports, which are **price inelastic**, may reduce a little (or not at all) despite the higher cost. This can cause a **deficit** in the balance of payments because **more** is spent on these items.

Practice Questions

Q1 What effect would an increase in demand for the pound have on its exchange rate?

Q2 What would be the impact of a decrease in the value of the pound on UK imports and exports?

Exam Question

Q1 Consider the impact on the UK economy of a rise in the exchange rate of the pound. [12 marks]

Exchange, exchange your life, trade it all...

It can be really tricky to get your head around all this increase/decrease stuff. Start by looking at one point at a time, thinking about what logically makes sense — for example, when there's an increase in the supply of the pound, this means there are more of them, so they're worth less (because they're less 'unique'). It's just common sense really. And a lot of words.

Free Trade and Protectionism

There are advantages and disadvantages of international trade to an economy. A certain level of international trade is good, as it raises the overall standard of living in a country, but there can also be downsides. **These pages are for OCR only.**

There are many **Advantages** to **International Trade**

1) **International trade** is the **exchange** of goods and services **between** countries (i.e. imports and exports).

2) Countries **can't** produce all the things they **want** or **need** — **some resources** such as gold are **unevenly distributed** globally, and some products can only be **produced** in places with the right **climate**. For example, the UK doesn't have the right climate to grow **oranges**, and it doesn't have any **diamonds** to mine.

3) This means that international trade can give countries **access** to resources and products they otherwise **wouldn't** be able to use — countries **export** goods in order to be able to **import** the things they can't **produce** themselves.

4) There's the added benefit that if a country **specialises** in the production of the things it's **best** at producing (especially compared to other countries), then **global** output is **increased** and **costs** are **reduced**.

5) By trading internationally, not only do consumers enjoy a **larger variety** of goods and services, but **competition** can lead to **lower** prices and **more** product **innovation**.

6) International trade tends to **improve** people's **standards of living**, by giving them more **choice**, and **better quality** and **cheaper** products.

There are **Several Reasons** governments use **Trade Barriers**

1) **Free trade** is international trade **without** any restrictions from things such as trade barriers.

2) However, free trade can have its **disadvantages** and governments might decide to use **protectionist policies** (see next page) to tackle these disadvantages.

3) Here are some examples of why governments might want to **impose** trade barriers:

To protect jobs
A government might feel there's a risk of too many **job losses** if domestic firms are **outcompeted** by foreign firms.

To protect infant industries
Industries that are just starting out, particularly in developing countries, struggle to compete with **international** companies. Governments might choose to impose trade barriers until the companies **are** big enough to compete. However, there's a **risk** that the industry may never become **truly** competitive, and in the meantime domestic **consumers** are stuck with **higher** prices, or **lower quality** goods.

To ban certain goods
The government may simply want to **ban** certain goods altogether because they consider them to be **bad** for **society** — e.g. firearms or drugs.

To avoid overdependence
Specialisation could mean an economy becomes **overdependent** on **one** industry — if something happened to **negatively** affect that industry, it would have a **severe impact** on the **whole** economy. For example, if a country's economy was dependent on **growing coffee** and a disease dramatically **reduced** the amount of coffee it could **produce**, this would have a **damaging** effect on its economy.

To protect against dumping
This is when companies sell goods abroad at a price that's **below** the production cost to try to **force** other countries' domestic producers **out of business**. They can then **raise prices** and **exploit** foreign consumers.

Free Trade and Protectionism

Governments try to **Protect Domestic** industries

Governments can use a range of **tariff** and **non-tariff** protectionist policies:

Non-tariff methods are just any barriers which don't involve actual tariffs.

1) **Tariffs** can be imposed in the form of a tax on selected imports. This makes imports more expensive, which helps **domestic** manufacturers to compete and raises **tax revenue** for the government.

2) **Quotas** can be fixed, which limit the **quantity** of a certain good that can be imported — any demand for the good **above** the quota will be **diverted** to **domestic products**.

3) **Embargoes** (bans) can be imposed on certain products — these are usually restricted to **extreme** cases, e.g. drugs or elephant ivory, but may also be for **political** reasons, e.g. if two countries are having a **disagreement**, they might impose embargoes on imports from **each other**. Embargoes tend to be **less** about protecting **domestic industries** and **more** about politics or enforcing laws.

4) The value of the currency can be **reduced** — this **raises** the price of **foreign** imports and **lowers** the price of **domestic** exports.

5) Tight **product standard regulations** can be imposed — foreign products which don't comply with the requirements **cannot** be imported. Product standard regulations could include things such as **high safety** standards, or **low emissions** requirements. These might be used for **environmental** or **consumer protection**, or to help to protect **domestic** industries that **can comply** with the **regulations**.

6) **Subsidies** can be given to domestic producers — this **reduces** the cost of production of domestic products, making them cheaper to buy, but subsidies can be **costly** to a government.

UK trade has seen a **Rise** in **Imports** and a **Fall** in **Exports**

1) The **general** pattern in UK trade since 2000 has seen exports **fall** and imports **rise**.

2) UK exports as a **percentage** of world goods export markets have **declined gradually** — this decline is similar in most other **major industrialised** countries, and is due to **competition** from **emerging** and **newly industrialised** economies such as China.

3) Imports have tended to **rise** for similar reasons — goods are often **cheaper** to buy from **less developed** countries. However, the country the UK imports the **most** from is **Germany**.

4) The **biggest** single market for **UK exports** is the **USA** — but just under **half** of the UK's exports go to countries in the **European Union** (EU).

5) Exports to countries such as **China**, whose economies are **growing** extremely quickly, are **rising**.

Practice Questions

Q1 Describe three of the benefits that international trade brings.

Q2 Give three ways a government can protect its economy.

Q3 Briefly describe the UK's changing pattern of international trade since 2000.

Exam Question

Q1 Evaluate to what extent free trade can be beneficial to a country's economy. [12 marks]

I'm free to trade whatever I, whatever I choose...

International trade has lots of advantages — but most governments impose some trade barriers to try to get a balance between the advantages that free trade brings and the need for protectionist policies to protect their own industries. Make sure you can discuss free trade and protectionism, including the different methods of protectionism that governments might use.

Conflicts Between Economic Objectives

There are conflicts between the four main economic objectives, so governments can't achieve them all at the same time. These pages talk you through some of these conflicts, and what a government can do. **These pages are for all boards.**

There are often **Conflicts** between **Government Objectives**

Particularly in the **short-term**, there are **conflicts** between the government's main objectives.

Inflation and Unemployment

1) When unemployment is **reduced** and the economy begins to **approach** full capacity, there are **fewer** spare workers, so **demand** for workers increases — especially the demand for **skilled** workers. This will lead to an **increase** in wages. The **extra cost** of higher wages may then be passed on by producers to consumers in the form of **higher prices**, which will cause **cost-push** inflation.

2) Low unemployment may cause consumers to **spend** more because they feel more **confident** in their **long-term** job prospects. This may lead to an **increase** in prices and cause **demand-pull** inflation.

3) So reducing unemployment makes it more **difficult** to keep inflation at the **preferred low rate**.

Economic Growth and Environmental Protection

Economic growth can put a **strain** on the **environment**. For example:

1) New factories and increases in production can raise levels of air and water **pollution**.

2) Increases in production will create **more waste**, which needs **disposing** of.

3) Economic growth will tend to increase the use of natural resources — this can be a major problem if these resources are **non-renewable**.

4) Ecosystems might be **damaged** or even **destroyed** by the **construction** of new factories, housing, etc. — in the most **extreme** cases, this can lead to the **extinction** of certain animals or plants.

Economic Growth and Inflation

1) A rapidly **growing** economy can cause large **increases** in **prices**, due to an increase in **demand**. This will cause a **higher** than desirable level of **inflation**.

2) Similarly, attempts to keep **inflation low** can **restrict** growth. For example, if **interest rates** are kept **high** to reduce inflation by **discouraging** spending (and encouraging saving), this can **restrict economic growth**.

Inflation and Equilibrium in the Balance of Payments

1) **Sometimes** the government's objectives for low inflation and equilibrium in the balance of payments will be **compatible**, but at other times they'll **conflict**.

2) For example, if **inflation is low**, this implies that prices are **rising slowly**. If prices rise **more slowly** than those in other in other countries, then **exports** to other countries will **increase** and **imports** will **decrease**. This would **increase a surplus** on the balance of payments, but **reduce** a balance of payments **deficit**.

3) Similarly, when low inflation is being **maintained**, **interest rates** are often kept quite **high**. High interest rates will **encourage** investment from abroad, which will **increase demand** for the domestic currency and therefore **increase** its **value**. This will make exports **more expensive** and imports **cheaper**, so **exports** will **decrease** and **imports** will **increase**. This would **reduce a surplus** on the balance of payments, but make a **deficit worse**.

Conflicts Between Economic Objectives

Governments have to make Trade-offs

Since there are conflicts between the main economic objectives, governments have to make **trade-offs** (see p.8) between them. This means they have to **compromise**, and decide to what extent they want to/can **achieve** each objective.

Mark made his feelings on compromise very clear.

1) The **Phillips curve** (see below) shows the **relationship** between inflation and unemployment. The curve below is just an example, but the original Phillips curve was based on data from the UK.

2) The Phillips curve shows that as **inflation** falls, **more** people become **unemployed**, and vice versa. This means that it's not possible for a government to **improve** one thing without **worsening** the other, so they have to make a **trade-off** between their **objectives** for inflation and unemployment. At any time, governments have to choose which objective is **more important**.

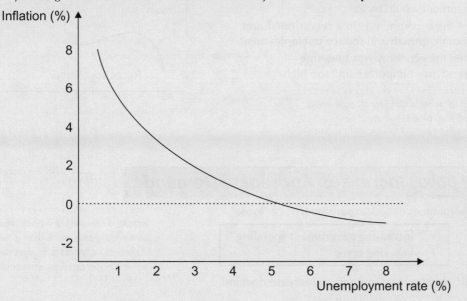

3) Another example of a **trade-off** is between protecting the environment and economic growth — governments impose **policies** to **protect** the environment (see p.102), but these often hold back economic growth. For example, tradeable pollution permits put a **restriction** on the amount of **pollution** firms can produce. These may mean that firms **can't** produce to their **full capacity** because they would **exceed** this pollution limit.

4) Ideally, governments want an **equilibrium** in the **balance of payments** and **low inflation** — but they may need to decide which of these is **more important** because if, for example, a government kept **inflation low** by using **high** interest rates, then this could **lower** exports and create a balance of payments **deficit**.

Practice Questions

Q1 Why might a government's objectives for economic growth and environmental protection conflict?

Q2 What does the Phillips curve show?

Exam Question

Q1 Discuss the possible conflicts between the four main macroeconomic objectives. [10 marks]

You'll need to make a trade-off between revision and your social life...

Unfortunately, it's not possible for a government to achieve all of their macroeconomic objectives at one time. Boosting economic growth and reducing unemployment go hand in hand, but they tend to lead to an increase in inflation and a worsening in the balance of payments. The result is that governments need to make a trade-off between the objectives.

Fiscal Policy

*The last section covered the different economic policy objectives that governments have. Now it's time to have a look at the government's toolbox for achieving these objectives. **These pages are for all boards.***

Fiscal Policy *is to do with* Taxation *and* Government Spending

1) **Fiscal policy** (sometimes referred to as **budgetary policy**) is all to do with **government spending** and **taxation**.

2) It can have both **macroeconomic effects** (i.e. fiscal policy can influence the economy as a whole) and **microeconomic effects** (i.e. it can influence individual firms and people).

3) **Traditionally**, fiscal policy has been used to influence **aggregate demand** (AD) — this is a **macroeconomic** effect.

4) The aim of managing demand in this way was to 'smooth out' the fluctuations in the **economic cycle**. In other words, the government would try to:
   - **boost demand** when the economy was in a **recession/slump** — to stimulate **economic growth** and **reduce unemployment**.
   - **reduce demand** when the economy was **booming** — to control **inflation** and avoid **imports** rising too high.

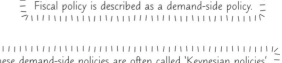
Fiscal policy is described as a demand-side policy.

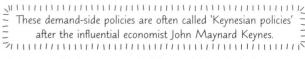
These demand-side policies are often called 'Keynesian policies' after the influential economist John Maynard Keynes.

See pages 92-93 for more about recessions/slumps, booms and macroeconomic objectives.

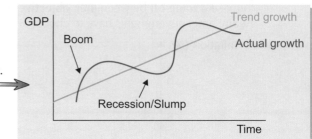

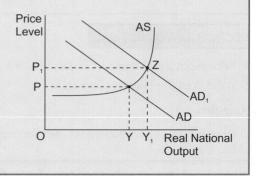

Reflationary *fiscal policy* Increases Aggregate Demand

Reflationary fiscal policy is sometimes called '**expansionary**', or '**loose**'. This involves one or more of:

- **increasing government spending**
- **lowering taxes**

Increased spending will often mean the government spends more than it receives in taxes — i.e. there's a 'budget deficit'. This will mean increased government borrowing.

1) In a **recession** fiscal policy becomes reflationary to **increase demand**. There are various measures the government can take:

- **Decreasing income tax** means consumers will have more disposable income to spend.
- **Decreasing indirect taxes** (such as VAT) makes goods less expensive (meaning consumers can buy more).
- **Increasing welfare payments** means that people with lower incomes will have more disposable income to spend.
- **Building new infrastructure** (e.g. schools, hospitals or roads) means more jobs and higher incomes, which also means that people have more disposable income to spend.

2) All of the above represent **lower withdrawals** from the circular flow of income (e.g. tax cuts means less tax leaks out of the circular flow), or **greater injections** (i.e. higher government spending or investment) — see p.80. The effect should be an **increase** in aggregate demand.

And don't forget the effect of the spending multiplier (see p.81), so any extra government spending leads to even greater increases in AD.

- A **reflationary** fiscal policy will shift the AD curve to the **right** — from AD to AD₁.
- The new **equilibrium** (Z) is at a **higher price level** (P_1) — this means that **inflation** will have **increased**.

  This is demand-pull inflation — see p.96.

- However, **output** has **increased** to Y_1 — meaning **unemployment** will have **decreased**, and **economic growth** will have occurred.

  See p.89 for more information.

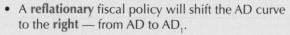

3) If an economy is experiencing a **negative output gap** (see p.93), these measures will reduce it by boosting aggregate demand.

Fiscal Policy

Deflationary fiscal policy Reduces Aggregate Demand

Deflationary fiscal policy is sometimes called '**contractionary**', or '**tight**'.
This involves one or both of:

- **reducing government spending**
- **raising taxes**

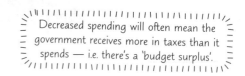

Decreased spending will often mean the government receives more in taxes than it spends — i.e. there's a 'budget surplus'.

1) In a **boom** fiscal policy becomes **deflationary** to **reduce demand**.
   Again, there are various measures the government can take:

- **Increasing income tax** means consumers will have less disposable income to spend.
- **Increasing indirect taxes** (such as VAT) makes goods more expensive.
- **Reducing welfare payments** means that people with lower incomes will have less disposable income to spend.
- **Reducing government spending** on new infrastructure means fewer jobs and lower incomes
  — this also means that people have less disposable income to spend.

2) All of the above represent **higher withdrawals** from the circular flow of income, or **smaller injections**.
   The effect should be a **fall** in aggregate demand.

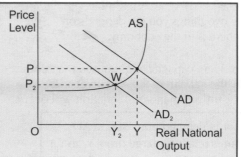

- A **deflationary** fiscal policy will shift the AD curve to the **left** — from AD to AD$_2$.
- The new **equilibrium** W is at a **lower price level** (P$_2$).
- **Output** has **fallen** to Y$_2$ — meaning **unemployment** will have **increased**, and the economy will have **shrunk**.

3) If an economy is experiencing a **positive output gap** (see p.93), these measures will reduce it by decreasing aggregate demand.

Changes in AD affect the Current Account of the Balance of Payments

1) When aggregate demand is boosted, the **current account** of the **balance of payments** worsens. A **current account deficit** will get **bigger** and a **current account surplus** will get **smaller**.

A balance of payments deficit (or surplus) is different from a budget deficit (or surplus).

2) This is because as people's incomes go up, they tend to spend more on **imports**.

3) The opposite happens when AD is reduced — the **current account** of the **balance of payments** improves.

4) This is because as incomes **fall**, so does spending on **imports**.

Practice Questions

Q1 What effect would a reflationary fiscal policy have on the AD curve?

Q2 When might a government use a reflationary fiscal policy?

Q3 Give one way that governments can implement a deflationary fiscal policy.

Q4 Describe why the boosting of aggregate demand can lead to a worsening of the balance of payments.

Exam Question

Q1 Which one of the following is an example of fiscal policy? Explain your answer.
A) An increase in the rate of interest.
B) A reduction in welfare payments.
C) An increase in the exchange rate.
D) An increase in the money supply.

[4 marks]

Quick, the economy's flatlining — we need reflationary measures, STAT...

Fiscal policy is all about government spending and taxation. To boost the economy you can pump in cash by increasing government spending and/or reducing taxation. To take demand out of the economy you do the opposite.

The Effectiveness of Fiscal Policy

In practice, the macroeconomic demand-side policies on the last two pages are tricky to use and have their drawbacks.
These pages are for all boards.

Fiscal policy is a *Tricky Tool* to Use

1) Managing **aggregate demand** sounds fairly easy, but in practice it's a **very difficult** thing to get right.

2) Government spending takes a **long time** to organise (lots of meetings and votes are needed before a decision can be made to spend any money), which means that the state of the economy may change by itself **before** any government action is taken.

3) Also, the government will often have **imperfect information** about the economy (i.e. information will be wrong or missing). This means the government might do the **wrong thing** because they're making decisions based on **inaccurate information** — see below.

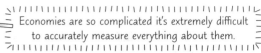
Economies are so complicated it's extremely difficult to accurately measure everything about them.

The *Effects* of *Increasing AD* depend on the *Current State* of the economy

1) An **expansionary fiscal policy** can help reflate the economy (i.e. **increase output** — a good thing), but at the same time lead to an increase in **inflation** (a bad thing) — see p.110.

2) **How much** of each of these two things you get depends on how much **spare capacity** there is in the economy.

Remember... this is shown by the slope of the AS curve — see p.88.

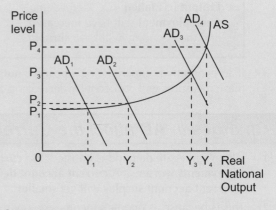

- If the economy has **lots** of spare capacity (e.g. unused machines and workers — shown by the flat part of the AS curve) and can **easily** increase supply, **little** demand-pull inflation will occur.

  > This is shown by the shift in demand from AD_1 to AD_2
  > — the increase in **output** is relatively **large** (from Y_1 to Y_2)
  > — the increase in **prices** is relatively **small** (from P_1 to P_2)

- But if the economy is working **close** to **full capacity** (e.g. few spare machines or workers — shown by the steeper part of the AS curve), then the results are different.

  > This is shown by the shift in demand from AD_3 to AD_4
  > — the increase in **output** is relatively **small** (from Y_3 to Y_4)
  > — the increase in **prices** is relatively **large** (from P_3 to P_4)

Basically, increasing AD now forces prices up because supply **can't keep up** with demand.

3) Using fiscal policy can also lead to '**stop-go cycles**':
- For example, a government might use fiscal policy to **boost** the economy during a **recession**. However, the economy could '**overshoot**' (i.e. grow too quickly), causing **high inflation**, before the government can change its policy.
- The government may then '**apply the brakes**' to the economy with a deflationary fiscal policy — which could lead to another recession... and so on.

Confidence can affect the impact of *Tax Cuts*

On p.110 it was assumed that **lowering taxes** will mean that consumers **spend more**, but this might not happen.

1) If people feel **confident** about their economic future (e.g. they're not worried about losing their job or the effect of future increases in their cost of living), then tax cuts for consumers are **likely** to **increase consumption** and lead to **economic growth**. This is because the extra disposable income from tax cuts is likely to be **spent**.

2) However, if people are **not** feeling confident, they may prefer to **save** the money from tax cuts instead of spending it.

Remember, saving is a leakage out of the circular flow of income, so it won't help the economy to expand.

3) Confidence is also crucial for businesses. A government would normally hope that giving firms a tax cut will encourage **investment** and increase the **productive potential** of the economy.

4) But if business owners are **not** feeling **confident** about their firm's future prospects, they could choose to **save** the money instead, or **delay** investing it until they feel that circumstances have improved.

The Effectiveness of Fiscal Policy

Government spending can **Crowd Out** private-sector spending

1) One possible effect of government spending is '**crowding out**'. This means that **government spending** just **replaces** private-sector spending (i.e. the spending would have happened anyway, but by the private sector).

2) For example, the government may **use resources** that the private sector would otherwise have used — e.g. the government might use materials or workers that the private sector could have employed.

This is most likely to happen when there is little spare capacity in the economy.

3) As a result there might be **no overall increase** in **aggregate demand**, which isn't what the government wants.

4) To pay for more spending, governments may need to **increase interest rates** to encourage people to lend them money. Higher interest rates will **discourage firms** from borrowing, so that will 'crowd out' private-sector investment.

The government's approach to fiscal policy has **Changed**

1) The traditional 'Keynesian' approach of 'smoothing out the economic cycle' can lead to various **trade-offs**. For example: • Increasing **aggregate demand** could lead to **higher inflation**.
   • Creating **more jobs** and **higher incomes** could lead to problems with the **balance of payments**.

2) Nowadays, this approach is used **less**. However, this doesn't mean fiscal policy isn't used — there are a number of ways fiscal policy can be used to help governments achieve their objectives:

Between 2008 and 2010 the government tried Keynesian demand-side fiscal policies to try to kick start the economy after the credit crunch.

(1) Fiscal policy is usually used to influence **aggregate supply** (see p.119). This is called **supply-side** fiscal policy — its aim is to increase the productive potential of the economy to create long-term economic growth. Successful supply-side policies **don't** cause **inflation** (p.119), and should **improve** the **current account** on the balance of payments. An example of a supply-side fiscal policy is offering **tax cuts** to entrepreneurs to encourage them to start up new businesses that will increase the **productive potential** of the economy.

(2) Fiscal policy is used on a **microeconomic** level to try to influence how **individual consumers** and **firms** behave. For example, **demerit goods** such as alcohol or tobacco can be **taxed** to try to persuade people to consume them less, and **merit goods** can be subsidised to increase their consumption. It can also be used to help governments achieve their **environmental policy objectives**. For example, the government could introduce '**green taxes**' that discourage the use of coal or oil, or provide **subsidies** to firms that use renewable energy (e.g. solar or wind power).

(3) Government spending can be directed at **specific regions** that need extra help. For example, if a region loses a big employer, the government could **invest** in that region to **create jobs**.

(4) **Progressive taxation** takes a **larger** amount of tax from people on **high** incomes than from those on **lower** incomes. This allows the government to **redistribute** wealth from those who are **better off** (i.e. more able to pay taxes) to those who are **less well off** — either in the form of benefits, or through the use of tax revenue to pay for the provision of merit goods.

Practice Questions

Q1 Explain one possible negative consequence of increasing aggregate demand.

Q2 Explain what 'crowding out' means.

Q3 Apart from increasing aggregate supply, describe two possible aims of fiscal policy.

Exam Question

Q1 Explain how an expansionary fiscal policy affects national output when an economy has little spare capacity. [8 marks]

Nothing's ever as easy as it looks when you're running an economy...

Even in theory, using fiscal policy to control an economy sounds quite tricky. In practice, it's probably even trickier than that. It's (probably) like driving a car where you can only look out the window to see where you're going once every few minutes, and then have to arrange a committee meeting to decide which way to turn the steering wheel. Not for the faint-hearted...

Monetary Policy

Monetary policy can be used to control the level of aggregate demand in an economy... but these days it's mostly used to control inflation. These pages describe the intended effects of monetary policy. **These pages are for all boards.**

Monetary Policy *mostly involves setting* Interest Rates

Monetary policy is described as a demand-side policy.

1) Monetary policy is all to do with controlling the **total amount** of 'money' in an economy (the **money supply**), and how expensive it is to **borrow** that money.
2) The **money supply** includes **notes** and **coins** in circulation, and also any money held in **bank accounts** that's available to be spent. Money can be **added** to the money supply when banks give **loans** to people and put money into their bank accounts.
3) Monetary policy involves manipulating **interest rates**, **exchange rates** and the **money supply** to affect aggregate demand.
4) The most important tool in the monetary policy toolbox is the ability to set **interest rates**. Changes to the interest rate affect **borrowing**, **spending**, **saving** and **investment**.

Monetary policy can be Contractionary *or* Expansionary

1) Broadly speaking, monetary policy can be **contractionary** ('tight') or **expansionary** ('loose').

Contractionary monetary policy acts to reduce aggregate demand using:
- a **high** interest rate
- **restrictions** on the money supply
- a **strong** exchange rate

The effect of this policy can be seen on the diagram below:

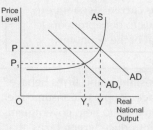

- AD shifts **left** from AD to AD_1.
- Prices **fall** from P to P_1.
- Output **falls** from Y to Y_1.
- This will result in higher **unemployment** and a slow-down in **economic growth**.

Expansionary monetary policy acts to increase aggregate demand using:
- a **low** interest rate
- **less restrictions** on the money supply
- a **weak** exchange rate

The effect of this policy can be seen on the diagram below:

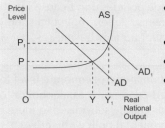

- AD shifts **right** from AD to AD_1.
- Prices **rise** from P to P_1.
- Output **rises** from Y to Y_1.
- This will result in lower **unemployment** and a boost for **economic growth**.

2) There's a **link** between the **three components** of monetary policy because changes in interest rates **affect** the exchange rate and the money supply. For example, a **high interest rate** can **restrict** the **money supply** as there's a **lower demand** for loans. It can also make the **exchange rate stronger** because there will be **increased demand** for the **currency** from people who wish to buy it and take advantage of the high interest rate (see p.115 for a full explanation).

Interest Rates *are set by the* Monetary Policy Committee (MPC)

1) One of the government's macroeconomic policy objectives is to have **stable prices** — in other words **low inflation**. To achieve this they can use the most powerful monetary policy tool — the **control** of **interest rates**.
2) In the UK the government **doesn't** set interest rates directly. Instead the **Monetary Policy Committee** (**MPC**) of the **Bank of England** sets interest rates in order to meet an **inflation target** that's set by the **government**.
3) The current target is an inflation rate of **2%** (as measured by the **consumer price index**, CPI). If the inflation rate is **more than 1%** away from this target then the Governor of the Bank of England must write to the Chancellor explaining **why** the target has been missed.

The Bank of England's official interest rate is known as the Bank Rate or Base Rate.

4) Changes in interest rates can affect the economy in many ways. For example, here are some effects of an **increase** in interest rates:

- The cost of **borrowing** money **increases** — so both people and firms are **less likely** to **borrow**.
- A lot of people with a **mortgage**, **overdraft** or **credit card** will have **higher repayments** — this means that those people will have less money to **spend**, so **consumption** goes down.
- **Investment** by firms may also fall, since most investments are made using **borrowed money**.
- Savers get a **bigger return** on their **savings**, so people are **likely** to **save more**.

An overdraft is when you borrow money from your bank when you run out of money in your account. They're a loan from your bank.

5) **Higher interest rates** mean that consumption and investment **fall** — causing **AD** to **fall**.
6) And by the same logic, if **interest rates fall** then **AD** will **rise**.

Monetary Policy

High interest rates Worsen the balance of payments current account

1) When interest rates are **high** in the UK, big financial institutions (such as large banks or insurance companies) want to **buy the pound**. This is so they can put their money into UK banks and **take advantage** of the high rewards for savers brought about by the high interest rates. This is likely to be a short-term movement of money and it's called '**hot money**'.

2) An **increased demand** for the pound means its **price goes up** — i.e. the pound's exchange rate **rises**.

3) Unfortunately, a **high exchange rate** makes UK exports **more expensive**.

> *See p.123 for the impact of exchange rates on a firm's competitiveness.*

- Suppose the **exchange rate** of the pound against the dollar is **£1 = $2**. And suppose a British firm makes pens that cost, say, £1.
- To buy one of these British pens, someone in the USA would first have to buy the pound. This would mean that the price of one of these pens in the USA is effectively **$2**, since it costs them **$2** to buy **£1**, and then they can spend this £1 on buying a pen.
- Now suppose the exchange rate **changed** to **£1 = $4** (i.e. the pound's exchange rate goes up, or the pound becomes **stronger**).
- Someone in the USA would now have to spend **$4** to pay for the same £1 pen. Remember, the pen's price in the UK **hasn't changed** at all — this **extra cost** to the person in the USA is **all** to do with the **cost** of **buying pounds**.

4) When this happens **exports go down**, **worsening** the current account on the **balance of payments**. (Remember though, this depends on the price elasticity of demand of exports and imports, see p.105 and p.117.)

5) For the same reason (but in reverse), **high** UK **interest rates** mean **imports** from abroad become **cheaper**. Again, this **worsens** the current account.

6) And remember... imports are a **leakage** in the circular flow of income, and so more spending on imports means a **reduction** in AD.

Low interest rates Improve the balance of payments current account

1) When UK **interest rates** are **low**, financial institutions will put their 'hot money' **somewhere else** where they can get a **better reward** from **high interest rates**.

2) This **lowers** the **demand** for the pound and its **exchange rate falls** (i.e. it becomes **cheaper** to buy pounds).

3) A lower exchange rate makes **UK exports cheaper** (remember... the UK price stays the same — it's the cost of buying the pound that changes), and so **exports rise**.

4) Imports become **more expensive**, so demand for them **falls**.

5) All of this leads to an **improvement** in the **current account** of the **balance of payments**.

The average price of hair products was on the rise — Mark couldn't care less.

Practice Questions

Q1 Who sets the interest rate in the UK?

Q2 Who sets the target rate of inflation for the UK?

Q3 Does expansionary monetary policy involve raising or lowering interest rates?

Q4 When interest rates are low, what effect does this have on the current account of the balance of payments?

Exam Question

Q1 Explain how a contractionary monetary policy might affect the current account of the balance of payments. [10 marks]

I've got a contractionary waistline policy to fit into my favourite jeans...

Well, that all sounds fairly straightforward then. If you think inflation's a bit low then decrease interest rates, but if you think inflation's a bit high then increase interest rates. How hard can it be? Well, in practice it's not quite as easy as I've made it sound. Read the next couple of pages to find out some of the difficulties. Eeeh... it's not as easy as it looks, this 'running an economy' lark.

The Effectiveness of Monetary Policy

Monetary policy sounds so simple... but it sort of isn't. These two pages are basically all about how and why all the things that <u>should</u> happen as a result of your monetary policies, sometimes don't. **These pages are for all boards.**

The **Monetary Policy Committee** (MPC) has a **Tough Job** to do

1) To achieve the **government's inflation target** the MPC needs to make a **decision** based on what it **thinks** will happen to inflation **in the future** — its policies have to be **pre-emptive**.

2) To make these predictions as accurately as it can, the MPC has to look at a lot of **economic data**. However, this data may not be very **accurate** and different sources may **contradict** each other — this makes it more difficult for the MPC to make accurate decisions.

3) One thing that's especially important for the MPC to look at is whether there's an **output gap**.

4) When the economy has lots of **spare capacity** (i.e. there's a negative output gap), inflation is **less likely** to **rise**. So the MPC could **decrease** interest rates.

> *Output gaps are discussed on p.93.*

- In this situation firms might **deliberately not** be working at **full capacity** because they're having **difficulty selling** their goods and their stock rooms are full — when this is the case they're unlikely to put their prices up.

- In a **recession** and during a **recovery** the MPC may decide to adopt an expansionary monetary policy — this could involve keeping **interest rates low** to try to encourage **growth** and **employment**.

5) But if the economy has **no spare capacity** (i.e. demand exceeds supply and there's a positive output gap), then that creates an 'upward pressure' on inflation. In this case, the MPC would be likely to **increase** interest rates.

6) By changing interest rates the MPC can cause **knock-on effects** which **conflict** with **government objectives**. For example, in tackling inflation the MPC can't raise interest rates to such a high level that they significantly harm economic growth and the level of unemployment.

Low interest rates **Don't** always stimulate **Spending** and **Investment**...

1) Low interest rates make it **cheaper** for consumers to **spend** and firms to **invest**, but that doesn't mean that this is definitely what they'll do. It often depends on **how confident** consumers and business leaders feel.

2) Interest rates are normally low when the economy is experiencing **low growth** or is in a **recession**. At times like these, people tend to be **uncertain** about the future, so they're **less likely** to want to **spend** their money.

3) In fact they may choose to **save** instead, even though the reward for saving is low.

4) Firms too will usually only invest if they're **confident** about their future income. If a firm has **few orders** and a **lot of surplus stock**, the last thing it's likely to want to do is spend more money. Even though money for investment is **cheap** to borrow, no one wants to **borrow** it.

...while **High** interest rates can lead to **Unfairness**

1) **High** interest rates pay **more** money to people who **already** have money in the bank, and **take** money away from those who have **borrowed** money.

2) In other words, high interest rates can **widen the gap** between the rich and poor.

3) This may not be something the government wants — there may be a **conflict** between the government's macroeconomic objectives.

It takes **Time** for interest rate changes to **Affect People's Behaviour**

1) The effect of changing interest rates is **not** felt straight away. For example, reducing interest rates **won't** usually cause a **sudden surge** in investment or house buying — it **takes time** to have an effect.

2) Firms **plan** investment projects **very carefully** — it can take months or years before the money is spent.

3) **House buying** can also take a long time — people first need to **find** a suitable home, and then the actual purchase can take a long time too.

4) **Fixed-rate mortgage** holders won't even notice the effect of an interest rate change until their fixed-rate period ends and their mortgage can then be affected by interest rate changes.

For a house that only needed 'minor improvements' it wasn't looking too great from the outside.

The Effectiveness of Monetary Policy

Interest rates **Don't** always **Affect** the **Balance of Payments** as **Expected**

1) **High interest rates** in the UK make the pound rise in value — so British goods become **more expensive overseas**.

2) When this happens you'd expect firms that usually buy British goods to buy from somewhere else. However, it takes **time** for buyers to find **alternative products**, and firms often have **contracts** with each other that may last for years, so foreign companies may continue to buy UK goods even if cheaper options become available.

3) This means that the demand for **UK exports** can be quite **price inelastic** (i.e. a change in price doesn't affect how much is demanded) — so the value of exports may fall by less than expected or they might even rise.

4) Also, if **inflation** is **high** in a country that's importing UK goods, then those UK imports might still be **competitively priced** despite the exchange rate rise.

5) When the pound is strong (i.e. the exchange rate is relatively high), **imports are cheaper**, and so become more popular. Normally, this increased spending on imports is considered to be **bad** for the economy, since imports are a **leakage** from the 'circular flow'.

6) However, cheaper imports are **good** for **UK firms** that **import lots** of raw materials and semi-finished goods (bits and pieces they need to make their finished goods, like a zip for a coat). For these firms, cheaper imports would **reduce their costs** (which should also mean lower prices for consumers domestically and abroad).

Rising interest rates **Don't** always **Reduce Inflation**

1) Higher interest rates will reduce **demand-pull** inflation.

2) However, if demand is already quite **low**, then **increasing interest rates** might not have as much of an effect on inflation as might be expected.

3) Firms may also have to **raise** their **prices** if they have to pay more interest on their **loans**. ← 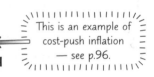 *This is an example of cost-push inflation — see p.96.*

4) Higher prices may cause workers to demand **higher wages** — leading to a **wage-price spiral** that pushes prices up higher (see p.96). So raising interest rates can make inflation **worse**.

Practice Questions

Q1 How could the amount of spare capacity in the economy affect what the MPC does with interest rates?

Q2 Why might some consumers choose to save at times of low interest rates?

Q3 Explain how high interest rates can widen the gap between rich and poor.

Q4 Why might a change in interest rates not have an immediate impact on levels of investment?

Exam Questions

Q1 Which one of the following is the Monetary Policy Committee most likely to consider when working out what interest rates to set?
Explain your answer.
A) The current GDP of the UK.
B) The amount of spare capacity in the UK economy.
C) The demand for UK exports.
D) The size of the 'gap' between the rich and poor. [4 marks]

Q2 The government of a country that is in recession has cut interest rates in an attempt to encourage consumers to spend and firms to invest. However, after three months, data suggests that saving has increased and firms have cut back their levels of investment.
Comment on why cutting interest rates during a recession may not help an economy to recover. [10 marks]

Q3 Explain how the volume of exports out of the UK is likely to be affected by an increase in the UK's interest rate. [10 marks]

I wouldn't fancy trying to do the MPC's job...

The MPC has to adopt policies that will take time to have an effect and which could have unintended consequences. I bet there's a car explanation for this — imagine trying to drive when turning the steering wheel causes the car to change direction... but only after a 5-second delay, and not always in the direction you wanted. This is (probably) what it's like to be in control of an economy.

Supply-side Policies

Right... supply-side policies — these are my favourites. They're also one of the government's favoured approaches to running an economy, so that's nice. **These pages are for all boards.**

Supply-side Policies can Increase what an economy can produce

1) In a nutshell, **supply-side policies** aim to **shift** the aggregate supply (AS) curve to the **right**. In other words, their aim is to **increase** the total amount that firms are **willing** to **supply** at a particular price.

2) There are various types of supply-side policies:

- Some involve increasing the **productive capacity** of the economy by increasing the **quantity** and **quality** of the **factors of production**. For example, some supply-side policies might aim to increase the **number** of people in work (e.g. by making it more difficult to claim unemployment benefits).

- Other policies might aim to increase the **productivity** of firms and their employees. For example, increasing **labour productivity** could be done by investing in **training** and **education** to make workers more skilled and efficient.  *See p.12 for more about productivity.*

- Governments can use supply-side policies to change **personal incentives**. For example, a reduction in **income tax** may encourage workers to work **longer hours** or work **harder** to get a promotion, and a reduction in **benefits** would give people more of an incentive to get a job.

- Supply-side policies can aim to make **markets** more efficient and competitive. For example:

Supply-side policies encourage 'marketisation' of the economy.

> ### PRIVATISATION + DEREGULATION
>
> - Many economists believe the **private sector** is more efficient and less wasteful than the **public sector**. So **privatisation** (when a firm or a whole industry changes from being run by the **public** sector to the **private** sector) is a popular supply-side policy with some economists.
>
> - **Deregulation** involves getting rid of rules imposed by the government ('red tape') that can restrict the level of **competition** or efficiency in a market. For example, regulations stopping private firms entering a market which contains only a state-owned monopoly could be scrapped, or governments could reduce the amount of 'red tape' and bureaucracy involved in getting planning permission. When there's more **competition** and **efficiency** in a market, **productivity** should **increase**.

> ### INCREASING THE FLEXIBILITY OF LABOUR MARKETS
>
> - A major supply-side policy in the UK in the 1980s was to **reduce** the **power** of **trade unions**.
>
> - Strong trade unions can negotiate **higher wages** for workers (which increase a firm's costs), and they can make it **harder** for firms to **lay off** workers.
>
> - Reducing the power of trade unions has resulted in a **more flexible** workforce. In practice, this means that **short-term, flexible** contracts are more common than they used to be, allowing firms to 'hire and fire' workers according to the current demands of the business.

Supply-side Policies can have Powerful effects

1) It takes time to see results from supply-side policies — they usually have most effect in the **medium to long term**. For example, the benefits of policies to improve **education** are usually felt many years after the policies were introduced.

2) Supply-side policies tend to be **microeconomic** — they affect the way individual consumers and firms behave (e.g. a policy might encourage a firm to train its workforce differently). But usually supply-side policies, such as privatisation and increasing the competitiveness within a market, work on a **macroeconomic** level.

3) Improving the supply side of the economy is not just down to the government — **businesses** can take the initiative and improve things themselves by investing in **new machinery** or paying for **extra staff training**.

4) In a **free market** it's in a firm's own interests to improve its **productivity** and **competitiveness**. When firms do this, the country's economy is helped too.

> - For example, supply-side policies introduced by a firm might increase its **competitiveness** and the **quality** of its products.
> - This could increase the quantity of products that the firm sells as **exports**.
> - This then improves the **current account** on the balance of payments.

Supply-side Policies

Supply-side policies help *Grow* the *Economy* without causing *Inflation*

This is the clever bit. In theory, supply-side policies create **economic growth** without **inflation**.

The effects of supply-side policies

- Supply-side policies shift the AS curve to the **right**, from AS_1 to AS_2.
- The economy is producing more — national output has increased from Y_1 to Y_2. This means there's been **economic growth**, and more people should have jobs.
- But **price levels** have **fallen** from P_1 to P_2 — so there's **no inflation**.

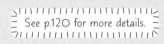

See p.120 for more details.

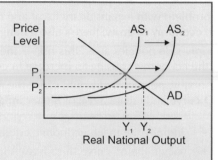

Supply-side *fiscal policies are currently more popular than* Demand-side *ones*

1) In recent times, governments have focused on implementing **supply-side fiscal policies** rather than **demand-side** ones.

2) Tax and benefit cuts have often been introduced to create **incentives** for **individual** economic agents (e.g. consumers and firms) to act in a way that will be good for the economy, and not to manage aggregate demand (AD).

   - For example, **income tax cuts** have been implemented to give workers an incentive to **work harder** rather than to **directly** increase people's **disposable income**.
   - Reductions in **business taxes** have aimed to provide an incentive for **entrepreneurs** to take more risks, invest in new machines and technology, and allow them to build successful, innovative companies.
   - Reductions in **welfare benefits** have aimed to increase people's incentive to **work** rather than stay on benefits.

3) If these supply-side policies are successful then **tax receipts** (i.e. the money the government gets from taxes) should go **up** rather than down. This is because:

   - **More people** are **in work** (meaning less money is spent by the government on welfare benefits).
   - People are **working** longer and harder (meaning they end up paying more income tax overall).
   - Businesses are more **successful** (meaning they have larger profits to tax).

4) So successful supply-side fiscal policies should **reduce** the size of a **budget deficit** (or **increase** the size of a **budget surplus**).

Practice Questions

Q1 How do successful supply-side policies shift the AS curve?

Q2 Explain how changing productivity can be a supply-side policy.

Q3 What is privatisation?

Q4 Explain why supply-side policies improve the current account on the balance of payments.

Exam Questions

Q1 Using a diagram, explain how supply-side policies can benefit an economy without leading to inflation. [6 marks]

Q2 Which of the following is most likely to lead to an increase in aggregate supply? Explain your answer.
A) An increase in income tax.
B) A rise in house prices.
C) An increase in training for workers provided by firms.
D) An increase in government spending on unemployment benefits. [4 marks]

Here's an incentive — have a cup of tea when you finish the page...

Supply-side policies are currently the favoured way to try to make an economy grow. That doesn't mean they're perfect in every way (as you'll see on the next couple of pages), only that they seem to have fewer unwanted knock-on effects than the other tools in the government's toolbox. To cut a long story short, they're important, and you need to know all about them for your exam.

The Effectiveness of Supply-side Policies

Supply-side policies are good... but they're not perfect in every way. **These pages are for all boards.**

Supply-side policies involve **Fewer Trade-offs** between objectives

1) A problem with expansionary fiscal and monetary policies is that while they might help the **economy to grow**, there's also a **danger** of **inflation rising** as a result.

2) Supply-side policies avoid this risk — they increase the **productive potential** of the economy, causing an **increase** in growth, jobs and output.

3) Normally, policies that would cause the **AS curve** to shift by increasing growth, jobs and output will **also** shift the **AD curve** and create a risk of **higher inflation** (see p.89). But successful supply-side policies can avoid this.

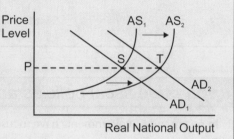

- Initially the macroeconomic equilibrium is at **point S**.
- When the AS curve shifts from AS$_1$ to AS$_2$ as a result of the supply-side policies, and AD increases from AD$_1$ to AD$_2$, the new macroeconomic equilibrium is now at **point T**.
- Prices haven't increased — supply has kept up with demand and **no demand-pull inflation** has been caused.
- And because supply-side policies aim to make firms more productive and efficient, the risk of **cost-push** inflation is also low.

4) Supply-side policies don't necessarily lead to increases in the **national debt** either.
   - A lot of expansionary fiscal and monetary policies involve **budget deficits**, where the government **spends** more than it receives in **taxes**.
   - However, many supply-side policies are implemented by the **private sector**. ← *Private investment by firms is actively encouraged by the government.*
   - And supply-side policies that make the economy grow also **increase tax receipts** — this helps **decrease** any budget deficits.
   - This means that there's less risk of private investment being '**crowded out**' (see p.122), as the government doesn't have to borrow so heavily to pay for its spending.

Supply-side policies can make an economy **Less Dependent** on **Imports**

1) Supply-side policies can make an economy **less dependent** on **imports**. If an economy can provide **high-quality** goods and services at **low prices**, people are less likely to buy imports.

2) Supply-side policies that keep UK exports competitive are vital for **future growth**.

3) **Foreign export markets** are becoming more and more important for UK firms. The economies of China and India are **growing quickly** and their **demand** for high-quality goods is **increasing**.

Thanks to the newly developed shrink ray the UK's annual exports to the USA could now fit into a single container.

Supply-side policies **Won't Work** in all circumstances

1) **Supply-side** policies are aimed at improving AS, but **without** sufficient AD, supply-side policies don't work.

2) For supply-side policies to be successful, they need **demand-side** policies to support any growth.

3) For this reason some economists argue that during a **recession**, when demand is weak, supply-side policies are **not** appropriate.

4) Supply-side policies also take **time** to work. Again, in a recession, the economy might need **more immediate** help. **Demand-side** policies can have a more immediate effect in these circumstances.

5) However, **supply-side** policies do make an economy more **resilient** and better able to **cope** with shocks. For example, in a recession, it's much better to have a **highly-trained** and **flexible** workforce.

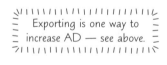

Exporting is one way to increase AD — see above.

The credit crunch in 2008 was a major shock to many economies — this is a situation where supply-side policies alone wouldn't have been appropriate.

The Effectiveness of Supply-side Policies

Supply-side policies still have their Downsides

1) Supply-side policies are **market-oriented** — they're based on the belief that **competition** in a **free market** will provide the **most efficient** outcomes overall. However, not everyone will agree that these efficient outcomes are actually **fair**.

> For example, one supply-side policy to **improve labour flexibility** would be to remove the **national minimum wage**. If this resulted in the AS curve shifting to the **right**, then the policy would have **worked**, but some people would probably be **paid less** than they would have if the national minimum wage was kept. Basically... supply-side policies **don't** mean that 'everybody wins'.

2) Some economists argue that supply-side policies **widen** the gap between the rich and the poor. It's argued that **entrepreneurs** and the **rich** are given **incentives** to make even more money, while those on welfare benefits are threatened with even greater **poverty**.

3) It's also claimed that supply-side policies **favour employers** over employees because policies that aim to make a workforce more flexible provide more benefits for employers than employees. Here are a couple of examples:

1
- One way to create a more flexible workforce is to **weaken** trade unions (see p.118).
- This is great for **employers** — for example, they'll be faced with less pressure to **raise wages**.
- Also, without any fear of **union action**, some firms might feel able to treat workers **unfairly**.

2
- Another way to create a more flexible workforce is to introduce laws making it **easier** to 'hire and fire' workers.
- It's argued that these laws also **favour employers** — they can more easily (and cheaply) recruit workers when they need them and get rid of workers that are less productive.
- However, there are potentially benefits for both **employers** and **employees**. For example, firms are **more likely** to take on workers in **good times** if they know that they'll be able to lay them off if times get **tougher**.

Practice Questions

Q1 Draw a diagram to show how supply-side policies can increase aggregate demand and supply.

Q2 Explain why supply-side policies can make an economy less dependent on imports.

Q3 Describe one situation where supply-side policies may not be the most effective way to improve the economy.

Q4 Why do some people claim supply-side policies favour employers over employees?

Exam Questions

Q1 Which one of the following statements is true of supply-side policies? Explain your answer.
A) They are short-term policies.
B) They make the economy less competitive.
C) They often involve the private sector.
D) They always cause inflation. [4 marks]

Q2 Evaluate the view that supply-side policies are always the best way to achieve the government's macroeconomic objectives. [25 marks]

Shift your AS — learn all about these supply-side policies...

I reckon there's another driving comparison that describes what it's like to use supply-side policies to try to control an economy. It's (probably) like driving a car which usually works pretty well, but whose steering stops working when you're headed towards a cliff, and in which some of the seats have lovely cushions while others are covered in sandpaper. Yes, it's (almost certainly) like that.

Conflict Between Policy Instruments

There you go... all you need to know to run an economy. Using your fiscal, monetary and supply-side policies all you've got to do is satisfy everyone's needs and desires. Easy. Except... well, read on... **These pages are for Edexcel and OCR.**

Fiscal policy can Conflict with Monetary policy

There are times when your fiscal policy can be trying to achieve **one thing**... while your monetary policy is trying to achieve the **opposite**. It's not even as unlikely as it sounds — there are some quite good reasons why this can come about.

1) To get the economy to **grow** the UK government might decide that it needs to use a **reflationary fiscal policy** to **increase AD**. It could do this by either reducing taxes or increasing government spending.

2) Either way, the government will probably have to **borrow** some money off the money markets. It can do this by issuing 'Treasury bills'.

> *Usually when people borrow money from the money markets, they're actually borrowing from large financial institutions like banks and other large investors like pension funds.*

> A **Treasury bill** is essentially a 'government IOU'.
>
> - You **lend** a government some money, and in return the government gives you a **certificate** promising to pay you back in, say, 3 months' time.
> - However, if you want, you can **sell** this certificate to anyone that wants to buy it. In this case, the government would pay **them** back the money shown on the certificate.
> - So these Treasury bills are quite '**liquid**' — they can be 'converted to money' quite easily by selling them.
> - And they're a **safe** place to invest too — a respectable government is **unlikely** to **default** on its debt and not pay back the money it's borrowed. This means that during a **credit crunch** (when investors don't really want to lend money, in case they don't get it back), investors will probably be more willing to lend to governments.

3) All this extra money spent by the government (or the money from tax cuts which other people will spend) could lead to a risk of **inflation** (see p.112).

4) This risk of inflation might convince the Monetary Policy Committee of the Bank of England to adopt a **contractionary monetary policy** (see p.114).

> *This is perfectly reasonable. After all, their job is to make sure inflation doesn't get out of hand.*

5) This would tend to **slow down** the economy (i.e. reduce output), which is **exactly the opposite** of what the government is trying to achieve.

6) And don't forget... all that government spending might '**crowd out**' investment by the private sector (see p.113), which could **decrease** the **productive potential** of the economy over the long term.

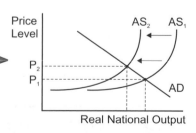

The conflict between policy instruments can quickly get out of hand.

Fiscal policy can Conflict with Supply-side policy

Sometimes, it can be **fiscal policies** and **supply-side policies** that are pushing in opposite directions.

1) Suppose a government wants to **increase aggregate demand** to get the economy to grow. It might decide to use a **reflationary fiscal policy** and spend money on, say, **health** and **education** — this extra spending will add to AD.

2) Making improvements to the health and education systems are effectively **supply-side** policies that will eventually lead to an improvement in **AS**.

3) The extra spending might lead to higher inflation in the **short term** (due to the increase in AD). But in the **longer term**, the increased AS should help reduce inflation (see p.119).

4) However, there will be a **conflict** between fiscal and supply-side policy if a government decided to use a **deflationary fiscal policy** to curb **inflation**.

5) As part of a deflationary fiscal policy a government could choose to **spend less** on **health** and **education** (which are two things governments tend to spend a lot on). This **could** lead to a shift to the left of the AS curve (from AS_1 to AS_2).

6) If AD **doesn't change** (or doesn't change by much), then this would result in **higher prices** (the equilibrium price level moves from P_1 to P_2). So, the government's deflationary fiscal policies have led to **higher inflation**, which is exactly the opposite of what it was trying to achieve.

Conflict Between Policy Instruments

Monetary policy can affect firms' Competitiveness in Different ways

A **supply-side policy** of a government might be to make firms **more competitive**.
However, a government's **monetary policy** may have an effect on the **competitiveness** of firms.

Contractionary monetary policy

- A **contractionary** monetary policy will probably involve a **rise** in interest rates.
- This will **increase** how much firms need to pay to **borrow** money — leading to **higher prices** and a **loss** of **competitiveness**.
- High interest rates may also lead to a **higher exchange rate** (see p.115).
- For firms that **import** their raw materials, this is a good thing — these raw materials will become **less expensive** and these firms will **remain competitive** despite high interest rates.
- However, a higher exchange rate will mean that firms which are **exporting** their products become **less competitive** internationally.

In this case, a contractionary monetary policy can act like a supply-side policy, as it makes some factors of production cheaper.

Expansionary monetary policy

- An **expansionary** monetary policy will probably involve a **reduction** in interest rates.
- This will **decrease** the cost to firms of **borrowing** money and this could lead to **greater competitiveness**.
- Low interest rates may also lead to a **lower exchange rate**.
- This will mean imported raw materials effectively become **more expensive**, increasing the **costs of production** for some firms (which could force prices to rise).
- However, the lower exchange rate will mean that firms which are **exporting** their products become **more competitive** internationally.

Making policy — you probably Won't keep Everyone happy

1) Whatever economic policy a government brings in, there will almost certainly be **winners** and **losers**. Some people and firms will **benefit**, while others will be **worse off**.
2) But exactly **how much** various people and firms will **benefit** or **lose** in the short and long term will be very **difficult** to predict.
3) Governments have to **prioritise** some objectives and focus their **policies** on achieving them. There may well be unwelcome **knock-on effects** elsewhere in the economy, but **balancing priorities** like this is ultimately what governments have to do.

Practice Questions

Q1 Explain how a government's reflationary fiscal policy can lead to a conflict with its monetary policy.
Q2 With the example of education, briefly explain how cutting government spending could result in inflation.
Q3 How might a contractionary monetary policy reduce firms' international competitiveness?

Exam Question

Q1 Evaluate three ways in which macroeconomic policy can be used to increase economic growth in an economy. [18 marks]

For this question think about how the policies might conflict with each other.

Running an economy is like walking a tightrope...

None of this means that trying to run an economy is impossible and so everyone should just give up and let whatever's going to happen just happen. But it does show that it's a difficult balancing act, and governments have to try to keep a lot of balls up in the air, as they try to juggle priorities (*must use more circus metaphors*)... and tame the lions of international competition.

Get Marks in Your Exam

These pages explain how you'll get marks in the exams. To do well you need to satisfy four different Assessment Objectives (AO1, AO2, AO3 and AO4), each of which requires different skills. Prove you've got the skills and you'll get the marks.

Make Sure *You* Read *the* Question Properly

It's easy to **misread** a question and spend 10 minutes writing about the **wrong thing**. A few simple tips can help you avoid this:

1) **Underline** the **command words** in the question (the ones that tell you **what to do**). Here are some common ones:

When you explain you need to **apply** your **economic knowledge** to the **context** you're given. The context could be a **specific market** or some **data**. E.g. *Explain why the price of beef changed in 2011.*

'Assess', 'Evaluate', 'Comment on' and 'Discuss' all mean roughly the **same thing**. They're about **weighing something up**. E.g. *Evaluate the success of reducing government spending to lower inflation.* You need to give a **balanced** answer — talk about all the **different viewpoints** on the subject.

Command words	Means write about...
Define	the **meaning** of the word
Explain	**why** it's like that (i.e. give reasons)
Analyse	something's **causes** and/or **effects**, and consider any **links** between them
Assess	the **advantages** and **disadvantages OR** the **arguments for** and **against**
Evaluate	
Comment on	
Discuss	

If you need to **define** a word, you need to give its **meaning**. E.g. *Define the term 'merit good'.*

Analysing requires you to **apply** your **own ideas** and your **economic knowledge** to show **why** you think something has happened or will happen. E.g. *Analyse the effect of higher interest rates on the economy.*

2) **Underline** the **key words** (the ones that tell you **what it's about**), e.g. productivity, sustainability, market failure.

3) **Re-read** the question and your answer **when you've finished** to check that your answer addresses **all parts** of the question. A **common mistake** is to **miss a bit out** — like when questions say 'refer to the data from...' or 'illustrate your answer with...'.

You get marks for *AO1 (showing knowledge)* and *AO2 (applying knowledge)*

AO1 and **AO2** questions usually start with words like "**Define**", "**State**", "**Give**", "**Explain**" or "**Calculate**".

1) **AO1** marks are for **content** and **knowledge**.
2) This means things like knowing the **proper definitions** for **economics terms**.

> To make sure you'll get marks for content, always give definitions of key terms you're using, or formulas if you're doing a calculation.

1) **AO2** marks are for **application** — applying your knowledge to a situation.
2) Numerical **calculations** are also marked as **application**.

You'll get more marks when you *Analyse (AO3)* and *Evaluate (AO4)*

AO3 marks are for **analysis** — thinking about benefits, costs, causes, effects and constraints. Analysis questions usually start with words like "**Analyse**", "**Examine**", or "**Explain why**".

1) Use your knowledge to **explain** your answer and give **reasons**. Consider **both sides** of the **argument** — you can only get **limited** analysis marks by looking at **one side**.
2) If there's data, say what the figures **mean**, talk about what might have **caused** them and say what **effect** you think they will have on the economy in the **future**.

AO4 marks are for **evaluation** — using your **judgement**. Evaluation questions usually start with words like "**Evaluate**", "**Assess**", "**Discuss**", "**Comment on**" or "**To what extent**".

1) **Weigh up** both sides of the argument — consider the **advantages** and **disadvantages** and say which **side** of the argument you think is **strongest**.
2) You **don't** need a **definite** answer. You can point out that it **depends** on various factors — as long as you say **what the factors** are, and say **why** the issue depends on those factors. Use your judgement to say what the **most important factors** are. The most important thing is to **justify** why you're saying what you're saying.

Get Marks in Your Exam

There are marks for the **Quality** of your **Writing**

1) For **all three** exam boards the **quality** of your **written communication** (QWC) will be assessed. Examiners will mark **specific questions** for QWC — in the **Edexcel** and **OCR** exams these questions will be **labelled** with an **asterisk** (*), and in the **AQA** exams these questions will be the ones worth **25 marks**.

2) Your QWC is **very important** because the examiner will decide whether to give your answer **more** or **fewer** marks depending on your QWC.

3) You have to write **formally** and **arrange relevant information clearly** — write a **well-structured essay**, not a list of bullet points. You need to use **specialist vocabulary** when it's appropriate, so it's well worth **learning** some of the **technical terms** used in this book.

4) You have to write **neatly** enough for the examiner to be able to read your answer. You also need to use good **spelling**, **grammar** and **punctuation** to make your meaning **crystal clear**. If your handwriting, grammar, spelling and punctuation are **so** far up the spout that the examiner **can't understand** what you've written, **expect problems**.

Impressive... but it won't get you any marks.

Jotting down a quick essay plan will help you to structure your essay.

Use the **Data** for **Data-response Questions**

That sounds **pretty obvious**, but there are some things you need to bear in mind:

1) If a question asks you to **refer** to a table of data, a graph, or some text, make sure you **use** it in your answer.

2) **Don't** just copy out loads of data — any data you use in your answer must be **relevant** to the specific point you're making.

3) If a question asks you to 'analyse' or 'explain why', you'll need to use the data as well as your **economic knowledge** to **back up** the points you make.

4) If you need to draw a diagram, do it in **pencil** so you can rub it out if you make a mistake. However, label your diagrams in **pen** so they're nice and clear.

5) Sometimes you might need to do a **calculation**. You can use a calculator to find the answer, but **write down** your **working out**. If you get the answer **wrong** you can still **pick up marks** for using the correct method.

Don't forget to include **All** the **Skills** in **Extended Answer Questions**

1) Essay questions need a bit of **planning**. Jot down a **rough outline** of what you want to say — remember, you need to make your answer **balanced**, so make a list of the **advantages** and **disadvantages**, or the arguments **for** and **against**.

2) **Diagrams** are a quick and easy way of explaining quite difficult concepts in your answers, but make sure you **explain** what your diagrams show and **always** refer to them in your answers. **Label** your diagrams properly so they're clear.

3) In an essay answer you need to show **all** the skills — **don't jump** straight to the **evaluation** part. So, if you're asked to evaluate the extent to which lowering the price of exports can bring about the recovery of the UK economy, you need to:

- **Define** what is meant by exports and recovery (this will get you your **AO1** marks).
- Explain how an increase in exports is **relevant** to the recovery of the UK economy (for **AO2** marks).
- Give the **advantages** and **disadvantages** of lowering the price of exports (for **AO3** marks).
- Finally, for the **AO4** marks, **weigh up** both sides of the argument and **decide** how successful, in your opinion, lowering the price of exports would be in helping the UK economy to recover.

Learn this stuff for some inflation of marks...

Of course, to do well in the exam you've got to know all that economics stuff inside out, but these pages will give you an idea of how you can put that knowledge to best use in the exam. Keep in mind that you don't just need to learn the facts for economics — you've got to prove to the examiner that you understand them and can apply them to various scenarios. So all very simple, really...

Do Well in Your AQA Exam

*These pages are most useful for students taking the **AQA** exam. But the sample exam question is worth a read no matter what exam board you're doing.*

AS Economics *is divided into* Two Examined Units

1) Unit 1 is called **Markets and Market Failure** — it introduces you to **microeconomics** and looks at how resources are allocated by markets and what happens when markets don't allocate resources efficiently.

2) Unit 2 is called **The National Economy** — it introduces you to **macroeconomics** and looks at the economic objectives of the UK government and how it tries to achieve them.

3) The exam papers for Unit 1 and Unit 2 have the **same format**:

> 1) You have **1 hour 15 minutes** for each exam.
>
> 2) **Section A** consists of **25 multiple-choice** questions worth **1 mark** each.
>
> 3) **Section B** contains **extracts** of information about two different scenarios — you have to choose **one** of these scenarios to answer questions about. Each scenario is followed by **four** compulsory **data-response** questions, worth **50 marks** in total. You have to show that you **understand** the information and can **analyse** and **evaluate** it.
>
> 4) There are **75 marks** available, so aim to get a mark **every minute** — this will give you a guide as to how long to spend on each question.

Here's an Example *of the type of* Extracts *you'll get in* Section B

There's a sample question and answer on the next page.

Extract A: Falling unemployment may lead to a rise in interest rates

The UK unemployment rate is continuing to fall according to the latest figures published by the Office of   1
National Statistics in January 2014. This is continuing a downward trend in the rate of unemployment
since October 2011. The current level of unemployment for November 2013 stands at 2.32 million,
down from a recent high of 2.68 million in October 2011, and represents a drop of 167 000 from
August 2013. Undoubtedly this is good news for thousands of people in Britain who now have a   5
job, but it does pose some questions for the Bank of England's Monetary Policy Committee (MPC).

The MPC has kept interest rates at 0.5% since March 2009 and the Governor of the Bank of England,
Mark Carney, announced in August 2013 that he would not consider a rise in interest rates until
the jobless level fell to, or below, 7% of the economically active population. With the recent
fall in unemployment, largely linked to stronger than expected growth in the economy, the UK   10
unemployment rate now stands at 7.1%. This has left several economists wondering if the MPC
will soon decide to raise interest rates once again, but with inflation standing at 2% at the end of
2013, there is no immediate need for the MPC to consider a large increase in interest rates.

Extract B: UK Quarterly Real GDP Growth 2011-2013

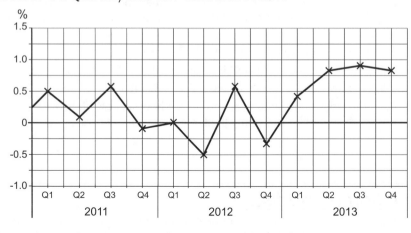

Do Well in Your AQA Exam

An *Example Extended Answer* to give you some tips:

Q1 Extract A (lines 11 – 13) states: 'This has left several economists wondering if the MPC will soon decide to raise interest rates once again, but with inflation standing at 2% at the end of 2013, there is no immediate need for the MPC to consider a large increase in interest rates.'

Using the data and your economic knowledge, evaluate to what extent a small rise in interest rates would affect the UK's rate of unemployment.
$\qquad$ 25 marks

The rate of unemployment is the number of people out of work as a percentage of the labour force. The demand for labour is a derived demand, which means that when the demand for goods and services is high then the demand for labour will also be high, bringing down the rate of unemployment.

> Definitions are great to use as introductions.

Interest rates are a tool that can affect how consumers spend and save, and how firms invest. High interest rates are a contractionary monetary policy, which means they tend to reduce consumer spending and investment by firms because borrowing is more expensive. Reduced consumer spending and investment by firms causes the aggregate demand curve to shift to the left and the rate of unemployment to increase (because labour is a derived demand). The size of the increase in unemployment would depend on where the aggregate demand curve was situated on the aggregate supply curve.

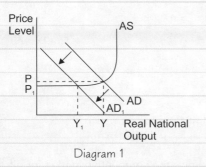

Diagram 1

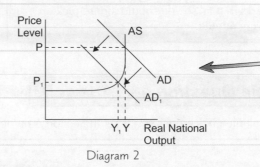

Diagram 2

> A relevant and accurate diagram can gain you up to 4 marks.

In diagram 1 the economy has a lot of spare capacity. If aggregate demand shifts left then the fall in employment is large compared to the fall in prices. When an economy has a lot of spare capacity it means that firms' stock rooms are full, and machines and workers are unused because consumption is low. Confidence in the economy will also be low and increasing interest rates so that spending and investment is more expensive will only shrink the economy. In diagram 2, where the economy is at full capacity, increasing interest rates and reducing aggregate demand has a bigger impact on inflation and a smaller impact on unemployment. Higher interest rates will slow down the demand-pull inflation that is putting prices up. There may be a small reduction in employment, but incomes and confidence in the economy will still be high.

> This is good analysis — just describing your diagram won't get you any extra marks.

Despite the sharp fall in the UK's unemployment, 167 000 between August and November 2013, the rate of unemployment is still quite high at 7.1%. This means that the UK economy has a lot of spare capacity, so the aggregate demand curve is likely to be situated somewhere like it is in diagram 1. Furthermore, although the UK economy has been growing steadily between Q1 and Q4 of 2013, many economists believe that it is still fragile. A rise in interest rates, even by a small amount, could hurt the economy and increase unemployment. Raising interest rates could also push up the value of the pound because it will attract 'hot money'. This would make UK exports less competitive, worsening the UK's large balance of payments deficit, and further reducing aggregate demand.

> Give data from the extracts to support your answer.

> Impress your examiners by making relevant references to the UK economy.

> Good evaluation like this will get you higher marks.

There are other factors that can affect the rate of unemployment which could reduce the impact of a rise in interest rates on unemployment. For example, government spending can stimulate the economy, especially given the multiplier effect. Also supply-side policies that make the workforce more productive and efficient could help to reduce the rate of unemployment.

> A sentence or two analysing and evaluating how these other factors might affect unemployment is needed here.

This essay starts off really well and would get around 18 out of 25 marks. The fact that it doesn't have a conclusion that makes a final judgement stops it from getting a higher mark. Also, it should analyse and evaluate the two other factors mentioned that could affect the rate of unemployment, rather than just tagging them on at the end.

Do Well in Your Edexcel Exam

*These pages are most useful for students taking the **Edexcel** exam. But the sample exam questions are worth a quick read no matter what exam board you're doing.*

AS Economics *is divided into* Two Examined Units

1) Unit 1 is called **Competitive Markets — How They Work and Why They Fail**. It introduces you to **microeconomics** and looks at how resources are allocated by markets and what happens when markets don't allocate resources efficiently.

2) Unit 2 is called **Managing the Economy**. It introduces you to **macroeconomics** and looks at the economic objectives of governments and how they try to achieve them.

Unit 1 Exam — 1 hour 30 minutes

1) **Section A** is made up of two-part questions — the first part is a **multiple-choice** question, and in the second part you have to **explain** why the answer you've chosen is correct.

2) There is a total of **32 marks** for Section A.

3) **Section B** contains two **data-response** questions — but you only have to answer **one**. You have to show that you **understand** the information and can **analyse** and **evaluate** it.

4) You can get **48 marks** for Section B.

5) There are **80 marks** in total so you should aim to pick up a mark roughly **every minute**.

Unit 2 Exam — 1 hour 30 minutes

1) The paper contains two **data-response** questions — but you only have to answer **one**.

2) There are **80 marks** in total so once again you should aim to pick up a mark roughly **every minute**.

Here's an *Example Question* and *Answer*

This question is like the multiple-choice ones you'll get in Section A of the Unit 1 exam.

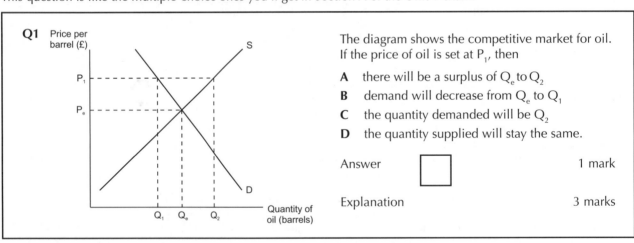

Q1 Price per barrel (£)

The diagram shows the competitive market for oil. If the price of oil is set at P_1, then

A there will be a surplus of Q_e to Q_2

B demand will decrease from Q_e to Q_1

C the quantity demanded will be Q_2

D the quantity supplied will stay the same.

Answer ☐   1 mark

Explanation   3 marks

Answer: B ◄ — You'd get 1 mark for giving the correct answer.

Giving a definition of the market equilibrium would get you 1 mark.

Explanation:

The market equilibrium is where supply and demand are balanced. For oil, this is at price P_e and quantity Q_e. When the price is increased and set at P_1, the quantity suppliers are prepared to supply changes to Q_2 — so option D is incorrect. Answer A is incorrect because the surplus supplied by the market at the new price is Q_1 to Q_2. When the price is increased and set at P_1, the quantity demanded decreases to Q_1 — so B is the correct answer.

Rejecting option D (OR rejecting option A) with a correct justification gets you another 1 mark.

An explanation of why option B is correct will also get you 1 mark.

This answer gets full marks. Even if you get the answer wrong, you can still earn explanation marks, e.g. you can be awarded 1 mark for a correct definition, or 1 mark for correctly rejecting an option. If you are unsure which option is correct, start by explaining as fully as you can which options are incorrect.

Do Well in Your Edexcel Exam

Here's another Example Question and Answer:

This question is similar to a data-response question you might get in the Unit 2 exam.

Figure 1 Average value of £1, in euros and dollars, over various one-year periods.

	euro (€)	USD ($)
2007	1.46	2.00
2008	1.29	1.88
2009	1.14	1.59
2010	1.18	1.55
2011	1.15	1.62
2012	1.20	1.60
2013	1.18	1.56

Q1 Explain the likely impact on the UK economy between 2007 and 2013 of the changes shown in Figure 1.

12 marks

The exchange rate is the value of one currency in terms of another. Figure 1 clearly shows that between 2007 and 2013, the value of the pound fell against both the euro and the dollar. In 2007 £1 was able to purchase 1.46 euros or 2 US dollars. By 2013, £1 was only able to purchase 1.18 euros or 1.56 US dollars. In both cases this is a fall in the pound of about 20% — a large amount.

Clear definition introduces the answer.

The data used here is relevant to the question.

When the pound depreciates, it makes the price of UK goods in foreign countries fall, and therefore UK exports become more competitive in foreign markets. The fall in the value of the pound makes it more expensive for UK consumers to import foreign goods. Therefore exports will tend to increase and imports will tend to decrease, leading to an overall increase in the UK's net exports.

This shows an understanding of why exports become cheaper for people in other countries.

As net exports is a component of aggregate demand (AD), the UK economy will expand — the AD curve will shift to the right. As long as there is spare capacity in the economy to meet the extra demand for UK exports, economic growth will occur in the short term without causing demand-pull inflation. The UK has a balance of payments deficit — but if exports increase and imports decrease, the current account of the balance of payments should improve.

Drawing an accurate diagram to show the shift would get some easy marks and support the analysis here.

However, the UK is a large importer of raw materials and semi-finished goods, so an increase in the cost of imports might lead to cost-push inflation due to the increased costs of production. Inflation has the opposite effect on net exports to the one described above — net exports would worsen. This would cause a fall in aggregate demand, and a worsening of the balance of payments.

This shows knowledge of economic theory.

If net exports improve, this will have a multiplier effect on aggregate demand. The initial increase in AD would create more jobs — causing a rise in the overall disposable income of consumers, and a second rise in AD as a result of increased consumer spending. This will continue to have a multiplying effect on the economy until all the initial money has leaked out of the circular flow. The creation of more jobs will also mean that unemployment will fall, and a rise in income will mean the standard of living in the UK will rise too.

It's important that you include the possible positive and negative impacts.

In the UK, as income increases, people tend to spend a proportionally larger amount of their income on imports — this would reduce the benefit brought to the economy (because the cost of imports is higher when the value of the pound has fallen).

Finish with a conclusion about what you think will happen.

In the long run, the likely impact of a fall in the value of the pound on the UK economy will be positive, but in the short run it might cause a balance of payments deficit because the UK imports more than it exports. Since 2013 the UK's economy has been growing again, which might in part be because the value of the pound has fallen (and stayed low), so the UK's exports have increased and its imports have decreased.

This shows knowledge of the UK economy.

This is a good answer that should get full marks. It shows a real understanding of exchange rates and the effect that a depreciation in the value of the pound has on UK exports and imports. It also explains the potential knock-on effects of these changes on the UK economy by discussing unemployment, living standards, economic growth and the current account of the balance of payments. Even when a diagram is not specifically asked for, it's often a good idea to include one if it's relevant, as it'll help you get some marks.

Do Well in Your OCR Exam

*These pages are most useful for students taking the **OCR** exam. But the sample exam questions are worth a read no matter what exam board you're doing.*

AS Economics *is divided into* Two Examined Units

1) Unit 1 is called **Markets in Action** — it introduces you to **microeconomics** and looks at how resources are allocated by markets and what happens when markets don't allocate resources efficiently.

2) Unit 2 is called **The National and International Economy** — it introduces you to **macroeconomics** and looks at the economic objectives of governments and how they try to achieve them.

3) The exam papers for Unit 1 and Unit 2 have the **same format**:

> 1) You have **1 hour 30 minutes** for each exam.
>
> 2) You have to answer all of the questions in each paper. The questions are data-response questions, so you have to show that you **understand** the information and can **analyse** and **evaluate** it.
>
> 3) There are **60 marks** available in each paper, so aim to get a mark **every one and a half minutes** — this will give you a guide as to how long to spend on each question.

Here's an *Example Question and* Answer

> **Extract A: Drought causes severe shortage of wheat**
>
> Two consecutive dry winters have led to a severe shortage of British wheat. Reservoir levels in the 1
> south of England have fallen to an all-time low and the government has enforced strict restrictions
> on the amount of water farmers can use for their land. As a result, the recent wheat harvests
> have been very poor and there is a serious decline in the supply of British wheat. The fall in the
> supply of wheat has forced many thrifty shoppers to switch to buying non-wheat-based products 5
> as they search for better deals. If this continues then many farmers could be put out of business.
>
> The government is considering a number of options to respond to this crisis. One possibility
> is that it could agree to relax the regulation on the growing of genetically modified (GM)
> crops, and encourage the use of GM wheat that's more resistant to drought. However, it
> is more likely that the government will introduce a wheat subsidy. This should provide 10
> some stability to the wheat market and help the farmers who are struggling the most.

> **Q1** Using a demand and supply diagram, comment on how the
> market for British wheat might be affected by the recent droughts. 8 marks

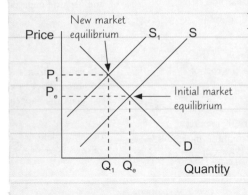

The diagram shows the likely effect of the recent droughts on the British wheat market. The initial market equilibrium before the droughts is at price P_e and quantity Q_e. However, British wheat yields are reduced by the lack of water, caused by the droughts and the subsequent government restrictions on water. The poor wheat yields have therefore shifted the supply of wheat to the left, from S to S_1. When supply shifts left, this causes an increase in the price, so demand contracts and a new equilibrium point is formed at price P_1 and quantity Q_1 — the new equilibrium is at a higher price and a lower quantity than the initial market equilibrium. Extract A also describes how demand for wheat has fallen because some consumers are looking for cheaper alternatives. The price elasticity of demand for wheat will affect how big this fall in demand will be. If demand for wheat is quite price inelastic, then the higher prices will not actually reduce demand very much.

This is a thorough answer that would get all 8 marks. The diagram is accurate and relevant to the answer — it's been used to support the answer rather than just drawn and forgotten.

Do Well in Your OCR Exam

An *Example Extended Answer* to give you some tips:

Q2 Discuss whether providing subsidies for British wheat farmers would be the most effective way of preventing them from going out of business.   18 marks

Subsidies are payments made by governments to firms or individuals. A subsidy lowers the costs of production, so the supply curve shifts to the right, causing a fall in the price and an increase in the quantity consumed. For example, in the diagram to the right, the subsidy shifts the supply curve from S to S_1. The price falls from P to P_1 and the quantity consumed increases from Q to Q_1. The subsidy per unit is shown by the vertical height $P_0 - P_1$.

A clear definition introduces the answer.

The provision of subsidies for wheat farmers would not only keep prices low for domestic and international consumers, but it would also keep wheat farming profitable, so that wheat farmers do not go out of business. If wheat farming became unprofitable, wheat farmers would be forced to stop growing wheat and find another crop that was profitable. As wheat is an important commodity and affects the price of bread and other key foodstuffs that people buy on a daily basis, this would mean that the UK would be dependent on imports for a staple food commodity, making it vulnerable. Subsidies would act as an incentive for farmers to grow wheat and increase output.

The use of a diagram makes it easier to explain the effect of a subsidy and will earn you extra marks.

This is a good explanation of the positive effects subsidies might have.

Subsidies are expensive and part of government spending — if the cost of the subsidies to the government is greater than the benefits brought by this intervention then this is an example of government failure. The money spent on subsidising wheat farmers also has an opportunity cost — it could have been spent on more productive projects that help to increase the productive potential of the economy. If farmers are encouraged to grow wheat, then fewer farmers will grow other things, so the supply of other farming products will fall and their prices will rise. The size of the impact of a subsidy will depend on how farmers react to it.

This point could be elaborated to make its meaning more clear.

Some people say that subsidies lead to government failure because they cause a misallocation of resources — that market forces are best placed to allocate resources efficiently, and subsidies interfere with this. Subsidies protect inefficient businesses, lowering their incentive to stay competitive.

This paragraph could have been explained more thoroughly.

A subsidy on wheat may have different effects in the short and long run. In general, the effect a subsidy has depends on the price elasticity of supply — in the short term, the supply of wheat is inelastic. The supply of wheat has been reduced, but the subsidies should reduce the price of the available wheat. In the long run, even if there continues to be a lack of water, the supply of wheat is more elastic, and subsidies will encourage more farmers to grow wheat.

This paragraph makes an important point about the price elasticity of supply.

The alternatives to subsidies that would help keep wheat farming profitable include nationalising the industry. Industries which are considered too important to leave to the free market are often nationalised. However, the argument against subsidies, that a free market is the best way to allocate resources, applies here too.

This paragraph should explain the benefit of nationalising.

Relaxing regulations on genetically modified (GM) crops may also be a solution in the long term. If a GM wheat crop that was more resistant to drought was used, the supply of wheat would increase. However, many people are against GM foods, so this may prove controversial.

These points should be elaborated to make them clearer.

There are many arguments against the use of wheat subsidies, but there are few realistic alternatives. The UK government tends to be more market-oriented, so is unlikely to consider nationalisation. GM foods are still too controversial. Subsidies may be a good short-term solution to reduce the price of the available wheat, but the government would need to take care that the long-term effects of subsidies were positive.

The conclusion could be more decisive and explain its points more.

This answer shows a strong knowledge of economic theory and some good analysis. It also makes evaluations as it goes along. Some points are a bit vague and could be explained to make their meaning clearer. It might have been a good idea to suggest another alternative — for example, reducing taxes on wheat. The conclusion could have been improved with a clearer judgement on the most effective way of protecting the British wheat industry. It'd earn about 15 out of 18 marks.

Answers

Section One — The Economic Problem

Page 5 — An Introduction to Economics

1   Maximum of 6 marks available. HINTS:
- Pick three factors of production that would be necessary for someone opening a new restaurant, and explain why each is important.
- E.g. 'Labour will be important, since a new restaurant will need people to carry out all the various tasks involved, such as cooking food, serving customers, managing the accounts, and so on'.

Page 7 — Markets and Economies

1   Maximum of 4 marks available. HINTS:
- Start by explaining the difference between a positive statement and a normative one, e.g. 'a positive statement is an objective statement which can be tested by looking at suitable evidence, while a normative statement expresses an opinion'.
- Then consider each of the given statements in turn:
  'Statement 1 could be tested by looking at evidence from different countries that have experienced recessions — you could see if there is actually any link between increased government spending and the speed of recovery. So Statement 1 is positive.'
  'Statement 2 can't be tested to see if it's true or not — it contains a value judgement which some people will agree with and others will disagree with. So Statement 2 is normative.'
- Don't forget to give your final answer... B.

Page 9 — Production Possibility Frontiers

1   Maximum of 4 marks available. HINTS:
- Explain that combinations of cars and butter that can be made using the existing resources are shown by points inside or on the production possibility frontier (PPF).
- W, Y and Z all show combinations that can be made using existing resources, since they all lie inside or on the PPF.
- But X lies outside the PPF, so this combination cannot be made using existing resources.
- So the answer is B.
2   Maximum of 5 marks available. HINTS:
- Start by defining the term opportunity cost, e.g. 'the next best alternative that you give up in making a particular decision'.
- Then explain that only combinations of cars and butter shown by points inside or on the production possibility frontier (PPF) can be made using the existing resources.
- Now you need to show an opportunity cost on this diagram. E.g. 'Suppose the combination of goods shown by point Y is currently being produced (20 000 cars and 9000 tonnes of butter), but it was then decided that more butter was needed. This could only be achieved by producing fewer cars. For example, if production were shifted to point Z, then this would mean 11 300 tonnes of butter would be produced, but with current resources only 10 000 cars could be produced. So the opportunity cost of producing an extra 2300 tonnes of butter is the lost production of 10 000 cars.'

Page 11 — Economic Objectives and Specialisation

1   Maximum of 4 marks available. HINTS:
- Start by explaining that specialisation and division of labour mean that people (and even whole economies) will focus on making the things they're good at making. This means they're not making for themselves all the things they want or need, so they'll need to get those things by trading.
- Then explain how using money as a medium of exchange simplifies trading, e.g. 'Using money as a medium of exchange allows trade between people and countries, even if they have no need of what the other actually produces. Money has value for a seller, so they are willing to exchange their products for money.'
- Finally, explain that this means people or countries are benefiting economically by doing what they're best at, while still obtaining everything they want or need.

Page 13 — Production, Productivity and Efficiency

1   Maximum of 4 marks available. HINTS:
- Explain what's meant by labour productivity, e.g. 'the amount of output produced per worker (or worker-hour)'.
- You can get marks for ruling out wrong answers. E.g. 'Option A might allow more output to be produced, but on its own this won't lead to improved

labour productivity, since the output per worker may not increase'.
- Then explain why you've chosen the correct answer, B. E.g. 'More specialisation may well improve the amount of output each worker produces, because people would be performing tasks that they are well trained for and have had a lot of practice at'.

Page 15 — Economies and Diseconomies of Scale

1   Maximum of 4 marks available. HINTS:
- State that what's being described in the question — firms may encounter 'diseconomies of scale', which is where the average cost per unit increases as a firm's output rises.
- Give examples of how diseconomies of scale can arise, e.g. 'Larger firms whose output has grown can suffer from increases in wastage and loss, as materials may seem in plentiful supply', or 'As a firm grows and its output increases, communication between workers may become less efficient.'

Section Two — Competitive Markets

Page 17 — Demand

1   Maximum of 4 marks available. HINTS:
- Start by stating what is likely to happen to the demand for tiles — 'The demand for tiles is likely to decrease in line with the falling demand for houses'.
- Explain why the demand for tiles is a derived demand.
- To maximise your marks you need to evaluate. So here you could say that if the housing market is in decline there would be less demand for tiles because fewer new houses would be built — so fewer tiles are needed. You could also say that there will always be some demand for tiles even when the housing market is slow (due to people redecorating and refurbishing etc.) but the fact that tile retailers are cutting back expansion plans suggests they have seen a drop-off in demand for tiles.
2   Maximum of 4 marks available. HINTS:
- Define what's meant by complementary goods, e.g. 'Complementary goods are goods that are often used together, so they are in joint demand. When demand rises for one good, then demand will also rise for the other good.'
- State what is likely to happen to the demand for crackers — 'The demand for crackers is likely to decline if the demand for cheese falls due to a price increase'.
- To maximise your marks you need to evaluate — so here you could say that people also buy crackers without cheese, so an increase in cheese prices may not have a dramatic impact on cracker sales.

Page 19 — Price, Income and Cross Elasticities of Demand

1   Maximum of 4 marks available. HINTS:
- The correct answer is B.
- This question is a case of calculating PED using the numbers you've been given. As it's a calculation there's only one correct answer and to get the marks for the explanation you need to show your working.
- $$percentage\ change\ in\ demand = \frac{200}{200} \times 100 = 100\%$$

  $$percentage\ change\ in\ price = \frac{-1.5}{3} \times 100 = -50\%$$

  $$PED = \frac{100}{-50} = -2.0$$

Page 21 — Uses of Elasticities of Demand

1   Maximum of 6 marks available. HINTS:
- Start by explaining what the negative XED means for the two goods — 'A negative cross elasticity of demand means that the goods are complements... a fall in the price of one will increase the quantity demanded of the other...'.
- Then you should relate this information to how the firm can maximise sales. As you know the products are complements, you could talk about how affecting the sale of one product will have an effect on the other product. For example, decreasing the price of product A could boost its sales and have the knock-on effect of boosting product B's sales.

Page 23 — Supply

1   Maximum of 4 marks available. HINTS:
- The correct answer is A.
- You need to explain why A is correct — e.g. 'A cut in the price causes a movement down the curve'.

- You should also explain why the other options (B, C and D) are incorrect — e.g. '...they would all cause the supply curve to shift as they cause an increase or decrease in the amount of the product supplied at every price'.
2 Maximum of 4 marks available. <u>HINTS</u>:
- The correct answer is C.
- For this question you need to work out which option would cause the supply curve to shift to the right. This is C because increased production speed results in increased output, which increases supply (and causes the supply curve to shift to the right).
- Also explain why the other options are incorrect. Options A, B and D all result in a decrease in supply and shift the supply curve to the left.

Page 25 — Price Elasticity of Supply

1 Maximum of 4 marks available. <u>HINTS</u>:
- There are several possible answers for this question.
- In general supply is more inelastic in the short run as at least one factor of production will be fixed (e.g. it takes time to expand banana plantations to allow for an increase in supply).
- More specific reasons include that bananas are perishable, so can't be stored for long, and take time to grow — both of which mean that suppliers can't respond that quickly to a change in price.
- Make sure you give two clear reasons for this question to get the marks.
2 Maximum of 4 marks available. <u>HINTS</u>:
- Your answer to this question is likely to focus on the fact that the firm employs 'highly skilled' workers to create hand-made furniture.
- For example, the firm may find it difficult to expand its workforce as it needs to find highly skilled workers and/or take time to train new unskilled staff.
- You could also mention that the furniture produced by the firm is likely to take a long time to make, which limits the ability of the firm to increase supply in the short run.

Page 27 — Market Equilibrium

1 Maximum of 4 marks available. <u>HINTS</u>:
- The correct answer is D because the equilibrium point moves when the demand curve shifts.
- A is incorrect as the equilibrium is where the demand and supply curves meet.
- B is incorrect as a fall in supply causes the supply curve to shift and the equilibrium point to move.
- C is incorrect because it is supply and demand which determine the equilibrium point, not the other way round.

Page 28 — Price and the Allocation of Resources

1 Maximum of 4 marks available. <u>HINTS</u>:
- Start by explaining what the price mechanism is — 'when a change in the supply or demand for a good/service leads to a change in its price, which in turn leads to a change in the quantity bought/sold, until supply is equal to demand'.
- Then talk about how price can act as an incentive — e.g. 'higher prices are attractive to firms because they can mean higher profits for the firm — this encourages firms to increase production/supply'.

Page 31 — Subsidies and Indirect Taxes

1 Maximum of 4 marks available. <u>HINTS</u>:
- The correct answer is D because this shows the area above the market price of the good if there was no subsidy.
- A, B and C are incorrect — A is the total cost of the subsidy, B is not part of the subsidy and C is the consumer gain from the subsidy.
2 Maximum of 8 marks available. <u>HINTS</u>:
- For this question it's a good idea to draw a diagram to show what happens when a tax is put on a product.
- Draw a diagram that shows how a tax shifts the supply curve to the left.
- Explain what the diagram shows — i.e. the price of the product increasing above the free market equilibrium price and the quantity demanded/supplied of the product falling.

Page 33 — Demand and Supply — Oil

1 Maximum of 12 marks available. <u>HINTS</u>:
- Explain the influence of a subsidy on price and demand for biofuels — e.g. it lowers the price of biofuel and increases demand for it.
- Draw a diagram showing how a subsidy on biofuels would shift the supply curve to the right.

- Explain what the diagram shows — i.e. the price of the product decreasing below the free market equilibrium price and the quantity demanded/supplied of the product increasing.
- Biofuels are a substitute for oil-based fuels, so explain how a reduction in the price of biofuel could affect the demand for oil (i.e. decrease it).
- Discuss other factors that could affect demand for biofuels and crude oil — e.g. if it is cheap and easy to switch to biofuels demand for them could increase hugely, but expensive switching, difficulties in use or limited uses could limit an increase in demand.

Page 35 — Demand and Supply — Agriculture

1 Maximum of 6 marks available. <u>HINTS</u>:
- Draw a diagram to show how a rise in demand for rice would shift the demand curve to the right. This would cause the price of rice to rise as the equilibrium point would shift.
- Explain the price rise by referring to features of your diagram. Your diagram should look like the one shown below.

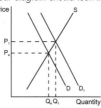

- You could also mention how rice is a major part of many people's diets, so an increase in price may not put people off buying it or get them to switch to alternatives — demand for rice is fairly price inelastic.

Page 37 — Demand and Supply — Labour

1 Maximum of 4 marks available. <u>HINTS</u>:
- The correct answer is C because an increase in staff productivity can encourage a firm to take on more staff to exploit this and maximise their output.
- A and D are incorrect as they increase costs for the firm. For option A the firm will need to spend money to purchase safety equipment. For option D the firm would spend money to provide extra staff benefits — e.g. a scheme that contributes to childcare costs.
- B is incorrect because at times of low demand for products they are more likely to reduce their labour force.

Page 39 — Demand and Supply — Metals

1 Maximum of 8 marks available. <u>HINTS</u>:
- For this question you can discuss a variety of different factors that can have an impact on housing prices in different areas.
- The supply of houses in an area impacts prices — large supply leads to lower prices. Supply depends on factors such as costs and availability of land, materials and construction workers.
- Government regulations — incentive schemes to build in a certain area may lead to a large supply of houses to buy and cause house prices to be lower than other areas without such schemes.
- Levels of employment play a role — in areas with high levels of unemployment house prices will be lower due to lower levels of demand.
- Desirability of an area — in a fashionable part of the country with nearby amenities and good transport links, house prices may be higher.
- Availability of cheap rental properties — this may reduce demand for houses to buy and therefore reduce average house prices.
2 Maximum of 6 marks available. <u>HINTS</u>:
- Draw a diagram to show how a decreased supply of the metal from country A causes the supply curve to shift to the left. Use your diagram to show that this shift causes the price of the metal to rise. Because supply and demand are likely to be inelastic, even a small decrease in supply will cause a big rise in the price.
- Your diagram should look like the one shown below.

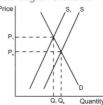

- Your diagram should be fully labelled and clearly show a price increase and decline in the quantity demanded.

Answers

Page 41 — Demand and Supply — Sport and Leisure

1   Maximum of 6 marks available. _HINTS:_
   • _Describe how free health care leads to a situation of excess demand, which means there is a shortage of health care available._
   • _Draw a diagram to show excess demand — the supply curve will be vertical as the supply of health care is fixed, and the price should be equal to zero._
   • _Explain why a zero price causes excess demand and what this means — e.g. 'the price mechanism can't act to ration resources or act as a signalling device, so there is not enough health care available to meet demand. To help ration health care, waiting lists may be required, but this could lead to people not being able to access the health care they need when they need it and negatively impact the standard of health in society overall'._

2   Maximum of 6 marks available. _HINTS:_
   • _Draw a diagram to show excess demand for the tickets — the supply curve will be vertical as the supply of tickets is fixed. Your diagram should look like the one shown below._

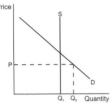

   • _Referring to your diagram, explain how at the price level shown there is an excess demand (Q_1 to Q_2) for tickets — the fixed supply of tickets is not enough to meet the level of demand for them._
   • _You can also mention how ticket touts may try to sell tickets for above the price that they were bought for._

Page 42 — Demand and Supply — Stock Market Shares

1   Maximum of 4 marks available. _HINTS:_
   • _Talk about the effect of the good news about sales on the demand for shares — e.g. 'favourable news about Gasoil plc's performance is likely to result in increased demand for their shares'._
   • _Mention how the level of confidence in the economy can have a significant impact on demand for shares generally — e.g. 'if there's an expected upturn or the economy is booming then demand for shares is likely to be high, but in a recession demand may be low due to uncertainty'._
   • _You could mention how the good sales figures may cause an increased demand for Gasoil plc's shares and this could lead to an increase in price — this increased price could then actually lead to a drop-off in demand. But also, an increase in the price of Gasoil plc's shares could result in an increased demand for the shares because the increasing share price acts as a signal that the company is doing well (and may continue to do well in the future) — this is appealing for people looking to buy shares._

Section Three — Market Failure

Page 45 — Market Failure: Externalities

1   Maximum of 8 marks available. _HINTS:_
   • _Describe what negative production externalities are, e.g. 'the external costs to a third party that are generated by the production of a good/service'._
   • _Explain that negative production externalities mean that the marginal social cost (MSC) is greater than the marginal private cost (MPC) and if only private costs are considered there is overproduction of the good/service — more of the good is produced than is desirable for society._
   • _You can draw a negative production externality diagram to help with your explanation (see p.44)._

Page 47 — Market Failure: The Impacts of Externalities

1   Maximum of 8 marks available. _HINTS:_
   • _Explain that there are negative externalities, such as pollution, that result from the production of some goods or services._
   • _Mention that producers only consider their private costs and will not consider the external costs of their activities to society._
   • _Say that if nothing is done by a government to ensure that these negative externalities of production are taken into account, then the level of production will remain above the socially optimal point (where MSC = MSB)._
   • _Briefly evaluate the impact of the negative externalities of production if a government did nothing to address them, e.g. 'If negative externalities, such as pollution, are ignored then it could have a major impact on society. Ignoring_

pollution could worsen public health, reducing workers' productivity, and governments may be required to increase their spending on health care.'

2   Maximum of 12 marks available. _HINTS:_
   • _Draw a diagram showing negative production externalities like the one below:_

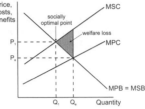

   • _To get all of the marks for this question you need to explain what your diagram shows. Make sure you correctly label the curves and axes._
   • _Make sure you explain how logging has a higher MSC than MPC and how, left to the market, the level of logging will be above the socially optimal point (where MSC = MSB)._
   • _Talk about how the free market level of production causes a welfare loss (you need to make it clear where this is on your diagram) and taking into account the negative externalities caused by logging will cause the price to increase (e.g. P_e to P_1) and output to decrease (e.g. Q_e to Q_1)._

Page 49 — Market Failure: Merit and Demerit Goods

1   Maximum of 6 marks available. _HINTS:_
   • _Give a definition of a merit good, e.g. 'Merit goods are goods which have greater social benefits than private benefits.'_
   • _Draw a diagram to show how merit goods are underprovided by the free market — this should look like the merit good diagram on p.48. Your diagram should show that the MSB curve is above the MPB curve and that the free market equilibrium is below the socially optimal level (where MSC = MSB) of consumption/production of the merit good._

Page 51 — Market Failure: Cost Benefit Analysis

1   Maximum of 4 marks available. _HINTS:_
   • _The correct answer is D. Explain the free rider problem and relate it to flood defences, e.g. 'As a flood defence system is a public good, it will be affected by the free rider problem. This means that the free market won't provide a flood defence system because consumers will be unwilling to pay for a service that they could get for free if other consumers paid for it.'_
   • _Option A is incorrect because sufficient knowledge to build adequate flood defences exists or could be acquired._
   • _Option B is incorrect because flooding only helps some forms of farming and isn't a reason to prevent the construction of a flood defence system._
   • _Option C is incorrect because a flood defence system is a public good and in a free market it wouldn't be possible to set a price for individuals to be charged that truly reflected the system's value to them._

2   Maximum of 6 marks available. _HINTS:_
   • _Explain the process of a cost benefit analysis (CBA) and the steps involved._
   • _Give examples of the costs that would be considered. Examples of private costs could be the cost of the railway lines and the additional trains required to run on the new rail link. Examples of external costs could be the damage caused to the countryside or a decrease in nearby property values._
   • _Give examples of the benefits to be considered. Examples of benefits could include a reduction in pollution as fewer people need to drive cars and less freight needs to be carried by lorries, or quicker commuting times, which could increase productivity._
   • _Then you need to point out that the government will assign values to the costs and benefits, and when all of the costs and benefits have been worked out, the net cost or benefit will then be calculated. You could also point out that if the project is seen as being popular (a vote-winner), then the government might go ahead with the project even if the costs outweigh the benefits (this is known as rent-seeking behaviour)._
   • _Keep your answer brief — you just need to discuss how a CBA might work, not give your opinions on a new rail link._

Page 53 — Market Failure: Monopolies

1   Maximum of 8 marks available. _HINTS:_
   • _This is a question about barriers to entry. Start by defining what a barrier to entry is, e.g. 'an obstacle that makes it impossible or unattractive for a new firm to enter into a market'._
   • _Explain some barriers to entry that might make it difficult to enter a market that already contains a firm with a monopoly._

Answers

- Examples include: the new firm may have higher costs than the monopoly firm, which can exploit economies of scale; the existing monopoly firm may have an established brand to which many consumers are loyal, which might mean that consumers are not willing to buy from a new firm with an unestablished brand; legislation may be in place to protect the monopoly firm, which prevents the new firm entering the market; and the market may have high start-up costs which might put off a new firm as these costs may be unrecoverable if the firm fails.

Page 54 — Market Failure: Immobile Factors of Production

1   Maximum of 4 marks available. <u>HINTS</u>:
- Give a definition of what an immobile factor of production is, e.g. a factor of production which cannot be moved from one location to another, such as land.
- Explain why immobile factors of production can lead to market failure. E.g. immobile factors of production can lead to inefficient allocation of resources (resources are often unused or underused), which means there's market failure.
- Give an example of where immobile factors of production can cause market failure. For example, a jobseeker may not be able to afford to move to a different area to get a job — this is an example of geographical labour immobility.

Page 55 — Market Failure: Imperfect Information

1   Maximum of 4 marks available. <u>HINTS</u>:
- Define what imperfect information is, e.g. 'Imperfect information is when buyers and/or sellers have incomplete knowledge of the price, costs, benefits and availability of products'.
- Give a couple of examples where this imperfect information causes market failure and the overprovision of demerit goods. For example, provision of alcohol, cigarettes and unhealthy foods.

Page 56 — Market Failure: Unstable Commodity Markets

1   Maximum of 8 marks available. <u>HINTS</u>:
- Describe what price instability is and that it can affect commodity markets, e.g. 'Prices are unstable when they have the ability to rapidly change by large amounts. This is often a feature of commodity markets...'.
- Mention that this price instability can lead to market failure.
- Explain reasons why market failure can be caused by price instability. For example, this uncertainty can restrict investment — this happens because firms are uncertain about possible returns on investment so they are less willing to make a large investment and may not invest at all. Another reason it causes market failure is that big rises and falls in prices can impact consumers heavily, particularly those on low incomes, who will be more heavily affected than people on higher incomes.

Page 57 — Market Failure: A Lack of Equity

1   Maximum of 6 marks available. <u>HINTS</u>:
- For this question you need to talk about a couple of different ways that the government may try to redistribute income more equally.
- You could talk about: the use of tax revenues to redistribute income to the people with low income (e.g. the elderly, sick and poor) via benefits, and to provide services for free (e.g. health care and education).
- Briefly evaluate the implications of the government redistributing income. For example, the redistribution may act to reduce efficiency in society as it can mean there is less of an incentive for people to work hard.

Page 59 — Government Intervention: Taxation

1   Maximum of 4 marks available. <u>HINTS</u>:
- The correct answer is B. This is because the tax causes the supply curve to shift left to S_1. The tax revenue is equal to the difference in price (= 25 − 15 = £10) at the new level of demand multiplied by the new equilibrium quantity (80), so the tax revenue is £800.

Page 60 — Government Intervention: Subsidies

1   Maximum of 4 marks available. <u>HINTS</u>:
- The correct answer is C. This is because the area ACFJ is equal to the difference between A and C (this takes into account the producer and consumer gain) multiplied by the quantity demanded when the subsidy is in place (equal to A to J). So ACFJ is the total cost of the subsidy to the government.

Page 61 — Government Intervention: Price Controls

1   Maximum of 8 marks available. <u>HINTS</u>:
- Draw a diagram that shows the setting of a maximum price like the one below.

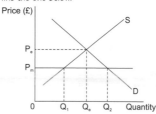

- Your diagram should have correctly labelled axes and clearly show a maximum price that is below the equilibrium price (e.g. in the diagram above P_m is below P_e).
- Give a complete explanation of what is shown on your diagram. Mention the equilibrium price and quantity and refer to the maximum price that has been set. You need to talk about the excess demand at the maximum price and indicate where this is shown on your diagram (i.e. Q_1 to Q_2 on the diagram above).

Page 62 — Government Intervention: Buffer Stocks

1   Maximum of 4 marks available. <u>HINTS</u>:
- The correct answer is B. This is the correct answer because farmers would be paid the minimum price (P_2) when supply is at S_1.
- Option A is incorrect as this is the price that would be received by farmers if there was no buffer stock scheme in place.
- Options C is incorrect as this is the price farmers would receive for the level of supply shown by S rather than S_1.
- Options D is incorrect because farmers would not receive this price for the level of supply shown by S_1.

Page 63 — Government Intervention: State Provision

1   Maximum of 6 marks available. <u>HINTS</u>:
- Start your answer by explaining that the state provision of health care means that it's likely to be free at point of use.
- There are several disadvantages that you could go on to explain. These include: state provision can mean there's less of an incentive to operate efficiently due to a lack of the price mechanism; state-provided health care may fail to respond to consumers' demands as there is no profit motive to determine the services offered; self-reliance of patients may be reduced if they know the service is there if they need it; and free health care can lead to excess demand and this can lead to long waiting lists for consumers.

Page 64 — Government Intervention: Regulation

1   Maximum of 4 marks available. <u>HINTS</u>:
- Start by talking about how regulations could be used to penalise firms that pollute excessively, e.g. 'Regulations could be put in place to limit the amount of pollution a firm could produce and they could be fined if they exceed this amount. This aims to correct the market failure of excess pollution.'
- You also need to explore why regulations might not always result in the correction of market failure. Some examples are: if the acceptable level of pollution set by the regulations is not low enough, it might not effectively correct the market failure caused by the pollution; if the punishment for breaking the regulation isn't large enough, it might not act as an effective deterrent meaning the firms don't change their behaviour; excessive regulation may encourage firms to move elsewhere, which could be bad for the economy; and the monitoring involved in regulations (e.g. measuring pollution levels) can be an expensive burden for governments.
- You need to make sure you discuss a couple of points in a bit of detail (but not too much, it's only a 4 mark question) and relate them back to the pollution example given in the question.

Page 66 — Government Intervention: Other Methods

1   Maximum of 6 marks available. <u>HINTS</u>:
- You need to explain that governments try to correct market failures that are caused by asymmetric information by providing more information to consumers with the aim of helping them to make rational decisions.
- Describe that in this example governments would try to give more information to consumers about the health problems linked to cigarette consumption in order to reduce the level of demand for cigarettes.

Answers

- *Give a couple of ways that governments could provide more information about the health implications of cigarettes, e.g. health warnings on cigarette packets and advertising campaigns to increase awareness of smoking-related disease.*

Page 68 — Government Failure

1   Maximum of 4 marks available. *HINTS:*
- *The correct answer is C. This is because the high cost involved in implementing the ban is an example of government failure.*
- *Options B and D are incorrect as they contribute to correcting the market failure associated with the banned substance.*
- *Option A is incorrect as the boosted opinion of the government hasn't contributed to a government failure.*

2   Maximum of 6 marks available. *HINTS:*
- *For this question you need to think about the effects the intervention would have and whether this actually addresses the market failure surrounding cigarette consumption.*
- *You should talk about how the desired impact of this intervention is to reduce demand for cigarettes and the negative externalities linked to their consumption (e.g. health problems).*
- *You also need to talk about the likely impact of the neighbouring country having cigarettes at a lower price, e.g. that people may purchase cigarettes from the neighbouring country to avoid the tax, and the consumption of cigarettes may not decrease as the government intended — this would be a government failure.*

Page 71 — Examples of Government Failure

1   Maximum of 4 marks available. *HINTS:*
- *The correct answer is C. The development of a black market is a possible consequence of setting a maximum rent as some people may be willing to pay above the maximum price to get a rental property.*
- *Option A is incorrect as maximum rents lead to shortages of rental properties.*
- *Option B is incorrect as the protection of tenants is not an example of government failure.*
- *Option D is incorrect as maximum rents aim to protect tenants from excessive rents.*

2   Maximum of 4 marks available. *HINTS:*
- *There are several different advantages you can talk about for this question. If you think about the problems associated with farm subsidies, there are several of these that would be eased if the size of payments were reduced.*
- *For example, reducing farm subsides could: reduce the oversupply of agricultural products and save money for governments if they have to store excess produce; and reduce the cost to the taxpayer.*

3   Maximum of 10 marks available. *HINTS:*
- *For this question you need to give arguments for and against road pricing.*
- *Arguments for a road pricing scheme include: a scheme could reduce the external costs linked to congestion (e.g. increased journey times) and the pollution (e.g. air and noise) it creates; revenue generated by the scheme can be used to contribute to projects that benefit society; and a reduction in health problems linked to traffic emissions inside the area covered by the scheme.*
- *Arguments against a road pricing scheme include: businesses inside a road pricing area may experience reduced trade because of the scheme; congestion may simply be shifted to areas not covered by the scheme — i.e. the road pricing may not actually reduce the external costs it aims to, just change their location; there may be underutilisation of road space in the road pricing area; schemes have an unfairly large impact on poor motorists; if the road pricing charge is too low then it might not have much impact on congestion levels.*
- *Include a brief evaluation of what you think about implementing a road pricing scheme to finish off your answer. It does not matter whether you are for or against, you just need to back up what you say.*

Section Four — Measuring Economic Performance

Page 73 — Measuring Economic Growth

1   Maximum of 8 marks available. *HINTS:*
- *Start by defining the GDP per capita.*
- *Give a few examples of why this comparison might not be accurate, e.g. 'GDP per capita figures don't take the hidden economy into account — the bigger the difference in the extent of the hidden economy between the two countries that are being compared, the less accurate the GDP per capita will be at making a comparison between their standards of living.'*
- *You could also mention what the GDP per capita doesn't take into account, e.g. income inequality between the rich and poor in a country, working conditions, number of hours worked per week.*

Page 75 — Measuring Inflation

1   Maximum of 6 marks available. *HINTS:*
- *Explain that the information given in the Living Costs and Food Survey can be inaccurate.*
- *Mention the point that certain households are excluded from the RPI.*
- *Discuss the fact that the basket of goods only changes once a year, so short-term changes are often missed.*

Page 77 — Measuring the Balance of Payments

1   Maximum of 4 marks available. *HINTS:*
- *State that one measure is the claimant count.*
- *Give one advantage and one disadvantage of the claimant count, e.g. 'The claimant count is the number of people who are claiming JSA, so it's easy to obtain the data. However, unemployed people who either choose not to claim JSA, or aren't eligible to claim it, aren't included in the claimant count.'*
- *State that the other measure is the Labour Force Survey.*
- *Give one advantage and one disadvantage of the Labour Force Survey, e.g. 'The Labour Force Survey is an internationally agreed measure for unemployment, so it's easy to use it to make comparisons with other countries. However, it's expensive to collect and compile the data.'*

2   Maximum of 4 marks available. *HINTS:*
- *Give a definition of the balance of payments.*
- *Explain that if the flow of money into a country exceeds the flow of money out of that country, it will have a balance of payments surplus.*
- *Then say that if the flow of money out of a country exceeds the flow of money into that country, it will have a balance of payments deficit.*

Page 79 — Measuring Development

1   Maximum of 12 marks available. *HINTS:*
- *Give a definition of the HDI — mention its three components and how each of them helps to measure the standard of living.*
- *Give an analysis of each of the three components — explain their limitations.*
- *Explain why the HDI is more accurate at measuring the standard of living than, e.g. the GDP per capita.*
- *Mention that other indicators would help to give a fuller picture, e.g. 'Other indicators could help to give a better picture of the standard of living in a country. For example, the number of mobile phones per thousand of the population — if there are lots of mobile phones, this suggests that people are paid enough to be able to afford them. Mobile phones also improve trading, which might lead to a higher level of economic development.'*

Section Five — Aggregate Demand and Aggregate Supply

Page 81 — The Circular Flow of Income

1   Maximum of 6 marks available. *HINTS:*
- *Start by defining the multiplier effect, e.g. 'The process by which an injection into the circular flow of income creates a change in the size of national income that's greater than the size of the initial injection.'*
- *Then explain that an increase in government spending will represent an injection into the circular flow of income, and how this extra money will go around the circular flow of income in the form of increased expenditure and income.*
- *Finally, explain that the size of the multiplier will depend on the size of leakages from the circular flow of income. So if a lot of money leaks out of the circular flow then the size of the multiplier will be quite small.*

Page 83 — Aggregate Demand

1   Maximum of 6 marks available. *HINTS:*
- *State that consumption is a component of aggregate demand, and how changes in consumption will affect aggregate demand, e.g. 'A rise in consumption will lead to an increase in aggregate demand.'*
- *Then, explain how high taxes affect consumption, e.g. 'High direct taxes (such as income tax) will reduce the amount of disposable income available to consumers, and high indirect taxes will increase the cost of spending. This means that high taxes are likely to lead to a fall in consumption and aggregate demand will be reduced.'*
- *And then explain how high interest rates affect consumption, e.g. 'High interest rates increase the cost of borrowing, which means that it's more expensive for consumers to borrow money to spend, and they make it more attractive for people to save their money. High interest rates may also reduce consumers' disposable income, as loan repayments and mortgages will become*

more expensive. As a result, high interest rates are likely to lead to a fall in consumption and a reduction in aggregate demand.'

2 Maximum of 6 marks available. <u>*HINTS*</u>:
*   Identify three things that will have an effect on investment, such as risk, business confidence and interest rates, and say what effect they will have.
*   The question asks you to describe three factors, so you don't need to provide too much detail.
*   Risk — if there is a high risk that an investment will not benefit a firm then it is less likely to invest.
*   Business confidence — if business confidence is high and a firm is doing well, then it is more likely to invest.
*   Interest rates — if interest rates are high then investment is likely to be reduced because the cost of borrowing to invest is higher.

Page 85 — Aggregate Demand

1 Maximum of 4 marks available. <u>*HINTS*</u>:
*   The correct answer is C.
*   You need to explain why C is correct — e.g. 'Government spending is a component of aggregate demand, so an increase in government spending will increase aggregate demand. A decrease in taxes will increase people's disposable income, so consumption (a component of aggregate demand) is likely to increase, which means aggregate demand will increase.'
*   You should also explain why the other options (A, B and D) are incorrect — e.g. 'Option B will cause aggregate demand to fall, and options A and D may result in a slight rise in aggregate demand, but they're less likely to lead to an increase in aggregate demand than option C.'

2 Maximum of 10 marks available. <u>*HINTS*</u>:
*   Start by defining exports, e.g. 'Exports are goods or services that are produced in one country and then sold in another.'
*   Then, identify two things that could increase the demand for a country's exports, such as the exchange rate or non-price factors.
*   The question asks you to explain two factors, so you'll be expected to give some reasons to support your answers.
*   Explain how the exchange rate may affect the demand for a country's exports, and remember to consider the price elasticity of demand — e.g. 'A fall in the value of a country's currency will reduce the price of its exports, so they'll be cheaper for other countries to buy and demand for them will increase. However, the level of an increase in demand will depend on the price elasticity of demand. For example, demand can be price inelastic in the short run, so if the UK's exchange rate fell, there may be a time lag before countries switch to buying exports from the UK instead of from another country. This means that in the short run, demand for a country's exports might not increase, or increase by much.'
*   Then go on to talk about the second factor, non-price factors — e.g. 'An improvement in the quality of a country's goods may increase demand for that country's exports, as people are often willing to pay more for good quality products. The level of the increase in demand may depend on who the country exports to — for example, demand for exports might be low if that country's main trading partners are quite poor or suffering from a recession.'

Page 87 — Aggregate Demand Analysis

1 Maximum of 10 marks available. <u>*HINTS*</u>:
*   Give a definition of the multiplier effect.
*   Use the multiplier effect to explain how an increase in government spending, e.g. on roads, hospitals and schools, would be likely to lead to a bigger increase in aggregate demand in general.
*   Draw a diagram to show how an increase in government spending will cause the aggregate demand curve to shift to the right.
*   Point out that the size of the increase in aggregate demand (and, therefore, the size of the shift to the right of the aggregate demand curve) depends on the size of the multiplier effect.
*   Explain that the size of the multiplier depends on the size of the leakages from the circular flow of income and the marginal propensity to consume, e.g. 'If the leakages in the circular flow are small and the marginal propensity to consume is high then the multiplier will be much bigger and cause a large shift to the right of the aggregate demand curve.'

Page 89 — Aggregate Supply

1 Maximum of 8 marks available. <u>*HINTS*</u>:
*   Draw a diagram to show a shift to the right of the aggregate supply curve.
*   Your diagram should look like the one shown below.

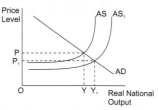

*   Referring to your diagram explain how a shift to the right of the aggregate supply curve (from AS to AS₁) means that output will increase (from Y to Y₁) and the price level will fall (from P to P₁). You should also point out that an increase in output will mean that unemployment will fall because labour is a derived demand. If more is being produced then the demand for labour will increase.
*   You should also mention that a fall in the price level will make a country's exports cheaper, so exports will increase and there will be an increase in a balance of payments surplus or a reduction in a balance of payments deficit.

Page 91 — Short Run and Long Run Aggregate Supply

1 Maximum of 4 marks available. <u>*HINTS*</u>:
*   The correct answer is B because the discovery of a new raw material would increase the factors of production that are available to an economy. If there are more factors of production available, in this case a new raw material, then the capacity of the economy will increase and the LRAS curve will shift to the right.
*   Options A, C and D are more likely to affect the aggregate demand curve or the short run aggregate supply curve as they will change the costs of production. None of these options will increase the capacity of the economy.

Section Six — Government Economic Policy Objectives

Page 95 — Economic Growth

1 Maximum of 5 marks available. <u>*HINTS*</u>:
*   Describe what the cycle is, e.g. 'the fluctuation of actual economic growth up and down'.
*   Explain what each of the different stages of the economic cycle are, i.e. boom, recession/slump, and recovery.
*   You could use a diagram to help you explain the different stages.

2 Maximum of 12 marks available. <u>*HINTS*</u>:
*   Start by defining economic growth, e.g. 'Economic growth is an increase in the productive potential of an economy.'
*   Give examples of the positive effects of high economic growth, such as a quick reduction in unemployment levels and an improvement in the standard of living.
*   Discuss the negatives of high economic growth, such as high inflation, pollution and economic instability. E.g. using a diagram, you could argue that if there is an increase in short run economic growth that causes the AD curve to cross the vertical part of the AS curve (or the LRAS curve) — there will be a rise in the price level but no increase in the actual productive potential of the economy.
*   Give an indication of the relative importance of the various positives and negatives.
*   The question asked you to 'evaluate' to what extent high economic growth is desirable, so make sure you conclude your answer clearly, e.g. 'In general, it's not possible to maintain high rates of economic growth. High short run economic growth which causes inflation and isn't increasing the productive potential of the economy will cause problems in the future. For example, if finite resources are being used too quickly, this will constrain future growth. High economic growth will bring certain short-term benefits, such as creating more jobs and reducing unemployment, but sustainable economic growth will be more beneficial to an economy in the long run.'

Page 97 — Inflation

1 Maximum of 12 marks available. <u>*HINTS*</u>:
*   Start by giving a definition of inflation, e.g. 'Inflation is the sustained rise in the average price of goods and services over a period of time.'
*   Give examples of the harm high inflation can cause, e.g. 'High inflation can reduce people's standards of living, especially those on fixed incomes. Prices are rising, but their incomes remain the same, so the real value of their money falls.'
*   Discuss the potential advantages of keeping the rate of inflation low, e.g. 'If a country's inflation rate is below the inflation rate in its competitor countries, it's likely to become more price competitive.'

Answers

- *Try to provide a thorough analysis of the positives and negatives, showing that you've considered the likely importance of each.*
- *You should also mention the difference between cost-push and demand-pull inflation. Demand-pull inflation tends to be less harmful, as it's caused by a rise in demand, whereas cost-push inflation is caused by an increase in the costs of production.*
- *Explain that deflation is a bad thing, and describe the effects it can have on the economy.*
- *Make a strong conclusion to your evaluation, explaining that a rate of 2% is considered desirable as some inflation is better than no (or negative) inflation, but that high inflation tends to be harmful.*
- *There are 12 marks for this question — make sure you provide enough examples and explanations.*

Page 99 — Unemployment

1   Maximum of 4 marks available. <u>HINTS</u>:
- *The answer is C.*
- *Give a definition of unemployment.*
- *Discount options A and D, e.g. 'Increased unemployment levels are likely to reduce the output of the economy, so option A is incorrect. The government is unlikely to reduce taxes on full-time workers, as the government will need to increase the money it spends on welfare benefit.'*
- *Explain that a rise in unemployment is likely to reduce consumption, as the unemployed will have less disposable income, so they'll spend less.*

Page 101 — The Balance of Payments

1   Maximum of 8 marks available. <u>HINTS</u>:
- *Give a definition of the balance of payments, e.g. 'The balance of payments measures international flows of money. It measures flows of money out of a country, e.g. to pay for imports, and flows of money into a country, e.g. from the sale of exports.'*
- *Define the four sections of the current account, and state whether the UK has a deficit or a surplus in each (as well as their relative sizes — i.e. large or small).*
- *Discuss the likely reasons for the UK importing more visible goods than it exports, such as high levels of consumer spending, a lack of price competitiveness and, until more recent years, the high value of the pound.*

Page 103 — Other Economic Policy Objectives

1   Maximum of 8 marks available. <u>HINTS</u>:
- *Start by explaining how firms might damage the environment, through, for example, carbon emissions or waste disposal.*
- *Explain that a government will try to measure the cost of the damage caused so they can attempt to internalise the externalities and encourage a change in the behaviour of firms.*
- *Describe the different methods governments might use to alter firms' behaviour, such as financial penalties, restrictions or bans.*
- *Give specific examples, e.g. 'Governments might use tradeable pollution permits — these restrict the amount of pollution firms can produce, but firms can buy/sell these permits between themselves.'*

Page 105 — Exchange Rates

1   Maximum of 12 marks available. <u>HINTS</u>:
- *Start with an explanation of what a rise in the exchange rate of the pound would be, e.g. 'A rise in the exchange rate of the pound means that one pound will buy more of a foreign currency.'*
- *Describe the effect of a rise of the exchange rate on each of the four macroeconomic objectives.*
- *Discuss the likely size and relative impact of the effect on each objective.*
- *Give an overall conclusion at the end, e.g. 'The likely overall effect on the UK economy of a rise in the exchange rate of the pound will be negative. UK goods and services will become less price competitive. This will tend to lead to a decrease in exports and an increase in imports, causing a possible fall in economic growth, rise in unemployment and worsening of the balance of payments deficit.'*

Page 107 — Free Trade and Protectionism

1   Maximum of 12 marks available. <u>HINTS</u>:
- *Start by defining free trade then explaining what trade barriers are.*
- *Give some advantages of free trade — these are advantages of international trade that doesn't have any trade barriers. E.g. countries can gain access to products that they can't produce themselves by importing them and*

consumers can have access to a larger variety of goods than only those which can be produced in the country where they live.
- *Give a few reasons why governments might want to impose trade barriers, such as to protect domestic jobs, to protect infant industries and to avoid overdependence, e.g. 'If domestic industries are outcompeted by international firms, it's likely that there will be domestic job losses. This means that governments might feel the need to impose trade barriers in order to protect these domestic jobs.'*
- *Make sure you conclude your answer, give your opinion on the extent that free trade is beneficial to a country's economy.*

Page 109 — Conflicts Between Economic Objectives

1   Maximum of 10 marks available. <u>HINTS</u>:
- *Start by saying that governments can't achieve all of their objectives at the same time — some of the objectives go hand in hand, but others conflict.*
- *Discuss the possible conflicts between different pairs of policy objectives.*
- *There are 10 marks available, so make sure you give plenty of details on each conflict you describe.*
- *You might want to include a sketch of a Phillips curve to back up an explanation of the conflict between inflation and unemployment.*

Section Seven — Macroeconomic Policy Instruments

Page 111 — Fiscal Policy

1   Maximum of 4 marks available. <u>HINTS</u>:
- *The correct answer is B. A reduction in welfare payments would be a decrease in government spending — changing the level of government spending is an example of fiscal policy.*
- *Options A, C and D are incorrect as they are all examples of monetary policy instruments.*

Page 113 — The Effectiveness of Fiscal Policy

1   Maximum of 8 marks available. <u>HINTS</u>:
- *Briefly explain how an expansionary fiscal policy can lead to increased output but also increased inflation — the amounts by which output and inflation increase depend on how much spare capacity there is in the economy.*
- *Draw a diagram showing an AD curve shifting to the right along an AS curve, like the diagram below.*

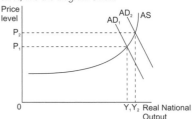

- *Explain that the economy has little spare capacity (e.g. few spare workers and production line capacity) when the AS curve is quite steep (the right-hand side of the curve). When this is the case it is difficult for supply to increase — so a small increase in output results in larger demand-pull inflation.*
- *Explain that this is shown on your diagram. When aggregate demand increases (e.g. from AD_1 to AD_2) the increase in output is relatively smaller (e.g. from Y_1 to Y_2) than the increase in prices (e.g. from P_1 to P_2).*

Page 115 — Monetary Policy

1   Maximum of 10 marks available. <u>HINTS</u>:
- *Explain what a contractionary monetary policy is likely to involve (i.e. a high interest rate, restricted money supply and a strong exchange rate) and what effect this might have on the economy, e.g. 'A contractionary monetary policy will cause aggregate demand to fall along with output and prices, which will lead to increased unemployment and decreased economic growth.'*
- *Now you need to explain what effect a contractionary monetary policy has on the current account of the balance of payments, e.g. 'Raising interest rates as part of a contractionary monetary policy can worsen the balance of payments current account. When interest rates are high, 'hot money' will flow into the UK as financial institutions look to make the most of the high rewards for savers. This 'hot money' will increase demand for the pound, pushing its price up — so the pound's exchange rate will rise. A high exchange rate will make UK exports more expensive, so exports will decrease, and the current account of the balance of payments will worsen.'*

Answers

- You could also add that a high exchange rate will mean that imports from abroad are cheaper to buy, further worsening the current account of the balance of payments.

Page 117 — The Effectiveness of Monetary Policy

1   Maximum of 4 marks available. <u>HINTS</u>:
- The correct option is B. It is very important for the MPC to consider the level of spare capacity in the economy. If there is lots of spare capacity then the MPC could lower interest rates without causing much (or any) inflation, but if there is no spare capacity then a lowering of interest rates could cause a high level of inflation.

2   Maximum of 10 marks available. <u>HINTS</u>:
- For this question you need to give some reasons why cutting interest rates might not lead to an increased level of consumer spending and investment from firms during a recession.
- You should mention that the level of confidence of consumers and firms has an influence, e.g. 'Consumers and firms might be uncertain about the future during a recession, so they might not want to spend or invest. Even if the government lowered interest rates to encourage spending and investment, consumers and firms may still choose to save more even though the reward for saving is low.'
- It's also worth mentioning that time is a factor, e.g. 'After 3 months, the cutting of interest rates may not have had a chance to impact the behaviour of consumers and firms — it can take time for consumers to make large purchases and firms to plan investments. So, the cutting of interest rates may help an economy to recover from a recession, but not in the time period that this data covers.'

3   Maximum of 10 marks available. <u>HINTS</u>:
- You need to mention what effect a rise in interest rates will have on the price of UK exports. E.g. 'An increase in interest rates means that the value of the pound is likely to rise due to the movement of 'hot money', and this will make UK exports more expensive'.
- You could then go on to explain what this means for UK exports, e.g. 'As UK exports are more expensive, this is likely to reduce demand for them. Firms that usually buy UK exports will look around for alternatives.'
- You should also look at the other side of the argument. You could argue that UK exports might not decrease rapidly after an interest rate rise, e.g. 'An increase in interest rates may not reduce UK exports straight away. It will take time for buyers to find suitable alternative suppliers and some will have long-term contracts with UK firms.' You could also argue that if inflation is high in a country where UK goods are being exported to, this might mean that UK goods are still competitive even though the pound's value has risen.

Page 119 — Supply-side Policies

1   Maximum of 6 marks available. <u>HINTS</u>:
- Supply-side policies aim to increase aggregate supply. For this question you should draw a diagram that shows aggregate supply increasing (the AS curve will shift to the right), like the diagram below.

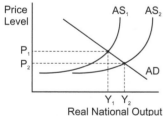

Real National Output

- Explain how the diagram shows that when AS increases there is no inflation. E.g. 'The diagram shows that when aggregate supply increases (from AS_1 to AS_2), output will increase (from Y_1 to Y_2) and the price level will fall (from P_1 to P_2). This increase in aggregate supply will benefit the economy — as it will increase output and, as a result, employment, while the fall in the price level shows that this will be achieved without inflation.'

2   Maximum of 4 marks available. <u>HINTS</u>:
- The correct answer is C. Supply-side policies aim to increase the amount that firms are willing to supply (at a particular price). One way of doing this is to increase the productivity of labour, which firms can do by increasing training for their workers.
- Option A is a contractionary fiscal policy which will reduce aggregate demand and option D is an expansionary fiscal policy which will increase aggregate demand, but neither policy is likely to affect aggregate supply.
- Option B may increase consumer confidence and cause aggregate demand to rise, but it is less likely to have an effect on aggregate supply.

Page 121 — The Effectiveness of Supply-side Policies

1   Maximum of 4 marks available. <u>HINTS</u>:
- The correct option is C. This is because many supply-side policies are implemented by the private sector.
- Option A is incorrect as supply-side policies have most effect in the medium and long term.
- Option B is incorrect as supply-side policies aim to make markets more efficient and competitive, not less competitive.
- Option D is incorrect as successful supply-side policies can avoid causing inflation.

2   Maximum of 25 marks available. <u>HINTS</u>:
- Start by defining what's meant by supply-side policies, 'Supply-side policies are policies that aim to increase aggregate supply.'
- Then, you need to say how supply-side policies can help a government achieve its macroeconomic objectives. You could argue that successful supply-side policies are a good way to achieve the government's macroeconomic objectives because they will lead to economic growth, a fall in unemployment and an improvement in the balance of payments, without causing inflation. You will then need to explain why this could happen.
- You could start by talking about economic growth and unemployment, e.g. 'When supply-side policies act to increase the productive potential of the economy, this will lead to increased growth and jobs. One way this can happen is by increasing labour productivity by providing greater training opportunities.'
- Then you could cover how supply-side policies can improve the balance of payments. E.g. 'Supply-side policies can help firms become more efficient, which will increase their output and the volume of goods that they export. This will improve the current account of the balance of payments.'
- You could then cover how supply-side policies can help governments achieve their objectives without causing inflation — you could use a diagram such as the one on p.120 to support your point.
- To gain evaluation marks you should discuss why supply-side policies might not be the best way for the government to achieve its macroeconomic objectives, e.g. 'During a recession it might not be appropriate to use supply-side policies because they take a long time to be effective and governments may need to act more quickly to increase economic growth and reduce unemployment.'
- You could also explain how some supply-side policies can make people worse off, e.g. 'Making the labour market more flexible could mean that workers can be fired more easily and be paid a lower wage — this is good for employers, but not for workers. Policies like this may help the government achieve its macroeconomic objectives but they could be unpopular with voters and may increase unemployment during a recession (when firms may lay people off).'
- At the end of your answer you should include a conclusion to sum up your opinions on supply-side policies. You should weigh up both sides of the argument, e.g. 'There are advantages of supply-side policies such as... but they have limitations, for example...' — you should back up your conclusion with the points that you discussed earlier in your answer.
- If you can demonstrate knowledge of the use of supply-side policy in the UK or elsewhere in the world this would help you achieve higher marks.

Page 123 — Conflict Between Policy Instruments

1   Maximum of 18 marks available. <u>HINTS</u>:
- First, you need to pick three different macroeconomic policies that could be used to increase economic growth, such as an increase in government spending on education, a decrease in interest rates and a reduction in unemployment benefits.
- Then you need to discuss the three policies and describe how they could be used to increase growth. For example, 'An expansionary monetary policy, such as lowering interest rates, can be used to increase aggregate demand and, as a result, create economic growth. Lower interest rates would make borrowing cheaper, which will encourage greater consumption and investment.' Make sure you talk about all three of the policies you have chosen.
- In your evaluation you should weigh up the pros and cons of the different policies — you could talk about things like time lags, the size of the multiplier effect, the impact of the level of spare capacity in the economy and any conflicts between the policies. For example, 'If the government chose to increase its spending on education, but also reduce its spending on unemployment benefits then, in the short run, the two policies may cancel each other out. If one policy increases government spending and the other decreases it, then this may lead to little change in aggregate demand and output.'
- To finish off your answer you could choose the policy which you think would be most effective for increasing aggregate supply. Use the points that you have covered earlier in your answer and your opinions to support your choice. Here is a good place to bring in any knowledge you have of situations where policies to boost economic growth have been implemented in real economies.

Glossary

accelerator process This is where any change in demand for goods/services beyond current capacity will lead to a greater percentage increase in the demand for the capital goods needed by firms to produce the extra goods/services.

actual economic growth A measure of economic growth which is adjusted for inflation.

aggregate demand The total demand, or total spending, in an economy at different price levels over a given period of time. It's made up of consumption, investment, government spending and net exports.
Aggregate Demand = C + I + G + (X – M)

aggregate supply The total amount of goods and services which can be supplied in an economy at different price levels over a given period of time.

allocative efficiency This is when the price of a good is equal to the price that consumers are happy to pay for it. This will happen when all resources are allocated efficiently.

asymmetric information This is when buyers have more information than sellers (or the opposite) in a market.

balance of payments A country's international transactions, i.e. a record of the flows of money into and out of a country.

budget deficit When government spending is greater than its revenue.

budget surplus When government spending is less than its revenue.

cartel A group of producers that agree to limit production in order to control the price of goods or services.

circular flow of income The flow of national output, income and expenditure between households and firms.
national output = national income = national expenditure

complementary good A good that is often used with another good — these goods are in joint demand.

composite demand This is when a good is demanded for two or more different uses. For example, milk can be used in the production of ice cream and chocolate.

consumer surplus When a consumer pays less for a good than they were prepared to, this amount of money is the consumer surplus.

cost-push inflation Inflation caused by the rising cost of the inputs to production.

cross elasticity of demand (XED) This is a measure of how the quantity demanded of one good/service responds to a change in the price of another good/service.

current account on the balance of payments A record of a country's international flows of money. It consists of: trade in goods, trade in services, international flows of income (salaries, interest, profit and dividends), and transfers.

cyclical unemployment Unemployment caused by a shortage of demand in an economy, e.g. when there's a slump.

demand-pull inflation Inflation caused by excessive growth in aggregate demand compared to aggregate supply.

demerit good A good or service which has greater social costs when it's consumed than private costs. Demerit goods tend to be overconsumed.

deregulation Removing rules imposed by the government that can restrict the level of competition in a market.

derived demand The demand for a good or factor of production due to its use in making another good/service.

disposable income Income, including welfare benefits, that is available for households to spend after income tax has been paid.

dividend A share in a firm's profits that is given to the firm's shareholders.

economic cycle The economic cycle (also known as the business or trade cycle) is the fluctuations in actual growth over a period of time (several years or decades).

economic growth An increase in an economy's productive potential. Usually measured as the rate of change of the gross domestic product (GDP), or the GDP per capita.

economies of scale The cost advantages of production on a large scale.

equilibrium Where the quantity supplied is equal to the quantity demanded.

equity This means fairness.

exchange rate The price at which one currency buys another.

externalities The external costs or benefits to a third party that is not involved in the making, buying/selling and consumption of a specific good/service.

factors of production These are the four inputs needed to make the things that people want. They are: land, labour, capital and enterprise.

fiscal policy Government policy that determines the levels of government spending and taxation. Often used to increase or decrease aggregate demand in an economy.

free market A market where there is no government intervention. Competition between different suppliers affects supply and demand, and as a result determines prices in free markets.

free trade International trade without any restrictions from things such as trade barriers.

frictional unemployment The unemployment experienced by workers between leaving one job and starting another.

government failure This occurs when government intervention into a market causes a misallocation of resources.

gross domestic product (GDP) The total value of all the goods and services produced in a country in a year.

Human Development Index (HDI) A measure of development that combines three equally weighted sections: health (life expectancy), education (average and expected years in school), and the standard of living (real GNI per capita).

imperfect information A situation where buyers and/or sellers don't have full knowledge regarding price, costs, benefits and availability of a good or service.

income elasticity of demand (YED) This is a measure of how the demand for a good/service responds to a change in real income.

inferior good A good for which demand decreases as income rises. For example, low quality food.

inflation The sustained rise in the average price of goods and services over a period of time.

interest The money paid to the lender by someone who borrows capital. This will often be a fixed percentage rate — known as an interest rate.

investment The purchase of capital, such as new machinery, in the hope that this will help generate an increased level of output. Investment can also mean buying shares from the stock market — this is done in the hope of making a future profit or receiving dividend payments.

joint demand This is when two complementary goods are consumed together.

joint supply This is when the production of one good involves the production of another.

long run A time period in which all the factors of production are variable so a firm can expand its capacity.

long run aggregate supply (LRAS) In the long run it is assumed that, because factors and costs of production can change, an economy will run at full capacity — so LRAS is the productive potential of an economy.

Glossary

macroeconomics This is the part of economics that looks at the economy as a whole. For example, trends in unemployment and economic growth.

marginal propensity to consume The proportion of an increase in income that people will spend (and not save).

market Where buyers and sellers exchange goods/services.

market failure This is where the price mechanism fails to allocate resources efficiently.

merit good A good or service which provides greater social benefits when it's consumed than private benefits. Merit goods tend to be underconsumed.

microeconomics This is the part of economics concerned with individual people, individual firms and individual markets. For example, it covers things like how changes in demand affects the price of a good in a market.

monetary policy Government policy that involves controlling the total amount of 'money' in an economy (the money supply), and how expensive it is to borrow that money. It involves manipulating interest rates, exchange rates and restrictions on the supply of money.

monopoly A pure monopoly is a market with only one supplier. Some markets will be referred to as a monopoly if there's more than one supplier, but one supplier dominates the market.

monopoly power The ability of a firm to be a 'price maker' and influence the price of a particular good in a market.

mortgage A loan taken out to contribute to the cost of buying a house (or other property).

multiplier effect The process by which an injection into the circular flow of income creates a change in the size of national income that's greater than the injection's size.

national output All the goods and services produced in a country in a year.

normal good A good for which demand increases as income rises. For example, clothing.

normative statement A subjective statement which contains some kind of value judgement — an opinion.

opportunity cost The benefit that's given up in order to do something else — it's the cost of the choice that's made.

output gap The gap between the trend rate of economic growth and actual economic growth. Output gaps can be positive or negative.

perfect information This is when buyers and sellers have full knowledge of prices, costs and availability of products.

Phillips curve A curve that shows the relationship between inflation and unemployment — as the level of one falls, the level of the other rises.

positive statement An objective statement that can be tested by referring to the available evidence.

price elasticity of demand (PED) This is a measure of how the quantity demanded of a good/service responds to a change in its price.

price elasticity of supply (PES) This is a measure of how the quantity supplied of a good/service responds to a change in its price.

price instability This is when a small increase or decrease in the quantity supplied of a good/service can have a large impact on the price. Price instability is a feature of many markets for agricultural products.

price mechanism This is when changes in the demand or supply of a good/service lead to changes in its price and the quantity bought/sold.

privatisation When a firm or a whole industry changes from being run by the public sector to the private sector. It is an example of a supply-side policy.

producer surplus When a producer receives more for a good than they were prepared to accept, this amount of money is the producer surplus.

production possibility frontier (PPF) A curve which shows all the maximum possible outputs of two goods or services using a fixed amount of inputs.

productive efficiency Outputting the desired amount of goods or services for the lowest average cost of production (this occurs on the PPF).

productivity A measure of how efficiently a company or an economy is producing its outputs.

protectionism When a government uses policies to control the level of international trade and protect its own economy, industries and firms.

public good A good which people cannot be stopped from consuming, even if they've not paid for it, and the consumption of which doesn't prevent others from benefiting from it (e.g. national defence).

purchasing power parity (PPP) An adjustment of an exchange rate to reflect the real purchasing power of the two currencies.

real income A measure of the amount of goods/services that a consumer can afford to purchase with their income — adjusted for inflation.

recession A period where economic growth becomes negative. Typically there are falling demand, low levels of investment and rising unemployment during a recession.

revenue The total value of sales within a time period. It can be calculated using the formula: price per unit × quantity sold.

seasonal unemployment Unemployment due to uneven economic activity during the year.

shareholders Individuals (or firms) that own shares in a company.

share A share represents a portion of a company's value — giving the share's owner a right to a portion of the company's profits.

short run A time period in which a firm's capacity is fixed and at least one factor of production is fixed.

short run aggregate supply (SRAS) This is aggregate supply when the factors of production are fixed.

speculation When things are bought (e.g. shares) in the hope that they will increase in value and can be sold for a profit at a later date.

structural unemployment Unemployment usually caused by the decline of major industry, which is made worse by labour immobility (geographical or occupational).

subsidy An amount of money paid by a government to the producer of a good/service to lower the price and increase demand for the good/service.

substitute good A good that can be used as an alternative to another good. For example, soya milk and cow's milk.

supply-side policy Government policy that aims to increase aggregate supply in an economy. For example, a policy to increase the productive capacity of the economy.

trade union An organisation of workers that acts to represent their interests, e.g. to improve their pay.

tax An amount of money paid to a government. It's paid directly, e.g. income tax, or indirectly, e.g. excise duty.

unemployment The level of unemployment is the number of people who are looking for a job but cannot find one. The rate of unemployment is the number of people out of work as a percentage of the labour force.

wage rate The price of labour, i.e. the rate of pay to employ a worker.

Index

A

accelerator process 83
actual growth 92, 93
ad valorem taxes 58, 59
aggregate demand (AD) 82-87, 94, 96
aggregate demand curve 86
aggregate supply (AS) 88-91, 94, 96
aggregate supply curve 88
agriculture
  buffer stocks 35, 62
  government failure 69
  market 34, 35
  price controls 61
allocative efficiency 28
asymmetric information 55
average cost curve 13

B

balance of payments 77, 92, 100, 101, 108
barriers to entry 52
basket of goods 74, 75
black market 61, 70
booms 72, 93
budget deficit 84
budget surplus 84
budgetigar 84
buffer stocks 35, 62
bureaucracy 67, 118

C

carbon offsetting 65
cartels 23, 32
circular flow of income 80, 81
claimant count 76
commodities 56, 62
Common Agricultural Policy (CAP) 69
complementary goods 17, 21
composite demand 17
contractionary monetary policy 114
consumer burden 31
consumer gain 30

consumer price index (CPI) 75, 114
consumer surplus 29
consumption 82
cost benefit analysis (CBA) 51
cost-push inflation 96
cross elasticity of demand (XED) 19, 21
crowding out 113, 120, 122
cyclical unemployment 98

D

deflation 74, 97
deflationary fiscal policy 111
demand 16-21
demand curve 16
demand-pull inflation 96
demand-side shocks 93
demerit goods 48, 49
deregulation 118
derived demand 17
direct taxes 58
diseconomies of scale 15
disinflation 74
division of labour 11
Doris 42

E

economic agents 5, 10
economic cycle 93, 110
economic development 78, 79
economic growth 72, 92-95, 108, 109
economic objectives 10, 92-109
  conflicts 108, 109
economic problem 4
economic stability 103
economies of scale 14, 15, 52, 53
emissions trading system (ETS) 65
environmental protection 102, 108, 109
equity 57
exam advice 124-131
exchange rates 104, 105
expansionary monetary policy 114
exports 84, 85, 120
externalities 43-47

F

factors of production 4, 54
fiscal policy 110-113, 122
fishing quotas 69
fly-tipping 46, 67
free market 6, 26
free rider problem 50
free trade 106
frictional unemployment 98
full employment 98

G

geographical immobility 54, 99
government failure 67-71
government intervention 58-66
government revenue 84
government spending 84
'green taxes' 113
gross domestic product (GDP) 72, 73
gross national income (GNI) 73

H

health care market 40
'hot money' 115
housing market 38
Human Development Index (HDI) 78, 79
hurdling 12
hyperinflation 74

I

imperfect information 49, 55, 112
imports 84, 85, 120
income 10, 57, 80, 81
income distribution 57, 102
income effect 16
income elasticity of demand (YED) 19, 21
index numbers 73
indirect taxes 30, 31, 58
inferior goods 17, 21

Index

Index